A PALER SHADE OF GREEN

A PALER SHADE OF GREEN

by

Des Hickey and Gus Smith

LESLIE FREWIN of LONDON

© Des Hickey and Gus Smith, 1972

First published 1972 by
Leslie Frewin Publishers Limited,
Five Goodwin's Court,
Saint Martin's Lane, London, WC2N 4LL

This book is set in Baskerville,
printed and bound in Great Britain by R. J. Acford, Ltd.,
Industrial Estate, Chichester, Sussex

World Rights Reserved

ISBN 85632 006 4

Contents

5

CONTENTS

Acknowledgements

In the preparation of this personalised history we are indebted to the following for their generous co-operation and patience during our lengthy tape-recorded interviews: Colin Blakely, Norman Cohen, Eileen Crowe, Cyril Cusack, Donal Donnelly, Hilton Edwards, Brian Friel, Richard Harris, John Huston, Denis Johnston, Marie Kean, Sean Kenny, Hugh Leonard, Joe Lynch, Tomás MacAnna, Donal McCann, Jack MacGowran, Siobhán McKenna, T. P. McKenna, Micheál MacLiammóir, Anna Manahan, Tom Murphy, Conor Cruise O'Brien, Denis O'Dea, Dan O'Herlihy, Milo O'Shea, Norman Rodway, Alan Simpson, and Brendan Smith.

We wish also to thank Hamish Hamilton, Ltd., for permission to quote an extract from Tyrone Guthrie's autobiography 'A Life in the Theatre' and the *Irish Times* for allowing us to quote from a letter of Sean O'Casey's which appeared in their columns.

We are indebted to Mrs. Eileen O'Casey and Brendan Smith for permission to publish letters of Sean O'Casey's relating to 'The Drums of Father Ned.'

We acknowledge the photographs supplied to us by the picture libraries of Independent Newspapers, Ltd.; the *Irish Press* and the *Irish Times*, and by photographers Dermot Barry and Charles Collins.

A special thank you is due to Mary Lavin for her advice and encouragement.

DES HICKEY AND GUS SMITH,
Dublin, March 1972.

Preface : *A search for fulfilment*

IN THE FIRST chapter of this book you will find a writer in his eighties preparing for yet another long journey from Dublin to New York, where he will contribute to magazines, begin a new book, and talk with his agent. This is the bizarre, but not uncommon, situation of the Irish artist, whether he be playwright, actor, director or designer, who cannot find artistic fulfilment within the confines of his own island. Padraic Colum, that old man preparing for the journey, was one of the first playwrights to leave Ireland in the early years of this century. Many were to follow him; some deciding to live permanently out of Ireland; others willing to commute with the theatrical and film centres of the world. A few rejected Ireland because of its frustrations, echoing perhaps the words of Joyce, 'I will not serve that in which I no longer believe . . .'

We find that the majority of those we have interviewed for this book left Ireland essentially in search of fulfilment and devoid of feelings of disillusionment. It may be that they realised that development and fulfilment could be sought only in exile, but whether the realisation of their dreams was achieved through a billboard on Broadway or in the West End or through a title on a cinema screen, it was necessary in each case that they should first leave Ireland.

Their reasons for leaving have been varied. Denis Johnston, whose plays influenced the Irish theatre in the late twenties and early thirties, left Ireland because he wanted to become involved with the new medium of television. Tyrone Guthrie went away to become an

9

actor and became instead a director and a pioneer of new theatres in Canada and the United States. Dan O'Herlihy took an architect's degree, but having acted at the Gate Theatre with Orson Welles he went off to join the Mercury Theatre in New York. Among a younger generation Sean Kenny also abandoned an architect's career in Dublin to become a theatre designer in London. Conor Cruise O'Brien made a career with the Irish Diplomatic Service and drew inspiration from the Congo for his play *Murderous Angels*.

In these pages we have not sought to deal with such personalities for their own sake. We have endeavoured, by presenting this book on two levels, to mirror the most significant events in the theatrical and cinematic history of Ireland since the turn of the century in the reminiscences of those who have helped to shape that history; and we have endeavoured also to show the private individuals behind the public faces.

We commenced to research the book early in 1969 and during the following two years interviewed the chief persons in this history, all of whom were willing to co-operate with us. In the end, our problem was to decide what material could be omitted; in a history spanning such a long period and involving so many outstanding figures this was a difficult problem. Nevertheless we have tried to convey through these edited interviews a definite course of theatrical and cinematic development, beginning with the Irish Dramatic Movement and the founding of the Abbey Theatre and continuing through the golden years of the Gate in the twenties and thirties, the doldrums of the forties, the new awakening in the fifties, which culminated in the establishment of the Dublin Theatre Festival and were enlivened by controversy, to the sixties when the new Abbey Theatre was opened and a group of writers and actors emerged who were, however, to make their reputations outside Ireland.

The reality in the beginning of the seventies is in the uncertain theatrical scene. Irish theatregoers are described by one actor in these pages as 'watchers in a funeral parlour'. A native Irish film industry remains a future hope. For Irish actors, writers, and directors the question has become one of survival. The Irish play-wright, according to Brian Friel, cannot hope to exist unless his work is performed abroad.

It will be seen that the Abbey Theatre figures prominently; this is not surprising when one considers that the modern Irish literary and dramatic movement developed from the establishment of the Abbey at the turn of the century. The dramatic movement created by W B Yeats and Lady Gregory has been a continuous one, except that Irish playwrights today are more likely to see their plays first performed in London or New York. Actors and directors no longer wait for the next Dublin production to be announced; they call their agents in other capitals. In a country with more amateur actors than Equity cardholders the professional theatre exists precariously. In Cork, a city of more than one hundred thousand people, there is no professional theatre company. Limerick, with fifty thousand inhabitants, can scarcely support its amateurs. Dublin looks more and more to the Abbey Theatre and to its future artistic policies. But revivals of naturalistic works by Lennox Robinson and George Shiels and adaptations of novels by Brendan Behan, Patrick Kavanagh, Frank O'Connor and Flann O'Brien delay the day when Ireland's national theatre can again be termed great. There is little wisdom today in the Irish writer or performer lingering in the Celtic Twilight; it is more sensible to view that twilight from a distance, sitting by the telephone and waiting, as Tyrone Guthrie might say, for a call from the Everywhere.

Yet Irish actors and dramatists are imbued with a curious loyalty. How else can one explain the appearances by Cyril Cusack, Siobhán McKenna and Micheál MacLiammóir at the Abbey Theatre, playing major roles for a salary of thirty pounds a week? But it is not necessarily loyalty that has brought home to Ireland those playwrights who will benefit from the tax exemption accorded by a new Government Bill. After eight years in London playwright Tom Murphy settled in Dublin in the spring of 1970; so did Hugh Leonard.

It would be reasonable to ask what place John Huston has in these pages. For a man steeped in the tradition of the American cinema,

Huston is now assuredly as much a part of Ireland as Kevin McClory, with whom he shares a love of the Irish countryside. Huston is today a naturalised Irishman, but his involvement goes deeper. He would seem an ideal pioneer for an Irish film industry. We have afforded him the last words in this book. By setting a traditional movement in contrary motion, Huston has become the first of the settlers, waiting perhaps for a new sunrise.

1

❧　❧　❧

Colum :　Life in a world of writers

ON A SUNNY September morning in 1969 a small, frail, greyhaired man opened the door to us in a terraced house in Edenvale Road in the Dublin suburb of Ranelagh. This was Padraic Colum on the day on which his novel, *The Flying Swans*, was published for the first time in Ireland, a writer who described himself as one of the originals of the Irish dramatic movement at the turn of the century, and who was its last survivor. Colum was the first Irish dramatist to express the peasant love of the land, and through the land the love of Ireland. The curtain line in one of his early plays, *The Land*, speaks of 'the Irish nation that is waiting to be born'.

One of the newspapers said after its first production in the Abbey Theatre in 1905:

> Mr Colum's dialect is admirable. It lives, which is everything. It is strong, coloured, subtle, and early rises into lyricism. The play has a curious formal excellence. It preserves absolutely the unity of time, the whole action being compressed into something less than two hours.
>
> No play yet produced in the Abbey Theatre has so gripped and held captive an audience. There have been fuller houses, but never

more enthusiastic. What we have been waiting for was a play that should be at once good and popular. Mr Yeats has proved a little too abstruse, and Mr Synge a little too bizarre, to get fully down to the hearts of the people. What distinguishes *The Land* and gives it a special value in the development of the Abbey Theatre is its spirit and subject. Mr Colum has caught up his play out of the midcurrent of actual Irish life.

Colum saw his nation born through revolution and revival, but his writings have been described as too pure to have been converted by political movements. His view of the peasant farmer was to be echoed by later Abbey writers such as Robinson, Murray, and Mayne. The world of O'Casey, however, was never Colum's.

When in Ranelagh he lived with his sister. He liked to talk to the people he met on his way to the local shops. Occasionally he went to the theatre. At the Abbey he could be found in company with Ernest Blythe and Richard Mulcahy, two former Ministers in the Free State Government. Since 1914 he had been a commuter to New York. A few days after the publication of *The Flying Swans* he flew again to New York. He never returned to Ireland; he died in Connecticut in January, 1972, at the age of ninety.

During our interview he was dressed in a grey tweed suit and sat upright on a sofa. He smoked occasionally, displayed a lively mind in conversation, and regretted that he would be in New York when Peter O'Toole played Shaw's *Man and Superman* in Dublin.

The small room in which we talked was filled with books. Near the sofa was an old black typewriter on which Colum liked to work every day, writing plays, poems and stories. 'I have plays in my desk which I haven't offered yet,' he said. He remarked on our punctuality when he met us at the door. 'You have come too early,' he commented.

*   *   *

I never want to live permanently in America or anywhere else, because by nature I am a wanderer. I first went to America in 1914 because I could not earn a living here; I had just married, and there was no living to be had in Dublin. I had done part-time editorial work for the *Irish Times* and the *Freeman's Journal*. I never got any money for my plays, although they were being performed at this time; or if I did, they were very small sums of money indeed. I was born in Longford, where my father was Master of the workhouse. He afterwards became Stationmaster at Sandycove, outside Dublin, and I went to the national school at Glasthule. I was the eldest of a family of eight.

Getting into the theatre as a young man was gradual. I was working in a railway clearinghouse, and becoming known to the Fays, and having a play of mine produced, *Broken Soil*, in 1903 at the Molesworth Hall when I was very young.

Yeats and Lady Gregory were not the original creators of the Irish theatre. The Irish theatre's creators were from political societies, Cumann na nGael and Inníní na hÉireann, and from the Fay Comedy Company. The Fay Company turned to Irish plays, and the first Irish play performed was AE's *Deirdre* in Saint Teresa's Hall, Clarendon Street, in April, 1902; and that was an exciting production because the Gaelic League spirit was very high at the time. Whenever a play was produced that mentioned the name Cuchullain the audience used to fill the theatre.

Yeats and Lady Gregory made up their minds that the only important dramatist we had in Ireland was Synge, and they were apt to overlook the work of a writer like George Fitzmaurice; they were impatient rather than eager when he showed a play to them.

I was therefore before them. They came into a theatre that Dudley Digges, the Fays, Máire Nic Shiúbhlaigh and Sara Allgood had already formed. At that time the theatre was so nationalistic that on our committee were Arthur Griffith and Maud Gonne.

I admired Griffith so much that I later wrote a biography of him. I did not know Michael Collins; I missed knowing him, and that is a great regret. De Valera I knew. He ruined things at that time, and he destroyed Clann na nGael. I think Griffith was the greatest statesman we had : a greater statesman than any of the others, because he saw that unless there was something to fall back on, the Irish Insurrection would be a waste. Griffith liked to compare Ireland with Hungary, but Hungary was a different country altogether. It had an aristocracy and a military élite that was powerful and completely nationalistic, which Ireland had not; but by creating this myth and urging us to start our own Government, whether we got Home Rule or not, Griffith gave Ireland something to fall back on after the Insurrection. It would have been all over, as with other insurrections, if Griffith had not created the idea of Dáil Éireann. That was Griffith's great contribution; but how shamefully he was treated.

The first play I wrote was an anti-recruiting play, *The Saxon Shilling*, which Willie Fay declined to stage. There was a suggestion that he wanted to attract another audience, apart from the nationalistic audience. When the Fay group decided not to put on my play, Arthur Griffith and Maud Gonne withdrew from the committee. It was as nationalistic as that. But, of course, Yeats was right. What was wanted was not a theatre confined to a single movement, but a regular theatre that would produce all our plays. But it must be remembered that every country, especially a country in the position of Ireland at that time, has to have an image of itself that it would like others to accept. The charge against Synge was that he was destroying this image. It was inconceivable in those days that an Irish farmer's wife would go off with a tramp of the roads, as in *In the Shadow of the Glen*. We lost very important actors because of the insistence that the play should go on: Dudley Digges and Maire Quinn left the theatre on account of this decision. Synge and I began at the same time, and I was not at all influenced by him. My great influence as a writer was Ibsen.

The most fruitful and exciting time in the Irish Dramatic Movement was before it became the Abbey Theatre. You must remember that the Abbey was given to Yeats by Elizabeth Horniman, but she had a wrong idea of Ireland altogether. She thought the Gaelic League would murder her. I remember the opening of the Abbey Theatre with the production of Yeats's *On Baile's Strand* on 27th December, 1904. The élite of Dublin was there, both Nationalist and Unionist. But then came the withdrawals from the Abbey.

I was very young and inexperienced at the time, and tremendously influenced by the older people, by the Fays and Yeats. Now Yeats was not by nature a dramatist; he made himself a dramatist. He was not one of those extraordinary poets who, when they have reached a certain stage, when they have found themselves, remain at that stage; Yeats changed constantly.

If you read the Victorian poets, Tennyson, Browning, Swinburne, and examine their collected works you will be disappointed after a while to find them saying the same things. Browning at the end was writing the same poems he wrote at the beginning of his literary life. But not Yeats; he continued to recreate himself. One of the ways in which he achieved this was through the theatre. He wanted to escape from the rhythms and the subjects he had been using. His father had always urged him to enter public life, and he was influenced by his father's advice. He speaks of trying to find a more manly energy. He found that energy in the theatre; but it was a deliberate choice. Although not by nature a dramatist, he wrote the best dramatic verse since the Jacobeans, since Webster. I think Yeats was very sincere about Ireland. Later he adopted what might be termed the Ascendancy point of view. He admired the Ireland of Grattan and Berkeley and the great Anglo–Irish writers.

On Lady Gregory's part there was a desire to have a man she regarded as a great poet in the theatre; and she herself had ambitions to be able to come into the Irish theatre. Yeats helped her in that. He was very good at helping young people and talking to them sensibly about their work. There was more intellectual excitement when men like Yeats and Arthur Griffith were around. One could meet them on the street and go into their offices to talk to them. When a poem of mine called 'A Poor Scholar' was published in Griffith's paper, the *United Irishman,* and I was working in the railway clearinghouse in Kildare Street, I remember going to see Yeats to talk about it.

One of the visions Yeats had – they changed from time to time, of course – was to create a powerfully-minded Irish population. He was fond of quoting Victor Hugo's words: 'The mob becomes a people in the theatre.' He was excited about his plays and would come down to rehearsals where he learned much from the Fays.

Willie Fay created the Abbey Theatre, but the talents of the two Fays fitted each other so well. Frank Fay was a wonderful elocutionist and could speak poetry splendidly; an art that has disappeared in Dublin today. I consider Dublin's public speaking the worst of any country I know: hemming and hawing and not enunciating words. Frank Fay would spend hours getting the line of a poem right. He cultivated the voice and would make the actors say 'oohs' and 'aahs' until their voices changed completely and they were capable of speaking verse.

I gave up my job in the clearinghouse in 1904. There was a splendid Irish-American named Thomas Hughes Kelly who gave me a scholarship that amounted to what I would have earned in the clearinghouse: £40 a year rising by increments to £100, so that I was able to go on with my writing. I never really made any money from my plays. In 1905 the Abbey Theatre presented what I called my agrarian comedy, *The Land*. But it was five years later before the theatre presented *Thomas Muskerry*. That was a great success. We had a fine cast: Arthur Sinclair, Sara Allgood, Maire O'Neill, J M Kerrigan, Fred O'Donovan. Sinclair played Thomas Muskerry. He was a disagreeable man, but one of the best actors I have ever seen, comparable to Coquelin, whom I remember.

When *Thomas Muskerry* was revived by the Abbey in the early sixties it was done so badly that it attracted practically no audience. That was in the Queen's, a terrible hole of a theatre. Of course, the workhouse has gone out of the consciousness of the people and the Abbey should have produced it as an historical play.

I was always an ardent nationalist. I was in the Volunteers and got my rifle at Howth. I was staying in the St Lawrence Hotel when the rifles were brought in. Eoin MacNeill, who was Chief of the Volunteers, was with us at lunch. He was very anxious about what would happen when we marched into town with the rifles. We were fired on at Bachelor's Walk. I would have been in the Insurrection had I been in Ireland; but I was able to do some propaganda work in America. I stayed in New York for three years at first, during which time I wrote reviews and lectured. I was then commissioned to go to Hawaii to study Polynesian folk tales and write books about them. I don't know what the word 'roots' means, but I like to be back in Dublin. I like to walk through St Stephen's Green and around the city streets, meeting people.

One evening I remember seeing this redbearded man in knicker-bockers walking vigorously along the street. I said to myself: 'Bernard Shaw is in Dublin.' That evening in the Abbey Theatre Lennox Robinson came to me and said: 'Mrs Shaw would like you to go down to the stalls to talk to Bernard.' I went down, of course, and Shaw said: 'This is my native town, yet it's the only town in the world where I have to send for somebody to talk to me.' During the intervals we talked about anything that came up. What impressed me was that although the play was a mediocre one, the great dramatic critic (and I regard Shaw as one of the greatest of dramatic critics) gave his full attention to the stage and became absorbed in the acting and in the play itself.

It was in the *salons* that Shaw, like Wilde, learned his conversation. In the Dublin of that time everybody who was important gave a special evening or afternoon. In Mespil House, where Sarah Purser was a great wit, you might find Professor Mahaffy or Stephen McKenna. One guest would be asked to recite a poem, another to sing or play music. But that cannot be any more. The *salon* depended on service and on the hostess being free to talk to you whilst the maid brought refreshments.

I knew Sean O'Casey and I was at the first production of *Juno and the Paycock* at the Abbey in 1924, which I liked; and I also liked *The Shadow of a Gunman*. But I do not like the plays he wrote after he left Ireland. Synge and O'Casey occupied two different worlds. There was more of our traditional poetry in the peasant life of Synge's plays than in the life of O'Casey's Dublin workmen. O'Casey's dialect never appeared to me to be real. It was Dublin speech, and I didn't quite accept it. He was not really influenced by what is called the Irish Movement. Writers like Yeats and Synge and myself were influenced by the ideas of the Movement – the language movement and so on, but O'Casey is the successor to Boucicault.

19

I knew Joyce here in Dublin and later in Paris, where I very often went to him to take dictation because his eyes were very bad. He was writing *Finnegans Wake*, and we used to talk about it, and it was a help to him if one could sit down and copy out things. Joyce's eyes were worse than O'Casey's, which were rather red-rimmed and unsightly. Joyce was very embittered. Oddly enough, it was a bitterness that went far back; it was a bitterness arising out of the Parnell affair. Joyce was only a boy at the time, but he was so precocious. He never forgave Tim Healy for answering Parnell's remark, 'I am the master of the Party', with the rejoinder, 'And who is the mistress?' He wrote a pamphlet in his teens denouncing Healy. Joyce used to work in the morning and would take time off in the afternoon. He liked having good dinners outside and had friends, but he enjoyed family life. I was working in Paris, where my wife was attending lectures at the Sorbonne, and I helped Joyce, although it was Samuel Beckett who was his secretary, though not a paid one. Whereas Joyce came from a nationalistic family, I don't think Beckett did. He did not have the same attachment to Ireland. It was not the same heartbreaking disruption on his part to leave the country as it was for Joyce.

The Beckett I knew in Paris was a very silent and I think a very troubled man. We often talked about Dublin. He was misled about the withdrawal of O'Casey's play *The Drums of Father Ned* from the Dublin Festival in 1958. This was a great misunderstanding on Beckett's part. O'Casey had a curious idea that he was being accused of anti-clericalism and that the bishops and everybody here were against him. There were to be religious services to start the Festival: a Mass, a Church of Ireland service, even a Jewish service. It was all nonsense to start like that. The Catholic Archbishop of Dublin very properly decided he wouldn't say the Mass. That's all there was to it. But it was blown up into an imaginary anti-O'Casey crusade led by the Archbishop, and it was taken up in New York that O'Casey was being persecuted. It wasn't like that at all. But Beckett was misled by the news. He withdrew his mime plays and said he would not return to Dublin.

Naturalistic drama can be done better today in the movies. In time the theatre will have to change and become completely poetical. I think Beckett has made a very able attempt to break with naturalism in *Waiting for Godot*; so has Ionesco in his Theatre of the Absurd. In breaking new ground, *Godot* is a work of genius, but I feel Beckett has reached a dead end and that his theatre cannot be developed further.

I am writing a series of plays in the convention of the Japanese *Noh* theatre. Yeats has done this, using mythological Irish subjects. I am writing *Noh* plays, but their subject is Irish history; although mythology is not excluded. The first play is *Moytura* about Sir William Wilde. The scene is Moytura, the mythical battleground for the powers of Light and Darkness. I have written plays too about Parnell, Joyce, and Casement, naming them after places, just as the Japanese plays were named after shrines: *Glendalough* about Parnell, *Monasterboice* about Joyce, and *Clogher* about Casement. I would like to go on writing such plays. I have written another, *Kilmore*, about the burial of Bishop Bedell, the Protestant bishop who translated the Bible into Irish and whose family feared that he would not be buried in Kilmore. But a splendid man, Colonel Myles O'Reilly, not only permitted the burial of the bishop there, but delivered an oration over his grave.

I think the play of mine that may last longer than any of the others is *The Fiddler's House*, which was originally *Broken Soil*. I think my best work is the novel *The Flying Swans*, which I dedicated to James Stephens. Stephens's early novel, *Mary, Mary*, sometimes called *The Charwoman's Daughter*, was a charming idyll of Dublin. I never walk in St Stephen's Green without thinking of Mary. I have lived in a world of writers, but I have been interested in painting more than in any of the other arts. I would like to know more about music, but unfortunately I began too late. Joyce, of course, knew a good deal about music, and so did Stephens. Joyce was a cultivated musician, and a great intellectual, although he avoided intellectual subjects in conversation. Beckett, too, is not intellectual in conversation.

How much of my writing will last? How would I know? It will last as long as somebody finds something in it. I have never made any money out of writing poetry, but I have written about a dozen books for children, beginning with *The King of Ireland's Son*; and I have written the classical stories, *The Odyssey*, and so on for children, and these are reprinted again and again, and I get an income out of that. I've managed to keep a bank account in Dublin and New York. My children's books have sold so well that I have reached the happy stage where all I have to do is to sign contracts and the books are republished and I get new royalties. New York is no more stimulating than anywhere else; as long as I have something to do, it doesn't matter where I am. I have always been a commuter. I have a good apartment in New York overlooking Central Park. My wife and I lived a long time there, and I pay a lower rent than I would for most apartments in New York. It's an apartment of five rooms, and my nephew lives with me, and looks after me to some extent, and I go walking in the Park. I belong to the American and Irish Academies of Letters.

I suppose my discipline was in learning poetry. When I was going along the road I could always say a poem. When I cannot sleep I always say a long poem to myself. That is a sort of discipline. A man does not look back over his whole life, but over his conscious life. I want to finish my recollections, and I have a long way to go yet; I am only half finished. I find the search for the right word is always hard. I am interested in clarity, and in conveying my emotions and feelings to the reader. Whether that is style or not, I don't care. I want to be charming and I want to be graceful if I can; but above all I want to be clear and to say what I want to say. In my life I think, on the whole, I have been calm. I have not quarrelled with people; at least I have not had public quarrels. Some people like quarrels, but they are a waste of time. I'm eighty-five, I think. I lose count. My wife was from County Sligo. That's her picture there, a painting done from a snapshot. I was at her grave yesterday in Howth. I would not like to live to be a hundred, to be feeble, and with all my friends gone.

2

❧ ❧ ❧

Cusack: Every week a different school

IN 1916, TWO years after Padraic Colum had first left for America,
Cyril Cusack, then a small boy, arrived in Ireland with his mother
and stepfather to begin an early theatrical career. When he came to
the Abbey Theatre from university in 1932 actors like Barry Fitzgerald and F J McCormick were living legends.

Despite his subsequent long career with the Abbey, most of
Cusack's work in films and much of his work in the theatre has been
undertaken outside Ireland: in Hollywood, New York, London,
Paris and Rome. When he returned to the London stage in Dürrenmatt's play, *The Physicists*, after a long absence, he called it 'my
second apprenticeship'. 'A thousand times welcome back', wrote
Bernard Levin. When he played Thersites in the film version of
Oedipus Rex, Freda Bruce Lockhart wrote that his performance helped
to break the British theatrical tradition of playing which 'often
reduces poetry to sound and scribble'.

Cusack's lifelong championing of Boucicault was vindicated when
he played *Conn the Shaughraun* at the World Theatre Season at London's
Aldwych in 1968. J C Trewin described his Shaughraun as 'a
Grumio crossed with Sam Weller and an Irish accent added' and

23

echoed Henry James's description of Boucicault's own performance in the part: 'simply exquisite'.

François Truffaut said of him when they were filming *Fahrenheit 451*:

> Cyril Cusack is the most restless actor I have known. He is a man of good nature and mildness. He can play his scenes in so many styles; he can be baroque, malicious, lyrical, but he can never be terrifying . . . While the accents of the solid English actors have begun to grate on my ears, the accent of Cyril Cusack the Irishman enchants me as much as does the accent of Oskar Werner.

Like the Redgraves, the Cusacks are a theatrical family. The eldest daughter Sinéad, who began her career at the Abbey Theatre, has appeared with her father in the films *David Copperfield* and *Toys*, and opposite Peter Sellers in *Hoffman*. Sorcha has won good notices for her performance in Pinter's *The Homecoming* at Trinity College, Dublin. The Cusacks' youngest daughter Niamh was given a tiny part in the film *I Was Happy Here*.

In London Cyril Cusack keeps a tall terraced house at Porchester Gardens because, he says, 'I spend so long in exile'; but when he returns to Dublin, where our meeting took place, it is always a renewal.

*   *   *

My commencement as a professional goes back to the days when with my stepfather, Breffni O'Rourke, we toured the little towns of Ireland. I was born in South Africa. My mother was Cockney and belonged to a theatrical family, most of them connected with vaudeville and music-hall.

I always say that I came back to Ireland in 1916; a very memorable year. For the next ten years or so I toured Ireland playing children's parts in melodrama. Every week I went to a different school. In those days we were able to play a full week in one of the very small towns or villages. I used to act at night and go to school during the day, and somehow I managed to graft a little education on to myself.

This eventually led to University College, Dublin, where I studied Politics, Modern History, and Roman Law. The idea was that I might go on for the Bar, but my compulsion was towards the theatre. My first appearance on the stage was in 1916 as Little Willie in *East Lynne* in Tipperary, and I first appeared in a film, *Knocknagow*, about the same time.

In 1932 I found myself in the orbit of the Abbey Theatre. I had done a little writing when I was in college, and had a few poems published; and I have pursued that minor talent through the years. I acted in a number of plays at college, including Wilde's *The Importance of Being Earnest* and Yeats's *The Pot of Broth*. We were rather enterprising in those days; we even had a public performance in the Gaiety Theatre.

During the holidays I worked professionally. By this time my mother and Breffni had gone to England and in the holiday period I used to work in various repertories, particularly Norwich and Windsor. My first appearance in London was at the Brixton Empire when I had a small part in Bennett's *Milestones*. I came on in the last act, and something happened between myself and the audience. I suddenly realised that they liked me. It was something I said, some innocuous line, and they laughed so sympathetically. That was one of the most memorable moments of my life. I felt the same thrill years later in Eugene O'Neill's play, *Ah, Wilderness!* in London. Likewise I derived something very special from the first production of O'Neill's *Moon for the Misbegotten* in New York.

Apart from my sporadic holiday experiences, I stuck to my last during the academic period. It was difficult to find a discipline for myself, as I was on my own. I have been on my own all my life except during those touring days with my mother and Breffni. I lived in Queen's Square, now Pearse Square, then the theatrical quarter in Dublin. All the professionals used to live around there, and the Queen's Theatre was a venue for us in those days. My mother worked there for about two years in melodrama and pantomime. We had had our own company, although we had toured with other companies in Ireland, including Jimmy O'Brien's. In the early days Jimmy O'Brien had a great name as an exponent of Boucicault.

I began with the Abbey in 1932 in a one-act play by A P Fanning called *Vigil*, which Lennox Robinson directed. I had gone along and seen Robinson and told him something of my background. He was sometimes rather vague and he put me down for two parts; one to be played by Cyril O'Rourke and the other by Cyril Cusack. Then I had a season or two with Hilton Edwards and Micheál Mac Liammóir at the Gate Theatre. I remember playing Paris in *Romeo and Juliet* to Mac Liammóir's Romeo.

My alma mater was the touring theatre, but the Abbey became my benevolent stepmother. During this period I made occasional appearances in London; in *The Playboy of the Western World* in 1938 and in *Ah, Wilderness!* in 1936, and then in *Thunder Rock* during the war. Between 1932 and 1945 I appeared in sixty-five plays at the Abbey. In those days it was practically a repertory.

Yeats was still alive, but not an active participant. Lennox Robinson was managing director, and then Frank O'Connor took over and later Hugh Hunt. It was somewhat erratic. I began to play away from the Abbey. I think, as has been said in Gerald Fay's book, I was not very happy with the artistic policy at the time. I felt very strongly that the Abbey, as the accepted national theatre, should attend the rural areas. Perhaps I felt this having come from the touring theatre. I also believed that the Abbey should be more enterprising in touring abroad. But apart from one visit to America during the time I was there, nothing of this was done. So I, being more ambitious in those days, formed my own company.

I had acted in some films during the war and with the money I earned I set up my company. My idea was to specialise in the best of Irish and classical theatre and to tour Ireland and travel abroad. This we did very successfully. We attended the first International Theatre Festival in Paris with *The Playboy of the Western World*. I had Siobhán McKenna as my Pegeen Mike, and a very good company that included Walter Macken, Jack MacGowran and Marie Kean. We were singled out with the Brecht company as the best offerings of the Festival. I took my company to Paris again in 1961 and was given the International Critics' Award as the actor of the season. We had played *Arms and the Man* and *Krapp's Last Tape*. Between times I made films in Hollywood and returned to subsidise my company with the money I earned. I must have made about fifty films.

After our return from the Paris Festival in 1961 I presented my own play in Dublin based on Kafka's *The Trial*. I called it *The Temptation of Mr O* and transferred it to a Dublin setting. It was written in rhythmical prose and Dublinese. I packed up my company after that.

In 1942 I had played opposite Vivien Leigh in London as Dubedat in *The Doctor's Dilemma*. At the end of the run I had a mishap, and I thought I would never play in London again, except perhaps with my own company. But in 1963 I decided I would no longer remain in banishment. I appeared in *The Physicists* with the Royal Shakespeare Company. It pleased me so much that after twenty years I was remembered. The critics received me with open arms. Milton Shulman headed his review: '*Cead Mile Failte*'. I remembered that Robert Atkins had asked me to play Hamlet about the time Gielgud was at his zenith, and I remember Hugh Hunt, who was associated with the Abbey at the time – it must have been 1936 – advising me not to accept. The Abbey offered me *The Playboy*. It was a choice between a career in England or Ireland. Because of my loyalty, I opted for *The Playboy*. My association with the Irish theatre was cemented by that decision. The only thing I would regret, perhaps, is that my attitude in theatre was more chauvinistic and less cosmopolitan than it might have been. Theatre has no national identity; it is something for the world, whether it is Irish, English or French.

I held on to the idea of presenting plays by Irish authors with my own company, extending the idea to include plays with Irish foundations, no matter what nationality the author might be – that and the classics. I think it was a fairly liberal decision. Sometimes my decision has been blotted out by other events, but it was part of a pattern, and the contribution of our company has inspired other people, even unconsciously, to travel along similar lines and perhaps extend the efforts we made. It has certainly been duplicated most effectively in the present-day policy of the Abbey Theatre. The Abbey, quite miraculously, has found an international footing on a larger scale than before.

I returned to the Abbey first of all as a shareholder at the invitation of the Minister for Finance – with twenty-four other people. In 1968 we revived Boucicault at the Abbey and then took the production to the World Theatre Season at the Aldwych. My interest in Boucicault goes back to my childhood days. I loved my period with the touring companies playing in melodrama. It is a nostalgic thing, I suppose. But the melodrama most emphatically has a place in the theatre, and Boucicault in the Irish theatre. Melodrama had been ridiculed and put out of court by intellectual and literary coteries. But it found its way back into the popular theatre. It is good theatre; theatre theatrical, not theatre of the intellect. A few people, including myself, suggested that Boucicault should be revived because of his value. Theatricality was beginning to leave the stage with the Wildes and particularly the Shaws, and, with the entry of theatre into the area of the intellect, theatrical effect was in abeyance. Yet even the classical theatre of *Oedipus Rex* is melodrama. Those who wish the Abbey to go on playing Synge and O'Casey to foreign audiences are casting old lines into the sea. The plays of Synge and O'Casey are overtired; but Boucicault's plays, with their strong sense of theatricality, will not tire.

Of all the parts I played at the Abbey I shall most remember Marchbanks in Shaw's *Candida*. I played it not from the head, but under certain directions from my being. It was a revelation to me that the audience was most enthusiastic about that particular performance.

I enjoyed playing in O'Casey. I followed Barry Fitzgerald as the Paycock when he went to America. I don't think I was a good Paycock; in fact, I was a very bad Paycock, an echo of Fitzgerald.

I liked playing *The New Gossoon* and *The Whiteheaded Boy*. Those characters were the naughty boys of that period. The Playboy is one of the most difficult parts for an actor. I played the part over a number of years, and I remember playing it in London when I was much younger and Alan Dent saying, 'This man would make a perfect Romeo.' In later years I found a different facet to the character, and when I finally played Christy Mahon in my own production in Dublin and Paris the part had a deeper emphasis.

When I was in Boston in a coproduction of mine, a play called *Goodwill Ambassador*, I had a call from a priest who had followed my career and wanted to meet me. So we met and he said: 'I remember you so well at the Abbey in *Maurice Harte*.' I said: 'But I never played *Maurice Harte*. That was F J McCormick's great performance.' He answered: 'I don't mean Maurice Harte at all. I mean the part of his young clerical student friend. I remember it as having been a very true performance.' But that sounds very self-applauding.

When I came back from England I played with Maureen Kiely in *The Barrel Organ* by Robert Collis. It was not the first time we had played together. A couple of years before the war we played in *The New Gossoon* at the Abbey. I remember I was very taken by her performance in the Collis play. At the end of the run we were married and later appeared together in productions of our own. I don't know that I would wish a theatrical career on my children. If they have the ability, the temperament, the character and the talent, then I should not be unhappy. But to maintain one's individuality, integrity and true personality in the theatre is a big task, because one is assaulted from all sides by trends of thought, some of them subversive, and one does not immediately recognise them as such. I have told my children of the hazards of acting. One particular hazard is that it can feed and inflate the ego with Dead Sea fruit instead of developing and consolidating an actor's true personality.

I may have been egotistic in my younger years. I was devoted to the work I was doing and fanatically attached to the tradition of the theatre by reason of my background. I love the theatre and theatre people, and my dedication may have expressed itself egotistically. In the theatre one is fed by fruity notices. Sometimes they are deserved and sometimes they are not; one has to sift the wheat from the chaff. One's performance is often heightened by the brilliance and generosity of other actors. It is a matter of interchange, of giving and taking.

I saw the film *Odd Man Out* recently in Rome, and though it was made in 1946 it stands up as an inspired film in many ways, with a remarkable performance from F J McCormick. I have always been happy and proud of my association with McCormick and Fitzgerald. In my film parts I have concentrated on veracity of characterisation. In the last few years I think my work in films has improved in some ways; it is more solid, less intuitive and perhaps technically better than it used to be.

I got my second wind with the part of the Secret Service Chief in *The Spy Who Came In From the Cold*. When I was first approached about the part I heard that it had been originally intended for Gielgud. Gielgud's mind and mine are totally different. I approached the film with no confidence that mine would be in any way a special performance; but it developed into something unusual. I met Richard Burton again in the film after many years. The first day on the film is always a bit nerve-racking, and I remember that we were both very nervous. I suppose neither of us knew exactly how he was going to pursue his part.

Afterwards I went with the Burtons to Rome for *The Taming of the Shrew*. I had worked with Richard Burton many years before in radio. We broadcast on a number of occasions for the BBC and struck up a mutual admiration society, although he was much younger than I. We were responsible for a unique event in radio history. Louis MacNeice had written a splendid dramatic poem called *The Dark Tower*. I broadcast in it twice, and then I was asked to do it again. But I was about to leave for Spain to film *The Spanish Gardener*, so instead MacNeice asked Burton to play my part, which he did. Then the BBC had a further revival of the poem, and Louis MacNeice divided his work in half; the first part used my voice and the second Burton's, both of us playing the same character.

After *The Taming of the Shrew* the Burtons had an idea that they might form a company of repertory film players. But the Italian woman director Cavani had seen two of my films and decided to ask me to play Galileo, because she thought there was no suitable Italian actor for the part. It was the longest part I ever played. The filming began in April and continued until November on locations in Bulgaria, Padua, Florence and Rome. Even then the film was unfinished from the director's point of view.

I was under the impression that *Galileo* would be in Italian. I asked for the script in Italian and made myself familiar with it. But when I arrived in Sofia I found that the majority of the cast were Bulgarian. I had no Bulgarian, and never will have. So I had to play in English whilst they played in Bulgarian. We rehearsed on cues, and I found myself *en rapport* with the Bulgarians, which made our acting better in a way because we were working on intuition. It taxed our ingenuity to respond to one another without understanding a word that was said; but the understanding was there just the same. Cavani has no English, but again there was an intuitive interchange of feelings and ideas, and sometimes values emerged that we might not have found if we had been speaking in the same tongue. When I filmed in *Fahrenheit 451* my French was minimal and the director, François Truffaut, had no English. It was said that my performance had considerable value because Truffaut and I had benefited through misunderstanding rather than complete understanding of what we were saying to each other.

Straightaway I would say that the directors I remember as being generally creative and most constructive so far as the actor is concerned are Carol Reed – of course, my first film was Reed's *Odd Man Out* – and Truffaut. In Reed's case this sympathy with the actor is drawn from his own background. He himself was an actor, and his family tradition goes back to Beerbohm Tree, to whom I think he is related. In Truffaut's case, it was his unhappy background which made him so human and sympathetic to actors. He had been a little waif, a stray. He had spent some time in reformatories. He used to steal and sell doorknockers to get enough money to go to the cinema. He had never, in fact, worked in a studio before he came to Pinewood. But he loved his actors, and his efforts and ours were engaged solely towards making a good film. He fell out with Oscar Werner, because Werner was afraid of fire. Many people are. We were sitting at one of those preproduction lunches when dear little François asked him to play the scene in which he uses a flamethrower, on my orders, to destroy his books. Werner said no; a definite, Teutonic no. He retired to his dressingroom and did not return to the set. I did the flamethrowing scene with a stunt man.

If Truffaut is a director who loves his actors, Zeffirelli is a mock actor who tells his actors how to perform. This upset me terribly, though Richard Burton kept telling me: 'You'll get used to it.' What a pity the Burtons never saw much of Ireland when they were filming here. I used to tell their chauffeur to drive along the coast road from their hotel to the studios in the early morning, but he would say: '*Non, non. Nous sommes trés pressé.*'

I have enjoyed working with most film directors. In the theatre I find direction less satisfying. I don't know why this is. When Carroll O'Connor was in my company in America I remember him saying to me: 'You're a director killer.' Perhaps this is because I like to exercise my individuality. The theatre director has acquired more power in the last couple of decades, and as an actor I sometimes rebel against this; not against the director as a person, but against the exercise of Pygmalion power over the actors to the exclusion of their personalities. I don't think this is necessarily ego on my part. There are certain things in life that one wants to do, should do or must do; and this occurs in the theatre, too. No two individuals operate in exactly the same way, and so the individuality of the director and the actor very often may clash.

In films the director is generally more concerned with the mechanics and the presentation of the actual picture. The individual performance is left more to the actor, particularly when the director is sympathetic to actors. You find sympathetic directors in the theatre, but the theatre director tends to envelop the personality of the actor. I cannot remember having trouble with a film director, unless, oddly enough, it was a television director.

I like to refer to Breffni O'Rourke as the epitome of the actor in the theatre. He was immersed in theatrical tradition. His mother had also been in the theatre. Like my mother, she began as a chorus girl before she went on the legitimate stage. I think I may have inherited the feeling of theatre from my mother and her side of the family. By association with Breffni I found a deepening of my regard and love for the theatrical tradition. I toured with him and watched him in so many different parts. Then I went to the Abbey and found actors like Fitzgerald, McCormick and others of that vintage period. In the

Abbey I absorbed another side of the tradition of theatre which had grown from the Fays.

I worked with Willie Fay and found in him an embodiment of theatrical tradition which goes back almost to the beginning of time. It is a very distinct tradition. I doubt if it has ever been fully expounded by writers, because they are engaged in another field of artistic activity. It is a tradition of legend, story and anecdote. The tradition of the actor is something apart even from high talent. An actor may be very talented and yet divorced from the tradition of theatre. I have found in small-part players who have been working all their lives in the theatre just as much inspiration as in an actor of great talent. In the British theatre there is a fine tradition, and from the many actors with whom I have worked there I have derived nourishment as an actor myself.

Acting is acting wherever it is or whatever the medium. Travelling outside one's own country is bound to broaden one as a person, and this applies very much to theatre. If one is responsive one can build upon experience and expand one's capacity. But I think it is important to draw from one's native soil. My native soil is the theatre, rather than any particular country; though I owe a debt to Ireland for the experience I have found by living here. I am a nationalist now in a very different sense from what I once was. In the development of countries there are periods, of necessity, I think, when one must remain centred on the development of oneself; and then one arrives at another point when one must become centrifugal and move out to find nourishment from other sources. I am a nationalist now in so far as I want to be able to give from what I have, and I would want us Irish to have sufficient to give and to contribute to other countries. I would like to contribute as an actor to the theatre of the world.

I think standards in Ireland need to be corrected from time to time. I think the more our people can see of theatre abroad, without separating themselves from their roots, the better they can appreciate and criticise our own theatre; but I don't think that foreign theatre should be brought in holus bolus. On the other hand, you find people whose experience of theatre is limited, and yet they can go to the

33

theatre for the first time and their vision is absolutely clear and their standards are innate. I have talked to the lady who does the cleaning for me and it has struck me that her appreciation of acting is very clear and true and stems from this quality in herself. The appreciation and recognition of an artistic criterion is based on the quality in oneself as well as experience, and I think it can be obfuscated by shallow distractions. There is an inpouring of distractions today which interferes with one's clarity of vision. It is something we must be very careful of in Ireland; it is happening all over the world and bringing with it a shuffling of standards.

I think that authority in Ireland is good in its intentions towards art. By subsidising theatre it is doing its best to give it the recognition and the stimulus it needs. But more important is the need for understanding and recognition from people with true artistic standards. The appreciation of what is good is more important than the money.

It worries me that we cannot make our own films. I think this is due to the acceptance of a standard that is wrong for us. I have always believed it should be possible to produce films in this country economically and artistically and to draw inspiration not from the spectacle films that the Americans produce but from an original source. I think we must find an economic art form in films, a new form of filmic presentation which could be a contribution to the outside work of cinema.

I am basically a religious man. The essence of religious experience and the purpose of religion is to find truth, and this applies to any form of living or work; to find truth and to get away from pretence. This is the paradox in the theatre. Outsiders sometimes think of the theatre as an area of pretence, but for me it is an area where one must seek truth. In formal religion, I accept Catholicism as the criterion and so far I have found no replacement. It is an area of adventure, of exploration in the search for God; and with all its ministerial defects it seems to me to provide the means towards finding the truth. The forms of Catholicism presented to me are stimulating; I do not say satisfying, because I do not think religion is intended to be satisfying. It promotes the divine discontent within oneself, so that one tries to make oneself a better person and draw oneself closer to God.

I have tried to explore the little talent I have for writing. I have produced a number of poems, and two or three plays which have been performed. Some of my poems have been accepted and one of them included in a publication called *The Best Poems of 1963*. I write when I have time, but it is another career. I have thought if I could possibly afford it – but I have a family of five – of giving up acting and trying to develop this other talent to its fullest. I would not say I have shot my bolt as an actor, but with the arrival of a new current of acting and playwriting the theatre has entered a new era, and I think that in my own career I have fulfilled so far as I can my talent as an actor. I sometimes hope that a part will turn up to which I can give myself completely. I would not reject it if it came.

3

❧ ❧ ❧

McCormick : 'Don't stay in Hollywood'

IN THE NEW Abbey Theatre there hangs a composite portrait of F J
McCormick titled 'The Empty Throne'. McCormick has had no
successor. In his autobiography Lennox Robinson recalled:

> A few years ago a thoughtful American woman spent her summer
> touring the theatres of Europe. She ended up with a few weeks in
> Dublin and finally said to me: 'I have seen one or two finer perform-
> ances than Mr McCormick's, but I have never seen such a versatile
> actor.'

McCormick's world was encompassed in a small theatre in the
capital city of a small country. He loved the Abbey so dearly that in
its lean years he sold his prized library to stay alive and remain a
member of the company. It was only in later years that he became
known to the world at large by playing a small part in the film
Odd Man Out. But by then he was a sick man, and his death in April,
1947, at the age of fifty-six was a shattering blow to the company of
players with whom he had spent his acting life.

Robinson called his death 'the passing of a player who was the
peer of Kean, Salvini, Irving, and any other great actor you can
think of'. McCormick was one of the extraordinary team which

launched O'Casey's first plays; but when leading members of this team, including Arthur Shields, Barry Fitzgerald and Sara Allgood, had left Ireland for America, McCormick stayed on.

Historians of the theatre may question whether his greatness has been diminished by his decision to remain in virtual obscurity. His widow, Eileen Crowe, continued as a member of the Abbey company. She lives in a small flat in a Dublin suburb and when she talks of 'Peter' she is talking of F J McCormick.

*   *   *

In 1931 a man named Otto Kahn advanced £1,000 towards an Abbey tour of America. On the first tour we did *John Ferguson* and *The Whiteheaded Boy*. Peter loved it. He was interested in everything, and America was something in those days. New York was a wonderful city, but most of us felt that if we were going to live in America it would be in San Francisco. When we returned in 1936 to make the film of *The Plough and the Stars* in Hollywood, Dudley Digges, who had already settled there and was very kind to us, said: 'Listen, don't stay in Hollywood when you finish the picture. Go home. They want you there. But if you want to come back later, then come back.' Of course, when we arrived home Peter and I didn't want to go back. Both of us were always home birds.

I had joined the Abbey School of Acting in October, 1921. During the time of the curfew the company was away touring. The Abbey had fallen on bad days and the theatre was closed. Michael Dolan was head of the School of Acting at the time. I think I had thirty shillings a week; the highest salary was four pounds a week – a ridiculously small salary to pay players. But there was no money. Seaghan Barlow, the stage carpenter, did wonderful work in making sets out of next to nothing, and he kept the theatre going, really. I was only six weeks in the School of Acting when I was given the lead in the revival of *The Revolutionist* by Terence MacSwiney. Sean O'Casey's first play, *The Shadow of a Gunman*, was produced in 1923

37

just after the players – Arthur Shields, Maureen Delany, Gertie Murphy (who married John McCormack's brother) and others – came back from their tour of America and Australia. I heard them talk about the strange man who went to rehearsals, and after the dress rehearsal went around and shook the hand of each of the players, thanking them for appearing in his little play.

I went to the first night of *The Shadow of a Gunman*. At the end of the first act I remember my hands were tingling because I had clapped so much, as had everyone in the audience. I went to the Green Room after the performance and found O'Casey sitting in a corner by himself, looking very frightened. I said to him: 'Are you the author of this play?' He said: 'Yes.' And I said: 'Heavens!' I just couldn't say enough enthusiastic things about it. The next day I had a very lovely letter from him saying that he hadn't realised when he talked to me the night before that he was talking to the Countess Cathleen and Norah Helmer. We became great friends afterwards, until the break-up. And then a lot of people weren't friends any more.

Like all the other players, Peter had to go away to make a living when the Abbey closed. He joined a touring company with *Paddy, The Next Best Thing*, and toured England as well as Belfast and Cork. As soon as the tour finished he came back to the Abbey. I remember seeing him in a play shortly after he returned. Several of us in the School of Acting regarded him as a matinée idol. We weren't friends at all in the beginning. I was playing the young girl entering the convent in *The Kingdom of God* by Martinez. In the second act she becomes a nun looking after a home for old men, and in the last act she is in charge of an orphanage. In this last act one of the former pupils of the orphanage, a matador, comes to present her with a bull's ear. Peter was stage manager, because in those days you could be playing big parts, as he and Arthur Shields were, and stage managing at the same time. He was so thorough in everything he did that he went out and bought a real bull's ear for this scene. Nobody knew of this until I opened the handkerchief which the matador gave me and saw the ear. Fortunately, it was the dress rehearsal. When we came off Arthur Shields attacked Peter for being so inconsiderate. But, of course, he was only trying to have every-thing exactly right. The two of them nearly had a fight, which was very unusual for actors in those days. I remember saying that day to someone: 'If Peter Judge was the last man in the world I wouldn't marry him.'

It wasn't very long afterwards that we became more than friends. We were married in December, 1925. Nobody had known of our plans. We told the others in the company only the night before we were married and asked them to come to the wedding. When I went to Lennox Robinson, he said: 'I was wondering when Peter was going to make an honest woman of you.' We were playing in *Grasshopper* that evening, a play translated by Padraic Colum from the German of Count Keyserling, and it was an embarrassing, but very lovely experience. The evening papers had got hold of the news, and I'm sure the audience applauded us for a full seven minutes.

I played Mary Boyle in the first performance of *Juno and the Paycock* in 1924. Peter played Joxer Daly. It was his great part. When Sydney Morgan played Joxer in London afterwards, he said: 'I can only copy McCormick.' But he liked *The Shadow of a Gunman* best; that was his favourite. After the first night of *Gunman*, Sean O'Casey said to him: 'That wasn't my character. But don't change him. He's much better than the character I wrote.' He and O'Casey were firm friends. O'Casey was quite different from any author the players had met. Peter was the one who befriended him and took him out to meals, partly because he was sorry for him, partly because he liked him and partly because he wanted to talk about the characters in the plays. He considered O'Casey a great playwright, but I remember someone in the Abbey saying to us: 'O'Casey is not a playwright. He's a reporter, and his plays will be forgotten in ten years.'

O'Casey wrote the part of The Covey in *The Plough and the Stars* for Peter, but he was cast as Jack Clitheroe. Peter had been very good to O'Casey in the early days, before he was recognised publicly. But on the fourth night of *The Plough* when the audience were in uproar and Peter, who was one of the cast, was trying to keep them quiet, he said: 'Don't blame the actors. We didn't write this play.' I think O'Casey never forgave him for that.

O'Casey had been a very happy man, but he became very bitter after the Abbey refused *The Silver Tassie*. Of course they should have put it on. After all, O'Casey had achieved great things for the Abbey with his first three plays. But his break with realism in the second act may have frightened them off. But we played it afterwards.

Peter was born in Skerries, where his father was the manager of a brewery. He went to the convent school and had a happy boyhood. He became a boy clerk in the Post Office in London and fed himself on rice which did terrible things to his digestion. His name was Peter Judge, but when he was moved to the Civil Service in Dublin he didn't want them to know he was acting, because they wouldn't approve of it, so he decided to take another name. I think F J McCormick was a name he saw on a poster. He was in the Abbey company before I joined them. When I came to the Abbey School of Acting he was away touring. Frank Fay had left many years before, but he was living in Dublin and they had engaged him to teach in the School of Acting. He selected me immediately and told me he would make my voice the talk of the world within six months. He had been touring England in Shakespeare and told me I must drop my 'h's'. We were rehearsing *The Shadowy Waters* and when I spoke the line: 'Why is the moon so pale?' Lennox Robinson asked me: 'What has the letter "h" done to you?'

'Mr Fay told me to drop my "h's",' I answered. The next day Yeats sent for me, and said: 'My compliments to Mr Fay, but would you please put back the "h".'

I remember the morning Arthur Griffith was buried. We had been rehearsing, and Lennox said to Michael Dolan and myself: 'We'll go down to Beresford Place to watch the funeral.' We went down, and at the head of the cortège was Michael Collins, a magnificent figure in his uniform. Lennox said: 'Oh, Michael, please give us a wedding for a change. We have had too many funerals.' A week later Michael Collins was dead.

I earned more money than Peter when I joined the company, because Lennox Robinson thought that I was the most wonderful thing that had ever happened. He gave me a rise, which I didn't appreciate at the time, and which was unfair. I had ten pounds and

Peter had five, which was ridiculous. Peter was interested in everything. He had a great interest in photography. He felt that every time a play was staged it would be sensible to take a photograph of the set to show the positioning of the furniture and props, so that there would be no dispute afterwards. He was asked by the management to take the photographs, and for taking them he got ten shillings a week. Actors would be asked to play big parts and stage manage at the same time. Peter was stage manager when he was playing Jack Tanner in *Man and Superman,* one of the longest parts in any play. How could they have asked him to do that? But they did. It was inhuman to expect actors to do that sort of thing, but they couldn't afford to pay a stage manager at the time.

Despite the small salaries the Abbey was a happy place in those days, and I don't think any actor wanted to go anywhere else. Peter was happy in his work, and we had a marvellous variety of parts. In later years we were cut down to kitchen comedies and kitchen tragedies, but in the early days we played practically all of Shaw and Ibsen. The players were extraordinarily content, much more so than people are now with larger salaries. I loved playing with Peter. There was no feeling of acting a part. He was the character he was playing and you were the character you were playing. When he played a big part my own part suffered very often because I would become so nervous and worried about him that I would almost forget what I was doing. As soon as he got news of a part, he studied all he could about it. He had a wonderful sense of humour and he was kind. On one occasion an actor was cast as Captain Boyle, who was a fine actor indeed, but completely unsuited to the part. On the first night Peter went down to the Abbey and played his own part with his back to the audience to help the actor, and when he was off stage he stood behind the window prompting him.

Peter liked to play classical parts, but costume plays were not always popular in the Abbey. He was magnificent in Shaw. He played Oedipus and Lear. One Sunday night we put on *Oedipus* for a charity audience in New York with just a curtain at the back of the stage. During an exit, Peter stepped off the stage into space, because it was so dark. But despite his fall he came on again and

41

finished the play. He received all sorts of offers at a time when we could have used the money, but he never wanted to leave the Abbey. When he finally appeared in the film *Odd Man Out* it made him an international name. They were making *Odd Man Out* and *Hungry Hill* at the same time, and he moved from one set to another. It was too much. Immediately afterwards they asked him to play in another film. I was so upset at the time that I don't remember the name of the film or the Irish location at which they were filming on the east coast. They were working nights and Peter had a gruelling time. He had to give it up.

Two Cities offered him a £2,000 yearly retainer and he was offered a five-year contract by Hollywood. He enjoyed making films, but the only thing that tempted him was an invitation from Olivier to play the First Gravedigger in *Hamlet*. He was very ill at the time, and Olivier offered to finish the film without Peter's scenes, and wait for him. Stanley Holloway played the part afterwards, and said he could not hope to be as good as FJ. On the day Peter died, the surgeon said to me: 'Which one of us wouldn't wish to go at the height of one's fame?'

When you consider the international exchange of actors today, perhaps Peter's full potential was never realised. But he was happy. He was happy playing all those wonderful parts. What upsets me is that his greatness is only for those who saw him and remember him. Nowadays, when so much great acting is preserved on film for posterity, all that remains of Peter's work is *The Plough and the Stars*, *Hungry Hill* and *Odd Man Out*. I don't remember him talking about the parts he would like to have played. Each part as he played it was his life for the time being.

4

    ✮   ✮   ✮

Siobhán McKenna : 'I modelled Joan on my mother'

DURING THE YEARS in which F J McCormick and Eileen Crowe were members of the Abbey Theatre company a younger theatrical couple came and went. Denis O'Dea and Siobhán McKenna decided to expand their work through films and on the stages of London and New York. The world saw Siobhán McKenna's Joan of Arc and Pegeen Mike. With Eithne Dunne and Marie Kean she became one of the postwar Abbey actresses to achieve recognition outside Ireland.

Like the McCormicks, Denis O'Dea and Siobhán McKenna had married during their time in the Abbey. His friends believe that O'Dea retired from acting when his stage and film careers were at their most rewarding. When we talked with him in his Dublin home the tall greyhaired actor recalled that he had entered the theatre through his internment during the Irish troubles. He had fought on the side of de Valera with the Irregulars against the Free Staters. In the internment camp the prisoners formed a dramatic society, using the tables in the dininghall placed together to make a stage, and presented such plays as *Meadowsweet* and *The Coiner*. O'Dea was eighteen when he was interned and on his release he kept the society active with some friends. It was now called the Republican Players Group, presenting plays around Dublin to raise funds for Republican prisoners' dependants.

It was suggested that he should join the Abbey School of Acting and that the society would pay his fees. His first appearance on the Abbey stage was in *The Woman* by Margaret O'Leary, in 1929.

'Arthur Shields was getting on in years and the company was short of juvenile leads. The American tours were approaching and Lennox Robinson told me to hold on. So I stayed, and went to America with F J McCormick, Barry Fitzgerald, Shields, Maureen Delany and other members of the company. That first tour has become a jumble in my memory, but I recall that we went to Los Angeles where actors like Ralph Bellamy asked if they could come on the stage for the crowd scenes of *The Playboy* in which Shields was playing Christy Mahon. John Ford came backstage to meet us all. At that time he was directing *The Informer* with Victor McLaglen. He asked me if I would come out to the studios and play a bit part. I got permission to play one of the gunmen in the film during the day and continue in the play at night. I did about five or six days' work, which was very remunerative at that time, and became friendly with Ford and appeared in a number of his pictures afterwards.'

O'Dea went out to Hollywood again with the Abbey company later in the thirties to appear in *The Plough and the Stars*. This time Barry Fitzgerald stayed on, but O'Dea said: 'I had no idea of settling there. I just wanted to be in Ireland.' The actor who influenced him in this was F J McCormick. 'I thought him the greatest actor on the Irish stage, indeed on any stage. I don't think he realised his potential in the world of theatre, or if he did he had my thing about being at home in Ireland. He wanted to be here, even though he had proved with *Odd Man Out* that the world was clamouring for him. He was still in the Abbey when Siobhán and I left.'

Yeats and Robinson also made an impression on him. 'I gave poetry recitals for them which included Yeats's poems. Yeats would come in and read his poetry. I thought him a very bad reader. He

44

droned and monotoned with his head moving from side to side. It was monotonous to me.'

O'Dea made films for Carol Reed, Henry Hathaway and, of course, Ford. He was with Marilyn Monroe in her first featured film, *Niagara*. 'I found her very conscientious. The studios were promoting her as a sex symbol and she played along with them so far as the public was concerned. She was a very hard worker and always knew her lines and was first on the set in the morning.

'You might have a little scene to yourself that involved some business, with only the camera crew around you. When it was over Marilyn would come out of a corner and walk over to compliment you. She was watching and learning, I think.

'The first day I met her was outside the city morgue in a Canadian town beside the Falls. I was playing a detective and she was arriving to identify a body. They indicated the car we were both to get out of. It was a long shot, so I walked down the street and got into the car, and she was sitting there. I told her "Miss Monroe, I'm Denis O'Dea". She said: "You're an Irish actor. Are you married?" When I told her I was, she asked: "Somebody well known!" "She will be well known," I answered. "That's very loyal of you," Marilyn remarked.'

When Siobhán McKenna was playing in *The Chalk Garden* on one side of Broadway and Denis O'Dea was in *The Righteous Are Bold* on the other side, Marilyn went backstage to meet Siobhán. 'Siobhán spoke to her about Ireland and invited her to visit us in Dublin. Marilyn said she would like to, and that she would keep in touch, but we never kept in touch.'

Today Siobhán McKenna and her husband Denis O'Dea live in a large Victorian house in Dublin with their son Donnacha, a Mexico Olympics swimmer; they have never set up home outside Ireland. Siobhán made an occasional return to the Abbey Theatre in the late sixties – as the Countess in *The Cherry Orchard* and as Cass in Brian Friel's *The Loves of Cass McGuire*. In the autumn of 1970 she achieved an especial ambition to present her favourite Irish writers to audiences outside Ireland when her one-woman show, *Here Are Ladies*, was staged first at Oxford and then at London's Criterion Theatre. It was after the run of this show that we talked with her.

*　　*　　*

Micheál Mac Liammóir used to say to me: 'What language do you pray in, Siobhán?' And I would always answer, 'In Irish'. I think it important that my father was born in Cork, my mother in Longford, that I was born in Belfast and grew up in Galway and that I now live in Dublin. I don't believe in provincialism; the whole of Ireland is very precious to me. In Belfast I had an Irish-speaking nurse, also called Siobhán, from Kerry, and my first language was Irish. My first visit to a theatre was in Belfast to see *Cinderella*. I remember everything was white and sparkling and I really believed I saw the pumpkin turn into a coach. The atmosphere we knew in Belfast was Gaelic; Belfast had the best traditional dancers in Ireland and we used to go to the Gaelic League. When the nuns there heard that we were moving to Galway they asked my parents to let me make my First Communion before I was taken to 'the pagan West'; and, of course, they were quite right because Galway is beautifully pagan. When we were living in Belfast I would spend my summers in Longford, where my mother and grandmother had been born. I remember Christmases in Longford with candles in the windows and walking to Mass. When we went to Galway I would divide my summers between Longford and Innishmaan on the Aran Islands and Carraroe in Connemara. I was seven when I first went to Innishmaan. They still talk there about the wild things I used to do like jumping off rooftops shouting: 'Tuig liomsa ag eitilt!' (Look at me flying!) It was the Innishmaan sport to see what wild donkeys could throw me, and not one of them could.

In Galway we lived in Rahoon, outside the city, in a great old rambling house called Fort Eyre. It was really the countryside and I used to go to school through the fields. My father was a great man for making you learn through fun. When we were small he would read to us in Irish and French and he would always start with a comic story like Jimín Mháire Thadhg; so one never baulked at another language, we just took it for granted. We always spoke Irish at home and we had an Irish-speaking housekeeper. Her name was Máire Ni Giolla Mhairtín, and when I first translated Barrie's *Mary Rose* into Irish I should have given her credit. She wouldn't speak one word of English. I remember discussing *Mary Rose* with her and asking her how one would say in Irish 'to lay a ghost'. She insisted: '*Ní beidh Bearla ar bith sa teach seo.*' (There will be no English in this house). I then had to make a literal translation for her and she agreed or disagreed, and that was the way I worked on my translation.

Not all of Galway was Gaelic. There was an enormously tall man named Claude Chavasse who wore a kilt and wouldn't speak one word of English. We used to go to the same sweet shop at Cook's Corner. He would ask for '*Bosca cipíní*' (a box of matches). The two ladies who ran the shop would be in despair and I would have to translate for them. People knew we were a Gaelic-speaking family and very often I would be pursued by the Henry Street kids as I cycled through Galway shouting: 'Siobhán Chavasse! Siobhán Chavasse!' I would be mortified and would say to my father: 'Oh, it's terrible what I have to suffer for this Irish language!' But really I never cared what anybody thought of me or my family, and I still don't. It was good training, because when you go into the theatre you must stop caring what anybody thinks of you.

In Belfast I would dress up in my mother's clothes and when I got a paintbox it wasn't on paper that I used to put the paints but on my face. In Rahoon there was an old barn and about a dozen of us children used to congregate there, some of us as performers, the rest as audience. We had a sort of stage rigged up with two old blankets for a curtain. We would begin by announcing: 'Today's story is . . .' and then we would make up our own dialogue spontaneously. I had a penchant for playing villains and my sister for heroines. At the Dominican Convent in Galway they used to annoy me by telling me I had a beautiful voice. They would put me into pious school plays. I remember having to play Charity. 'Love on and falter not, for he will come. Love is all-powerful, so do not fear.' I used to get the giggles. I told the nuns I didn't like those parts, so we kids put on our own play and invited them to the performance. We made them pay. They were amazed because the play was not lovey and sweet and religious.

I was expelled from school because I went out to the University rag. I was then sent to the St Louis Convent in Monaghan where they told me to choose and direct a play, although they could not have known anything about my barn acting. They always put me in school operettas, although I couldn't sing. A priest who used to come to perfect the productions told me when I was sixteen that I would make a marvellous comedienne for the Abbey Theatre. My father was outraged at the thought. I never wanted to be an actress; it was just part of one's childhood fun. But when I went to Galway University on a scholarship I joined the city's Gaelic theatre – the Taibhdhearc. I played Lady Macbeth at the age of seventeen with a round face and two long plaits. My very first performance was an Irish princess in a pageant. Walter Macken, who was directing the theatre, said to me afterwards: 'You died so gracefully.' When he asked me if I would do *Mary Rose* I told him I would translate it but not play in it. I was a clown, I said, and couldn't possibly play Barrie's heroine. Yet people still talk about *Mary Rose* in Galway, because once I played the part I really believed I had been stolen away by the fairies. We all believed it at the Taibhdhearc and Walter Macken got a real fairy tree for the production.

My mother's attitude towards the theatre was mine, but my father thought I had brains; he believed I had the makings of a mathematician. I did well at mathematics, but I suspect it was because of his teaching and not my ability. I could not bear arithmetic and still can't; this shows in my acting because I enjoy rehearsing rather than performing. I enjoy the problem time in rehearsal, especially with a new play. People tell me to do the classics, but I feel I have an equal duty to present-day writers. In a way I don't care if a new play flops because the author and the actors have been brought one step further. I like an author to be around, although most actors don't. Sometimes I'll tell an author what I think he means and he may say:

'You're absolutely right.' A good author is writing half the time under inspiration and doesn't analyse what he is writing.

Although I liked having Brian Friel around for *The Loves of Cass McGuire*, he thinks it is up to the actors to a great extent. After the dress rehearsal he said: 'I wonder, should we cut some of those stories Cass tells?' I told him: 'If you cut her vulgarity you won't touch anyone's heart. You wrote this character and those stories came out. If you cheat by removing some of them she is not a whole person. I heard those stories when I was a youngster; they are corny and very innocent; but it is why Cass tells them and how she tells them and to whom she tells them that is important.'

I came to the Abbey Theatre from Galway in 1944. The first English play in which Denis and I appeared together was *The End House* by Joseph Tomelty. Two years later we were married and we began making films. While Denis was in *Hungry Hill*, I was in *Odd Man Out*. When I arrived at the Abbey Theatre Barry Fitzgerald, Sara Allgood and others of that period had gone and, unfortunately, Yeats and Lady Gregory had gone. But I feel that the actors who were there when I arrived were far greater because they were now professionals and had the best of both worlds. I am not denying talents such as Barry Fitzgerald's, but I had never seen him on the stage and couldn't imagine him being anything like F J McCormick. McCormick was the greatest actor I have ever clapped eyes on. And when I saw May Craig in *The Words on the Window Pane* by Yeats, who had directed her in the play originally, she was overwhelming. And there were other extraordinary people like Cyril Cusack, Brid Ni Loinsigh, Liam Redmond, Harry Brogan, Fred Johnson, Denis and Mick Dolan, who in his own way was as perfect as McCormick. There were so many talented people that I could never understand how I managed to get my nose in edgeways.

When I first went to the Abbey it wasn't in my nature to call anybody 'Mister' or 'Missus' or 'Miss' because it was the Galway tradition always to call people by their first names to show that one loved them. My father was always called Eoin. But I respected the Abbey Players and if I went up to the Green Room and a senior player, as they were termed, was there I would think twice before

49

I went in. They called me 'Miss McKenna', which I found very strange and foreign, and then I remember Mick Dolan suddenly calling me 'Siobhán'. You had to earn your place.

During my first year at the Abbey I was asked to star in a film, *I See A Dark Stranger*, which Deborah Kerr later did. I went to McCormick and he advised me: 'Please stay for at least three years. You could become an overnight star, but I also think you could become a real actress.' I turned the part down, although it was a leading part, and my first screen appearance was to be a tiny one in *Hungry Hill*. I was able to do it during the Abbey holidays when Denis did *Odd Man Out*. We had arranged to get married in Galway at this time and when they wanted to build up my part in *Hungry Hill*, I made the excuse that I wanted to go to Paris with my father because he hadn't had a holiday for a long time.

In those days I used to read the notices. If I got a good notice I would be up the stairs to Ernest Blythe's office. I used to get five shilling rises and within the space of two years I was on top salary. When I was earning two pounds five shillings a week my flat was costing me fifteen shillings and that was simply because my landlady in Northbrook Road liked me.

She gave me a marvellous room with wood panelling and a big fire. I never told my father and mother what I was earning. I had come up to Dublin to study for my MA and had drifted into the Abbey. My mother used to send me farm eggs because they were fresh; she never realised she was sending me my food. I would live on bread and butter and egg and tea and on payday treat myself to a bun in the Country Shop in Stephen's Green. When I became ill my cousin came to see me. I had been in bed for three days and when she opened the cupboard it was bare.

You had to supply your own clothes at the Abbey for modern plays. Eithne Dunne, who used to play sophisticated parts, had left when I arrived and they probably thought: 'Well, here's a girl who could dress herself.' May Craig was generous to me and I shall not forget her kindness. She would give me her pearls, and when I played the Woman from Rathmines in *The Plough and the Stars* she gave me a long fur coat and made me a hat with a feather in it.

McCormick and Cusack and Denis were in that production. When I played a very sophisticated part I wore my little black dress and May, who had been sent a present of a hat by friends in New York, said: 'I have the perfect thing for you, Siobhán.' It was a toque of little flowers in pink, mauve and blue which she set on one side of my head. I remember it so well. But I told her: 'But you can't give me this. You haven't worn it yet. People will say "Look at May Craig in the hat Siobhán was wearing in that play!"' So she went out and bought pieces of tulle and a kind of crown and turned it into a new hat for me.

I think actors should go abroad for experience. In those days once you left the Abbey you didn't come back, and that was much too harsh. Yet when Denis and I got married and went away to make films they were very amicable. We never left the Abbey officially. We were never rebels. We have both gone back to play there. When we were offered contracts in Hollywood, Denis thought it might be pleasant for a while, especially to have one's own swimming-pool and all that. But I wouldn't consider it. I had heard the stories about Sara Allgood and Barry Fitzgerald, of how they had gone out for one picture and found the life so comfortable that they hadn't come back. Apart from Barry Fitzgerald, the great ones settled down to playing little parts. Years later I went to Hollywood to make a television film. It was neither city nor country and the smog was terrible. I thought: 'My God, where did I get my wisdom?'

My early films were made in England. When I came to make *The Adventurers* with Denis Price and Jack Hawkins there was a slump in British films and budgets had been cut. They were trying to do scenes in one take, and as this was a period story and my hairstyle had to be exact, they kept rushing me in and out under hair-dryers. In a previous film, *The Lost People*, I had worn rags, so for *The Adventurers* they gave me a dozen dresses, all boned, all uncomfortable, and, considering I was supposed to be a doctor's daughter in Africa, unpractical. I was in agony. My character would really have had only a couple of blouses and skirts, but I was changing costumes three times a day and trying to discard the dresses with the wardrobe girl. They insisted on my wearing a glamorous make-up, which was also very untrue. I swore I would never make another film. That's it, I thought. I had never left the theatre, but now I felt I should play in Shakespeare. I had earned a reputation in London in a play by Anouilh, *Fading Mansions*, for Olivier. But to establish oneself as a respected actress in England one must play Shakespeare. I went to Stratford-on-Avon for nine months and have never regretted it.

Having done my stint at Stratford, I thought I would return to Dublin and work at home again. I had played Pegeen Mike in *The Playboy of the Western World* at the Edinburgh Festival with Liam Gannon as a wonderful Christy Mahon. It occurred to me how marvellous it would be to do the play with Cyril Cusack, who had been the Playboy in an Abbey production in which I played Sara Tansey.

At this time Cyril had been asked to bring a play to the Paris Festival. I got in touch with him and Brendan Smith and we decided that *The Playboy of the Western World* would be a good choice for Paris. Cyril Cusack had a reputation for being difficult, but when people asked me during rehearsals: 'How are you getting on with Cyril?' I didn't really know what they meant. I suppose they considered that I, too, was temperamental. After Paris, we toured Ireland with *Playboy*. In some small towns the people believed they were coming to see a cowboy film.

It was during that tour that our manager, Bill Ryan, told me that Hilton Edwards and Micheál Mac Liammóir were in the doldrums. They were not attracting audiences. The whole shape of theatre was changing at the time; everything was much more costly and you could not afford to have a flop. Hilton was very honest. 'I don't bring them in, dear,' he said. 'Just the old ladies rattling their teacups.'

He asked me to join him in a season. We played *The Loves of Four Colonels* and *Anna Christie*, and we took *Anna Christie* off to packed houses. We began to think of another play. Hilton went home and read the whole of *St Joan* over lunch. But I suggested *The Apple Cart* because there was a better part for Hilton in it. 'We'll do *St Joan*,' he said.

They hadn't got much money. Michael O'Herlihy, who designed the sets, was given a fiver to spend. He collected old flats they had stored away and painted them black and grey with blobs of red and gold which would pick up the light in certain scenes, and he added a font here and a platform there. The rest was Hilton's lighting.

They took the play off after five months. I was fascinated by the character of Joan. I had already played the part in my own translation at the Taibhdhearc in Galway. I had made some films at the time and Seán Ó Horáin, a good friend, asked me to come back to the Taibhdhearc. At this time Ingrid Bergman was in a play by Maxwell Anderson about an actress playing St Joan, and Seán asked me if I would do the play for Galway; but I told him I would do Shaw's *St Joan*. The Taibhdhearc was always looking for ways to avoid paying royalties; at that time the actors weren't paid, the theatre just didn't make any money and they had a subsidy so tiny it could only be called love money. When they asked Shaw for his permission he wrote back to say that anybody who was mad enough to translate his plays into the Irish language, of course, didn't have to pay royalties. I sat down and began to translate the play; it took me four or five weeks. Shaw was dying at the time and I had a desperate longing to go over to Ayot St Lawrence to see him. That is a strange thing about the Irish. It may sound theatrical, but Shaw died on the night I finished translating the Epilogue. A week later we were in rehearsals.

I had become interested in *St Joan* when I was studying the Hundred Years' War at school. When we came to the last chapter of the history book, which was written by Professor Liam O'Briain, who was to play a great part in my life, we read that the Hundred Years' War was not to end until a young girl named Jeanne d'Arc came on the scene at the age of seventeen. I thought this very abrupt and couldn't wait until the following year to find out more about her. I didn't have much pocket money, yet I went down and bought the second volume of the history book in Galway. I was fascinated and I have been reading about Joan ever since. When I first came to play the part I modelled Joan on my mother who had this extraordinary intimacy with God. She would be talking and would suddenly turn away from us and say: 'Now, look here, I have never refused anything You asked me. I am just insisting that You do this one thing for me.' She would talk to God quite frankly, and extraordinary things would happen. My father went from Belfast to Galway as a University lecturer in mathematics and when the Chair of Mathematical Physics became vacant my mother told him: 'You must go for that, Eoin.' 'Don't be silly woman,' he answered, but he went. My mother told him he would get thirteen votes. 'Don't be talking through your hat,' he said. 'I'll get about eight.' But she insisted: 'You'll get thirteen because I've heard thirteen Masses this morning.' That evening about six o'clock we were sitting down to tea when there was a knock at the door. My father, all nerves, went to open it and we heard a voice saying: 'Congratulations.' My mother rose like a queen from the table and sailed out to ask: 'How many votes?' My sister Nancy and I were stunned to hear: 'Thirteen.' It was all totally real to my mother. Shaw's definition of a miracle is something wonderful to those who witness it and simple to those who perform it. I am sure it has something to do with prayer, and prayer could be just wishing. My mother had this extraordinary faith and complete acceptance, which used to get on my father's nerves sometimes. I remember him turning to her one day when she said: 'Welcome be the will of God', and remarking: 'Greta, do you know what it is? If this house fell down on top of us you would say "Welcome be the will of God." ' And my mother insisted 'I would, because there would be nothing else you could say.' She was like Joan; you couldn't answer back because she had this remarkable commonsense.

I think Shaw was Joan. I would love to have seen him play her in a school production. I think he understood her awfully well. Like her, he had this enormous honesty; he always went straight to the point and didn't bother being polite in inverted commas. I think he fell in love with Joan, as I did. Sometimes people would compliment him on a wonderful line in the play, as when Cochon asks Joan during the Trial Scene if she is in the state of Grace. She answers: 'If I am not, may God bring me to it. If I am, may God keep me in it.' A brilliant answer, but the lines are from the Trial papers in Paris. Shaw used to pretend to be jealous when the great lines his friends picked out were the words Joan had actually spoken. He once said that he had written the play as though Joan were looking over his shoulder. When I translated the play into Irish Joan spoke for me as if she were a Connemara girl. The only time I found the translation difficult was in Act Four when Joan isn't on and they talk about her in a sort of intellectual argument.

I think Hilton Edwards made a grave mistake in doing a television film at the time he was asked to bring the play to London. I was disappointed because I liked the Dublin cast so much. Jack Mac-Gowran's Dauphin was every bit as good as my Joan. He fitted in with everything Shaw had asked for, even to his knobbly knees. In all the productions of *St Joan* in which I have played, and I have been in about seven productions in different parts of the world, I do not think that first Irish cast was ever excelled.

Just before we took the play off in Dublin in 1954, John Fernald of the Arts Theatre came over from London to invite me to play at his theatre. I suggested he should present *St Joan*. He said it would be extremely costly and that he could not take over the Irish cast. A couple of months elapsed before he telephoned to say: 'I've got the money if you can play for twelve a week.' My father remarked: 'My secretary earns that.' I said: 'Yes, but your secretary can't play St Joan.'

I had been paid twelve thousand pounds for my first featured film, *Daughter of Darkness*. Now I went back to play for 'twelve a week'. London was even more enthusiastic than Dublin. Churchill came to see the play one evening; he was a great Shaw fan. I remember the actors saying: 'Winston is out front.' I tried to keep calm. I asked, 'What's that got to do with me?' They said: 'Well, he IS a great man.' I said: 'I know he's a great man, but I hate being told so.' Then I heard on the tannoy a murmur from the auditorium and suddenly there was silence. I could hear the audience rising to its feet and cheering. My legs were like water. I thought, yes, he is a great man. He was sitting in the front row because he was so small he could not have seen over anybody's head. The dreadful words I had to say about the English in the play seemed to be directed at him.

For years, whenever I have been in London, I have gone to Ayot St Lawrence and walked round Shaw's house and the grounds. I always feel sad that he is not there. Shaw has never been a great success in Dublin, yet Shaw revivals in London always seem to succeed. It's ironic. I think people in Ireland have written such inaccurate things about Shaw that other people believed them. When we were neutral during the war he came to our defence; and he came to the defence of Roger Casement. When a Dublin dustman sent him a little silver shamrock, Shaw wrote to him: 'You should not spend your money on me. But I shall put your shamrock on my watch chain, and there it shall remain until I myself drop off it.'

After something like seven months *St Joan* was taken off in London playing to standing audiences. I was to go to America with the play, but by then they were doing Anouilh's *Joan* and they were afraid that one play might kill the other. Instead, I did *The Chalk Garden* by Enid Bagnold first, and that ran for twelve months until it was taken off because the producer had a row with the theatre. There was a rule that after the end of a run you could not work for six months, but Equity waived the rule when I wrote to tell them that I was not an employee, but an employer of fifty actors. *St Joan*, I said, would not be done without me. So we did the play and the Americans packed the theatre. When I played Joan in Paris, Micheál Mac Liammóir was the Dauphin. I wanted Jack MacGowran for the part, but Micheál told me he could be the greatest Dauphin. 'You just have a thing about Jackie,' he said. I read the reviews with great trepidation. This was Joan's own country, but even *Figaro* said I was right for the part.

Most people don't realise that actors are never smug even when they are in a big success. When I first played St Joan in London at the Arts Theatre I was very depressed in spite of the reviews. I had a terrible longing to know what Shaw himself would have thought of my performance. One night I went into the theatre and saw stacks of letters on my dressing-room table. I suddenly picked up one of the letters, for what reason I don't know, and it was from a man who dealt with manuscripts. He had seen my performance and thought I might like to have as a little gift a page of a letter written by Shaw to

Gabriel Pascal. It was to the effect that he had considered me for a film of *St Joan*, which I could not understand because he had never seen me and I had never met him; but he had written: 'Nonsense. Get in touch with Siobhán McKenna.' His secretary had written 'Shuban' and Shaw had crossed this out and written in 'Siobhán' with Gaelic a accent. I said: 'Oh God, this is my answer. Shaw has spoken to me.' Then Lady Astor, who had been a great friend of Shaw's, came in to see the play. She was in tears after the performance. She said to me: 'If only the old boy could see you.' Wendy Hiller, whom Shaw had directed, wrote me a letter. She said I had done everything in the play that Shaw had asked her to do, and now she understood exactly what he had wanted. All this may sound vain; I do not mean it that way, but the people who knew Shaw meant an awful lot to me.

I will always put the theatre before anything else. Acting on the stage may not be as permanent as acting in films, but it's satisfying to be able to work in your own country. My living in Ireland has conflicted with offers from abroad. When they used to offer me seven-year contracts I always turned them down. No, I would think, this is not what I am about. I love my country and the Irish with all their faults. Even a strongminded person like me could perhaps have been turned into somebody else in Hollywood, and I did not want that. Nationalism is an extension of loving your own first. I once had a television discussion with James Thurber and Noël Coward on humour, of all things. I was here in Dublin, Thurber in New York and Coward in the Bahamas. Ed Murrow was linking the programme but we could not see one another. I like Noël and we have had a few good evenings together in New York. We were getting on fine when I heard him say he was fond of the Irish, although they were unreliable like veal. I said: 'Like what?' He said: '*Veal.*' I said: 'Sorry, Noël, I can't hear you.' 'VEAL!' he repeated, and I roared with laughter. He then said that there were thugs and corner boys among the Irish who delighted in blowing up little old ladies posting letters in English letterboxes. I'm afraid he got it from me then. I told him I knew of no little old ladies who had been blown up and that those he called thugs and corner boys were idealists, many of them teachers. There was a furore from the Stormont Government and questions in the House of Commons. Lord Brookeborough, the Stormont Prime Minister, said he would like to put me across his knee and spank me. The newspaper people were 'phoning and calling at my door and the news bulletins on the radio kept referring to 'the Irish actress', Siobhán McKenna'. Donnacha would look up from his homework and say to me: 'I don't know why they take so much notice of you.'

Noël and I are still friends. I don't care what anybody says about me, but to label the Irish as being unreliable like veal is just not true. I had lunch in Stormont recently, and when I went up the steps they were staring at me but when I came down they were beaming because I hadn't blown them up. I dislike violence, but I like truth.

I love all our writers because they spoil you. If you are brought up on a diet of Irish writers, other writing seems a famine by comparison. I think M J Molloy is our most exquisite stylist in the theatre since Synge, but I think some of our writers today are a little repressed by what they think people will say of them. A schoolteacher imagines if he writes a book he cannot teach school any more. The old Gaelic literature was marvellously honest and Rabelaisian and yet had a spiritual content. We are in a transitional stage as a people, because when you meet the Irish in a pub you know they are not the sort of people to be repressed.

When I came to Dublin first I could afford only the gallery in the Gaiety and it was crowded with 'shawlies' and students. Hilton and Micheál brought them in with Shakespeare. But these days for a great part of the year only variety can fill our theatres. I once played St Joan in the round in Philadelphia, and I think this is the direction in which theatre is moving. I would like to see Sean Kenny design a great theatre in the round for Ireland. I think that would be good for our playwrights who are still writing for boxes.

Downstairs there's a roomful of scripts. I often look at them and wonder how many I would like to have done. I thought about Juno for twenty years before I allowed myself to play the part. I modelled my Juno on a Dublin lady who used to work at the Gaiety Theatre and who always wore brown. I feel guilty that I have not played more often in Gaelic. When a London critic once wrote that I promised to become Britain's greatest tragedienne, I became very upset, apart from the fact that I like comedy as much as tragedy. But Denis said: 'Oh, you are very foolish.'

5

❦   ❦   ❦

Johnston : 'Did you know Yeats ?   And did you lunch with Shaw?'

DENIS O'DEA HAD portrayed Darrell Blake, the young revolutionary, in the first production of *The Moon in the Yellow River* by Denis Johnston at the Abbey Theatre in 1931. F J McCormick was Dobelle, the Englishman who had come to live in Ireland, and Eileen Crowe his eccentric sister, Columba. The play was directed by Lennox Robinson.

This period, from the late twenties to the middle thirties, in the Dublin theatre was notable for a profusion of interesting dramatists: Robinson, Paul Vincent Carroll, George Shiels, T C Murray, Louis D'Alton, St John Ervine, Frank O'Connor and Brinsley Mac-Namara. Shaw's plays were popular, so were O'Casey's. *The Moon in the Yellow River* was the second play written by Johnston, a versatile young lawyer and theatre producer. He was, however, unhappy with that first production, just as he was dissatisfied nearly forty years later when the play was revived in the new Abbey Theatre. He complained to us, with a hint of frustration, that he had not been invited, although in Dublin, to attend the rehearsals. He did not wish to direct the players in any way, but would like, he said, to have talked about the production with the director, 'They made very little of my play,' he said, 'and I am disappointed'.

In a voice which betrayed a trace of American he talked to us with great lucidity, sitting in an old bungalow he had rented with his wife in the Dublin suburb of Foxrock. A tall, greyhaired figure, approaching seventy, Johnston displayed an outstanding memory for personalities and events. Even then he was planning a return to lecturing in an American college during the summer.

Denis Johnston has written six plays, in addition to his books *In Search of Swift* and the autobiographical *Nine Rivers to Jordan*, for which latter book he drew on his experiences as a war correspondent. Many Dubliners expected that he would become a director of the Abbey Theatre. In 1962, when strongly favoured for the appointment as Director-General of the Irish broadcasting and television service, he was passed over in favour of a Swede.

When not lecturing in America, Johnston lives in Alderney in the Channel Islands. In a preface to his collected plays he wrote: 'It is necessary to correct a widespread impression, put about by unscrupulous enemies, that I died of some unspecified disease in the summer of 1933.'

Revivals of his plays have been infrequent in Dublin; until its revival in 1970, *The Moon in the Yellow River* had not been performed on the Dublin stage since the forties. Unlike most of the dramatists of his time Johnston was not totally involved with the Abbey. His first play, *The Old Lady Says No!* had its first production by Hilton Edwards' and Micheál Mac Liammóir's Gate Theatre, of which Johnston became a director in 1931. He remains one of the few surviving dramatists who contributed to the Irish theatre in the twenties and thirties. As late as 1958 the Abbey presented his play about the 1916 Rising, *The Scythe and the Sunset*, which a few months earlier had been given its first production at Cambridge, Massachusetts. Denis Johnston intends to go on writing; he intends, too, to live in Ireland again one day.

* * *

I had no ambition to be a literary man. I assumed that I would be a lawyer; my father had been a lawyer and he wanted me to be a lawyer too. But when I went to America about the age of twenty-two to study law at Harvard I became interested in the theatre. I had been at school in Dublin from 1908 until the beginning of the First World War when I spent a year at a school in Edinburgh from which I was brought back, probably because of food rationing. My father came from Magherafelt in County Derry and my mother from Belfast, and my mother's people from Cork; but I myself am a Dubliner.

I was always a theatregoer, but I became interested in theatrical production when I went to America. I read a lot of plays when maybe I should have been reading law. Eugene O'Neill was being discovered about that time and I had discovered Shaw. Until then I had played the usual sports and rowed in boat crews. I suppose I was a late starter. When I came back from America and began studying at King's Inns I joined the Dublin Drama League and acted and later directed for them. I am a very bad actor; I don't think I'm a bad director; and I was more interested in the processes of direction than acting. When I began 'devilling' in London I met Sean O'Casey and we used to go to the London Gate Theatre together. He told me his views on the theatre and I told him mine. He was a very amusing person and the best company you could possibly ask for. O'Casey held the centre of the stage as he was entitled to do. He was a very good mimic, acting out the stories he told you. He was really Joxer Daly. It rather irritated me that a man of such enormous ability should write in his later days a play like *Within the Gates*, in which he tried to make use of the technique of Expressionism which he and I had discovered together in the London Gate Theatre. His attitude towards those who criticised him was childish in many ways, as were his views on politics. But O'Casey was a very likeable person and his cynicism towards Ireland was that of a man who loved his country but wanted it to be more to his heart's desire.

It was in London around this time that I saw Claude Rains in George Kaiser's play *From Morn Till Midnight*, which I subsequently directed at the Peacock in Dublin. I think that must have been one of Dublin's first experiences of Expressionism. When I returned from London around 1927 I was called to the Irish Bar. I continued to direct plays for the Drama League. I directed Barry Fitzgerald and F J McCormick and actors of that sort and was subsequently to direct them in *King Lear* at the Abbey Theatre. That was the Abbey's first effort at Shakespeare. Some people said that Yeats invited me to direct *Lear* because he had refused to present *The Old Lady Says No!* But it wasn't for that reason at all. It was because the Abbey had never played Shakespeare and wanted a director who could approach the play from a new angle; at least that is what Yeats told me. I used to sit near him in the Abbey Theatre. To me he was a major poet with a floppy tie. It never occurred to me at the time how remarkable it was to be sitting beside him. George Russell was just a nice old man with a beard: the 'hairy fairy' as he was called. I don't drop names as a rule, but in America, where I have been teaching for a good many years, I find myself being regarded with awe by people who ask: 'Did you actually know Yeats? Did you really have lunch with Shaw? What was Lady Gregory like? What was George Russell like?' It must have been an unusually interesting time, but to me all these people were merely citizens of Dublin like myself.

When I wrote *The Old Lady Says No!* in 1926 nobody would stage it. Eventually it was Shelagh Richards who persuaded Hilton Edwards and Micheál Mac Liammóir to produce it. They had to be persuaded, because the play was hard to follow on the page. It wasn't written with any idea other than that a director would want to see what would happen if he attempted certain techniques on the stage. The play was written without any didactic motive; the last thing that emerged from the writing of *The Old Lady* was the point of the play. I had already written a couple of one-act plays as an experiment but *The Old Lady* was the first play I sent to anybody with the idea of having it produced. I had originally submitted it to the Abbey and they received it in a very friendly fashion. Yeats did a lot of work on the script. One of my precious possessions is the first draft of *The Old Lady* with Yeats's marginal notes all the way through and lines crossed out and other lines substituted. He told me that audiences would not accept more than an hour and a quarter of the play, so I got it down to an hour and a quarter. Eventually Yeats said to me, 'The play has too many scenes.' Then he thought for a long while, and added, 'And the scenes are too long.'

Yeats did his best for *The Old Lady*, but I have never resented the fact that the Abbey turned the play down. I don't think it was their kind of play; it was definitely a Gate play. I had a deep respect for Yeats for his canons of good taste. When one is young one tends to overwrite. In the first draft of *The Old Lady Says No!* there is the line, 'I have written my name in letters of fire across the page of history.' Yeats crossed this out and substituted, 'I shall be remembered.' I didn't use his corrections, but I recognised the fact that I was overwriting. Despite my respect for Yeats's good taste, I had no particular respect for him as a constructive dramatist. I was aware that he had attempted techniques on the stage which could not be done. Lady Gregory was a much better dramatist, but I didn't much like her personally.

When *The Moon in the Yellow River* was first produced at the Abbey it was gently sabotaged. A very good company can disassociate itself from a play which it doesn't much like. Six or seven years later the Abbey gave a good performance of that play, but when they first produced it Lennox Robinson took it exactly as it was written. It surprised me that he didn't alter a line. The play required sensible alterations, but it may be that Lennox didn't understand it, or perhaps thought it very good. It was on this occasion that Lennox asked me if I wished to use my own name as the author of the play. At that time I was a practising barrister and it was regarded as unprofessional for someone at the Bar, unless he was a complete beginner, to engage in any other business. We looked across the street to the Metropolitan Hall and saw that somebody called E W Tocher was holding a revivalist meeting. I said to Lennox: 'Let's have him on both sides of the street', so we used E W Tocher's name instead of mine on our programme.

During the next five years I moved to and fro between Dublin and London, continuing my practice at the Irish Bar and righting the wrongs in film scripts in London. During those years I wrote *A Bride for the Unicorn*; it was produced in Dublin by the Gate Theatre and

John Huston at his home at St. Cleran's in County Galway.

[*To face page 64*

Hilton Edwards as Herod in Conor Cruise O'Brien's play *King Herod Explains* at the Dublin Theatre Festival.

Richard Harris on location in Mexico for *Major Dundee* with producer Jerry Bressler (*left*).

Eileen Crowe with Harry Brogan in George Shiels' play *Grogan and the Ferret* at the Peacock Theatre, Dublin.

subsequently presented in America. I also wrote a play called *Storm Song* which was produced at the Gate; that was an attempt to write a popular play, something at which I am not very good. In 1936 I joined the BBC. I had seen television coming. It was a medium that few people knew anything about, but I am very much better with things that are just beginning than those that have become routine. I knew I wouldn't get into the BBC by asking: 'Please, may I become a television director?' So I took the first job that came my way, which was a radio scriptwriter with the BBC in Belfast. After a year and a half I was sent to the Corporation's staff college in London. It was then I flung my bomb and announced that what I was really after was television. They said: 'Certainly. Glad to know you. Come on in.' So I went to Alexandra Palace as one of the beginners in television. I was one of the first to write original plays for television. Until then everybody had been adapting existing plays. The idea was that you took a play and said to yourself: 'How can I get it into this keyhole?' That's what they were doing when I started writing plays for the medium. It was exhausting, but exciting. Everything that is now accepted as commonplace was being discovered. Day and night we used to argue violently about the presentation of a play on the small screen. One school of thought believed that television plays were movies on a small screen; another school believed that they were plays viewed through a keyhole. I maintained that television drama was visual broadcasting. Unfortunately, the war came and when it was over I went back to television not as a director but as a programme director.

I became a war correspondent when the war was at a low water mark, after the disasters in the Middle East and the attack on Stalingrad; so that when I arrived in Cairo everybody was packing to go home. I don't know if war changed me as a writer; it certainly changed me as a person. It clarified my ideas about many things and made me discover myself in a way I would never have done otherwise. Of course, war was abhorrent to me; there was nothing more harrowing than the discovery of Buchenwald. On the other hand there was a sense of liberation. The few weeks after Alamein when we were chasing across North Africa, living on enemy loot, were most exciting.

I sent my communiqués by cable, which was not a good way of doing it, or on recordings which I made in the field in a recording truck. The recordings were taken to Cairo by a dispatch rider and put on the air to London where they were re-recorded and then broadcast. At that time there was a controversy in the BBC as to what was a correspondent's job. It amounted to this: Should one stay behind with the generals, sending back situation reports based on the best possible information, or should one go forward to see what it was like? I chose the second course; Richard Dimbleby was the great exponent of the first. I maintained it was insufficient to interview pilots after they had been on a mission; one should go on a mission oneself with them or, better still, carry recording gear on a mission. Quite contrary to instructions I used to get my engineer to take my equipment apart so that I could carry it on a raid and make a running commentary as the flak came up. That is what is memorable to me. Of course, such procedures became commonplace before the war was over. Everybody did it. However, I don't think anybody had done it before me.

I was one of the first correspondents into Buchenwald. I had always taken the line, very common to my generation, that there is no real difference between right and wrong; and now one suddenly came upon the dehumanisation of the race; it was not a question of anger or spite, or anything of that sort, but of absolute evil. That was a profound experience for me.

After the war I came back to London and stayed long enough with the BBC to get the television service going again on what seemed to me to be practical lines. I liked the BBC to the very end, but I disliked London after the war, and I think it would be fair to say that I disliked England after the war. There was a terrible sense of futility and frustration. It seemed a hangover for a country which had just won a war and should not have been behaving in that way. I wanted to get out.

In 1948, I went to America where I worked for the Theater Guild, adapting scripts and doctoring plays. Then I did what everybody does sooner or later in America: I taught college. I found it stimulating. I was a newcomer as a teacher. I was forty-five when I started and each time I went back during the succeeding years I would add whatever I had forgotten in previous years. I was teaching mainly in Ivy League girls' colleges. I found these girls insistent on arguing with you; which I would never have dared to do as a student. This was one of the qualities I liked in them.

I still return to America to lecture. I don't go to the theatre there unless there is something I particularly want to see. I don't much like most of the plays they are writing these days. Some plays I would go to see as a matter of course, but I don't enjoy playgoing as a rule. When I first went to America I was impressed by O'Neill's works and by his extraordinary powers of experiment. I don't think he had much to say, but I liked his plays and I liked the man himself. When I met him in his latter days in hospital he was a lovely person, relaxing and entertaining. There was no performance. You talked to him without wondering what you ought to say. I don't much like Arthur Miller's plays, although I think *Death of a Salesman* is a brilliant work from the point of view of technique. It is a good play to use to teach students how to write drama. The playwright who interests me more is Albee. He has a facile mind. But I don't think his dialogue is as good as Pinter's, which is quite fascinating.

In the thirties *The Moon in the Yellow River* was produced on Broadway before it was seen in London. It had what the agents call a mixed reception; it was appreciated by half the critics and cursed by the other half. The publicity for the play consisted of the publication in parallel columns of opposite views by the critics. When the play had its first production at the Abbey Theatre it received a good notice in the *Irish Times*. I sent the notice to Bernard Shaw and asked if I could see him. To my great surprise I was invited to lunch. I suppose he considered me as somebody coming from the same stable as himself.

I went hoping to discuss my play with him. We talked at great length about his re-writing of *Coriolanus*, about how *Caesar and Cleopatra* had been produced in Vienna and various other matters. It was only when I was going down in the lift afterwards that it struck

67

me that what we had not discussed was my play. I thought to myself that it only goes to show that great men won't do anything for you: they ask you to lunch and nothing happens. But it was the opposite with Shaw. Most celebrities would have said that they greatly enjoyed my play and that they must do this and that, and then done nothing. Shaw never mentioned my play, but he had it staged at the Malvern Festival that summer. That was how it arrived in England after its production at the Abbey. It was presented at Malvern by the Birmingham Repertory and was then brought to London by the Malvern Festival people, first to the Westminster, where I directed it myself, and it then transferred to the Haymarket and later to the Duchess. *The Moon in the Yellow River* was well received in London by the kind of audiences I wanted to like it; it was not received well by the kind of audiences I am not concerned about. That may sound an arrogant statement, but I do write for a certain type of audience.

When I met Shaw on later occasions he used to talk about O'Casey to me. He had a great regard for him; a rather absurd regard in some respects. He would say to me that the second act of *The Silver Tassie* was one of the greatest pieces of writing for the stage. To my mind it is an interesting act, but not among the greatest ever written. It is Expressionistic, and Shaw liked that.

Shaw's whole life was an act, really; a very good act. He was not great company. I always imagined that Shaw would be a wonderful person to talk to, but at the time I came to know him Shaw was an old man, and you had to be careful that he didn't think you were trying to get something from him. He was surrounded by people all of whom were trying to get something from him, and you had to take time and trouble in reassuring Shaw that you wanted nothing. Once you satisfied him on this point he would relax; but you had to do this, and that was tiresome. I prefer celebrated people with whom you do not have to act. However, they are very few, though there are some. De Valera is one, for instance. I have always found 'Dev' extremely easy to talk to because you never have to act in front of him.

During my formative years I was influenced greatly by H G Wells, particularly by his *Outline of History*. I was also influenced considerably by Wilde and, of course, enormously by Shaw, as most of us were. We were all standing on Shaw's shoulders. Having got over the initial annoyance of not knowing quite what he was talking about, one realises that Shaw is so plain and so obvious that nowadays one finds him a bore.

In the middle twenties the Abbey was an influence. At some stage in our lives we discover the world of the spirit through books or personalities. Having been a conventional schoolboy and undergraduate I made this discovery through the Abbey Theatre. I was a hanger-on in the Green Room. I knew all the actors, and it was much more easygoing at the Abbey than it is now. You could walk into the theatre and up to the Green Room to talk to your friends and nobody would stop you. After a play I would sit up all night talking with 'Boss' Shields whilst we ate bacon and eggs in his room.

It has always been my great ambition to sit on the Abbey's Board of Directors. To this day I have never made it. On one occasion I was asked if I would come back to the Abbey and be their director; it was the very time I had accepted a job as a television director at the BBC, and I would not have wanted to give up the chance of going into television. I think the Abbey didn't invite me to join the Board because various people had said no. I think Yeats would have let me in. I don't think Lady Gregory would, and I believe Lennox Robinson was largely responsible for my not getting into the Abbey. I think Yeats was both a great poet and a great man. He was undoubtedly a colossal figure. The more one reads his later writings the more important they seem. It is the other way round with Shaw. Yeats's *Sailing to Byzantium* and his later plays, *Purgatory*, a very difficult but fascinating play, and particularly his comedy *The Player Queen*, are works of importance to me. Yeats and Eliot grow in my mind just as Auden does the opposite. Yeats and Lady Gregory had the remarkable gift of creating a writers' theatre, which is the best kind of theatre. The trouble with the Gate, although it did brilliant work, was that it was run by actors for actors.

One of the peculiarities of Dublin is that it produces a large number of competent actors. They must be directed, and more than that they must have a producer. In my day there was Yeats and he, as I said, established a canon. Yeats could say to any writer: 'You can't do that.' And the writer would go away with his tail between his legs. Nobody can say that today. There are many writers today just as good as T C Murray or Brinsley MacNamara or George Shiels who were writing the standard works performed all through the twenties and thirties. One looks back on that period and thinks: 'Wasn't it marvellous?' But what sort of plays were they doing? *Look at the Heffernans*. Many such plays were good in their own way and writers are writing good plays in their own way today, but they have to be better.

Looking back on life I like the fact that I have been associated with theatre people. Actors and actresses are the best company I know. I liked Barry Fitzgerald very much and 'Boss' Shields was a good friend of mine. McCormick was not an awfully interesting person off the stage – he was very concerned with the condition of his stomach and he loved his radio – but he was a very good sort. But it is rather distant from me now. For the past few years I have lived in Alderney in the Channel Islands and each time I come back to Dublin I find it has changed just as the rest of the world has changed. Each time I return I park my car further and further from the centre of town and each time Dublin seems less entertaining with fewer interesting people.

I was brought up as an oldfashioned Home Ruler. My father stood for Parliament in the 1910 election as a Home Rule Liberal and I always assumed that liberalism was the basis of all political thought. I believed that progress must be good and conservatism bad. I talked a good deal about politics in the Cambridge Union. I became President of the Union on the strength of my attack on the Black and Tans, which appealed to the English conscience. On the strength of one speech they swept me into the Presidency. I became a little cynical at the time of the Civil War and since then I have not been interested in politics. During the 1916 Rising our house in Lansdowne Road was occupied by rebels who held it for three days.

We were on good terms with them, despite the fact that they would not let us go. They were nice fellows and I was deeply moved by 1916. In fact, I tried to join the IRA and couldn't get in. You just couldn't turn up at Harcourt Street and ask to join them; they would tell you to go to hell. Since the Civil War I haven't been stirred by nationalistic feelings. I love my country, and I love my city particularly. I consider myself a Dubliner more than an Irishman. I don't feel a stranger in America; I don't feel a stranger for one moment in England. When I talk to an Englishman it never occurs to me that I am an Irishman; but I talk in a different way to a Dubliner because we have a common background which means an awful lot to me.

I went away from Ireland because I wanted to get into television, but I don't think I have ever left Ireland. To tell the truth, I keep coming back every year. What draws one back to Dublin is what draws one to the bedroom. It's the place where you are born, where you make love and where you die. It's not a place to work in. People who spend their lives trying to work in Dublin become frustrated in a great many ways.

I am always interested in what I am doing at the present moment. At the time I wrote *The Moon in the Yellow River* I thought of nothing else. If you write a book or a play and feel when you have finished it that you have absolutely nothing more to say, then it is probably very good. I have never attempted to write a novel; that's too literate a job for me. I am more interested in writing for performance. I like the co-operation you can get from a good director and actor. I was lucky at the Gate where, as rarely happens to a writer, a director came along and gave my play more than I had given it, and then an actor came along and gave it more than the director. That was the combination of Hilton, Micheál and myself. The Gate let the air into the Irish theatre. Those little theatres would still be staging *Autumn Fire* without the example of the Gate.

I take a long time to write a play. I am affected by the reception a play gets and am always ready to be told that I am no good. From time to time I have been sat upon, and then I have stopped writing for a while. I write everything five or six times. My first draft is terrible; nowadays, in fact, I just gallop through that first draft. I do my second and third re-write in intelligible English. I don't write at regular hours. I am much too irregular a person to be able to write for two hours in the morning or two in the afternoon. I write a lot, but I don't write in a regular way. I'm too peripatetic. At the moment I'm moving my home; perhaps to America, possibly back here. I like to move around. I'm a jigger.

6

❧ ❧ ❧

Edwards and Mac Liammóir: We must be talking . . .

FORTY-TWO YEARS after Micheál Mac Liammóir and Hilton
Edwards had founded the Dublin Gate Theatre they received belated
recognition from the Irish Government in the form of a subsidy. In
1928 Mac Liammóir had designed a dark curtain for the stage of their
new theatre on which an energetic figure flung open golden gates.
Whilst the Abbey Theatre, the national theatre, offered mostly
native Irish plays, the tireless partners began their seasons in a pocket
theatre adjoining the Abbey, throwing open those golden gates to
present world theatre to Dublin audiences. Their repertoire ranged
from Sophocles to Shakespeare and from Molière to Mac Liammóir
himself, whose early plays, *Where Stars Walk* and *Ill Met by Moon-
light,* brought the Celtic twilight into the modern drawing-room.

Mac Liammóir had been a child actor (he appeared with Noël
Coward in *Peter Pan*) who became a stage designer and later returned
to acting, playing a new part at the Gate every two weeks; but it
was not until years later when he took his solo performance, *The
Importance of Being Oscar,* abroad that the world became aware of his
extraordinary artistry. Whilst Mac Liammóir toured with Wilde,
Hilton Edwards, actor and director, was directing Brian Friel's plays

73

on Broadway. To Edwards, also, international recognition came belatedly.

But Ireland, often accused of rejecting its great ones, rose to the occasion on Mac Liammóir's seventieth birthday in October, 1969. Congratulatory messages and telegrams arrived at the early Georgian house in Dublin's Harcourt Terrace, which is adorned with books, paintings and antiques, and in which our conversation took place. Mac Liammóir said to us: 'D'you know, I rather mourn it. It is *they* who are celebrating my birthday for me.'

* * *

MICHEÁL MAC LIAMMÓIR: Hilton and I did not meet until the latter part of the twenties – 1927, to be precise. For me the twenties are extremely significant; not on account of my own life only, but because they were the outstanding aesthetically inventive decade. Certain decades have an edge to them; and the nineties were a decade in which astonishing things happened and astonishing people appeared and disappeared. The nineties are remembered for their frivolity and called the 'Naughty Nineties' and the 'Yellow Nineties'. They were truly remarkable years. What was invented and discovered in the nineties was being perfected until the First World War. After the war it seems to me that the twenties emerged primarily as a sort of 'The job's done, boys. Let's have a drink' period. This was the prevailing mood of the lighter side of the twenties. But serious things happened as well. Expressionism was discovered in Germany, and in Russia too. The German movement came mainly from the agony of losing the First World War. Since then little completely new has been stated; in fact, there has been a return to the pre-twenties technique of realistic drama. But the twenties invented a new form of presentation in the theatre. They also discovered Sean O'Casey in Ireland. I think he's an overrated man; but that's my personal opinion, and nothing to do with the truth,

74

necessarily. The twenties saw the perfection of the Diaghilev Russian ballet, the discovery of Jean Cocteau in France and the final flowering of Madame Colette. America came into its own in the twenties. The Negro came into his own in the arts. Extraordinary things happened politically. Communism and Fascism were both invented in the twenties to our everlasting sorrow. But they were extremely significant. It was not merely a decade of gramophones and cocktail parties, low waistlines on the ladies and the first short skirts to be seen for a long time. That is why it seems comic now. All new inventions seem comic at first. There is nothing more amusing than the sight of an old-fashioned gramophone or an old-fashioned motor-car. The twenties saw all that, and culminated for me in the great turning point of my life when circumstances made me decide to return to the stage which I had left in 1917.

In 1916 we were an Irish family living in London. We had gone there in 1907. I am just as old as the century, so it's very difficult for me to lie about my age. Our opinions, like those of most Irish families, transplanted or not, were sharply divided. I and two of my sisters were violently for the Insurrection; my father and my two other sisters were very much against it. My father was an old-fashioned Redmondite who said: 'This is the end of all our hopes.' My mother, like many Irish mothers, was blissfully indifferent and said: 'Ah well, you never know who's going to come out top.' She took it in an inevitable and very womanly way and didn't really care much one way or the other. My people were from the South, and we talked of nothing else but the Insurrection of course. I remember one evening especially when my younger sister Peg and I heard that Countess Markievicz had been sentenced to death. We collapsed into each other's arms in tears in the dining-room. I remember that well, though I was only a boy at the time.

I returned to Ireland the following year and came to live in Dublin; it was not my first visit to Dublin. We lived in Howth, which I still love more than any place on the earth's surface. But that again is a personal opinion. It is a place where important years of my life were spent between the ages of seventeen and twenty-one. Then came the twenties, which for me were mainly spent in Switzerland, Germany, France and Italy for reasons of health – illness, rather. I did not see America until the thirties when I went there for the first time with Hilton.

In 1927 I met Hilton, as I tire not of telling the world, apparently. I am always talking of how we met on the steps of the Athenaeum in Enniscorthy on 17th June, 1927. He was a compelling stranger, and we decided to make a theatre together.

HILTON EDWARDS: Micheál talks about the birth of Expressionism. I would point out that Expressionism was never at home in the theatre. It eventually found its true place in the cinema where it became part of montage. But I am in complete agreement with Micheál's view that there seems to be nowadays, apart from the permissiveness of morals, no new invention in the theatre since the twenties. We appear to have travelled in a series of circles. Even in the plays of today the themes of the twenties are revived; people like Dürrenmatt seem to me like twenties' writers. There has been no new form in the theatre since then. Now that we have come to copulation on the stage in America I am wondering where we can go from there. I would suggest that in a few years' time it will be quite obscene to show the top of one's nose on the stage. In which case, with my nose, I shall have to retire completely.

I had been to Ireland in 1921 for five weeks with the company of Charles Doran. I then spent five years at the Old Vic, and during an interim I was in a play called *The Dybbuk* produced by Robert Atkins, my Old Vic director, at the Royalty Theatre. A member of the cast, George Owen, asked me if I could find an actor to go to Ireland to assist Anew McMaster in a Shakespearean company. McMaster's leading man had fallen ill. I had no intention of leaving my native London. I asked various friends of mine, and they didn't feel like going either. So George Owen suggested: 'Why don't you go yourself?' My mother had lately died and I had six weeks to spare between engagements, so I went over to McMaster's company for five weeks, playing such parts as Iago and Macduff and Claudius. I met Micheál in the company and very soon afterwards, although it

76

was lovely summer weather, caught pneumonia. I missed my next engagement in England and didn't feel like going back in my condition. McMaster asked me if I would stay on. It had been a very pleasant tour, so I stayed. I found that touring the small towns of Ireland in the winter was a different proposition to touring them in the summer. Having caught pneumonia in the summer, you may guess what awaited me in the winter. However, during this time Micheál and I warmed ourselves by making plans for the Gate Theatre.

I wanted a theatre anywhere; Micheál particularly wanted one here in Ireland; so we decided to make it here. I rather regret that we called it the Gate. With me in *The Dybbuk* was Peter Godfrey, who had run the Gate Theatre in London. When Micheál and I planned to make a theatre I went over to London to clear up my affairs and bring back my personal effects. When I told Peter Godfrey about our project he said: 'Why a new theatre? Why not start another Gate and we can exchange plays?' It seemed a good idea at the time, but it didn't work out because we discovered that England was much further away from Ireland than its mere geographical distance. Plays suited to him were not suited to us: and although our association remained very friendly there was really no connexion between the theatres. We exchanged only one play. So the Dublin Gate survived longer than the London Gate. I still regret its name because I feel I have been instrumental in adding another provincial attainment to Ireland; and we already have the *Irish Tatler and Sketch*, the *Irish Times*, the Irish Derby . . .

MAC LIAMMÓIR: . . . and the Prom concerts.

EDWARDS: However, that's the name. It was partly as a reaction to my tour with Anew McMaster that I wanted to start the Gate. I had played Shakespeare with Charles Doran's company for a year in England and Ireland; I had played Shakespeare for five years at the Old Vic; and now I was playing Shakespeare again with Mc-Master. Being a young man – I was twenty-four – I wanted to get into the contemporary theatre. But Micheál and I realised that the only way to achieve this was to create a theatre of our own.

77

Although we left his company, we maintained very friendly relations with McMaster. He was a magnificent, heroic, Nordic figure with a God-given voice and a natural sense of poetry. He was not always at his best in modern plays; he was an extrovert in the classic mould with great artistic generosity, one of the last of the actors with the grand manner. Had it not been for a series of fortuitous circumstances he would have remained in London, and Ireland would not have had the benefit of his performances.

I never saw his James Tyrone in *Long Day's Journey Into Night*, which he played mainly in America, and which must have been a McMaster I didn't know. He was essentially a costume actor, almost I would say (and I don't say this with any sense of denigration) on an operatic scale. He played Shakespeare primarily for its music.

MAC LIAMMÓIR: He was related to me by marriage. I had known him since he was about twelve years old. When he was a young man he was magnificent-looking, with all the attributes which Hilton has described. I think he was made of the glamour of the theatre. He was a true child of Harlequin. His world outside the theatre was curiously unreal. He was what the world agrees to call completely mad. He was quite dotty in many ways and always over-life-size. A woman once complained to me: 'All you theatrical people seem a little over-life-size,' to which I retorted: 'All you non-theatrical people seem to be a little under-dress-rehearsal-size,' which to me is completely true; theatre people have a slight exaggeration of manner, just as they have an instinctive projection of voice.

EDWARDS: It is the theatrical person's function to project, and the non-theatrical person's function not to project, but to receive.

MAC LIAMMÓIR: That mainly applies to these islands. You will find that English-speaking people find French and Italian people, for example, 'affected' – by which they mean that they seem over-life-size to them. In France or Italy, however, the actor is not so remarkable as in the Anglo-Saxon world.

EDWARDS: That is because these islands suffer respectively from the results of Oliver Cromwell in England and from your present bishops in Ireland –.

MAC LIAMMÓIR: Oh, what a statement –.

EDWARDS: Factual.

MAC LIAMMÓIR: Shakespeare is the only thing that the peasant race understands. The peasant race is far closer to classical drama than to modern claptrap-urban plays about business situations and financial crises and so on. They are much closer to that ancient world that produced *Oedipus* and *Hamlet*. But it would be impossible to bring Shakespeare to the Irish peasant today because of the faint corruption of the world of the cinema and television which has brought expert cheapness to the small towns. In 1924 when Mc-Master began his Irish tours the people, except for lamentable shows of tenth-rate melodrama, were virginal. The folk imaginations which had supplied Yeats and Lady Gregory with all they wanted were there.

EDWARDS: They didn't know, for instance, how the Trial scene in *The Merchant of Venice* was going to end. Therefore it had all the thrills of the trial of *Madame X*. I suggest that the Greek physician was more real to the Irish mind than a character played by Robertson Hare. McMaster played Othello over a span of twenty-five years. In the early sixties we wanted him to play Othello in the Dublin Theatre Festival. We wanted something for McMaster to play in, and we thought of his greatest part. But in the course of rehearsals he had what amounted to a heart attack. He died quite suddenly. Not that McMaster wanted to appear in the play; he had played Othello so many times before; but we thought the time had come to show McMaster in Dublin again, perhaps for the last time, in his greatest part.

MAC LIAMMÓIR: I would agree it was his greatest part: although I believe he was magnificent in *Long Day's Journey Into Night*. It has always been an astonishment to me that when the Abbey Theatre put that play on (and made a failure of it, incidentally) they did not invite McMaster as a guest artist to play the part in which he had

79

been so successful in America. He was quite available. He was not interested in anything outside the theatre, really, but he adored the eccentricities of Irish country life and its sudden strange extravagances, and the charm and easiness and humour that you don't find in England.

EDWARDS: Would that all the men were as mad as he.

MAC LIAMMÓIR: Yes, oh, yes.

EDWARDS: Had it not been for those circumstances of a personal nature that had taken McMaster away from England and brought him to Ireland, the Irish would never have been able to afford a man like him. He chose to stay here, and was willing to make sacrifices, as indeed Micheál and I were, for very different reasons. He geared himself to playing here, and eventually did well financially.

MAC LIAMMÓIR: I think it only fair to say, Hilton, that he was curiously unambitious from the normal theatrical point of view.

EDWARDS: He acted what he wanted to act.

MAC LIAMMÓIR: Another actor of his stature would want to play in London, Paris, New York or Berlin, depending on the language of his birth, and nothing else would satisfy him. On the other hand if, like Cyril Cusack, Siobhán McKenna or I, he has a nationalistic bug in his blood, he would say: 'No, I want to play here in Ireland.' Mac was not like this. Once he could get on his feet and act, it didn't matter whether he was in London or Ballingarry so long as he was there with an audience. He did love this wild, fresh appreciation of the type of audience which Hilton has described; an audience that finds Shakespeare's Trial scene as exciting as an Agatha Christie.

The twenties in Dublin were dominated by the Abbey Theatre because of the discovery of O'Casey. The Abbey was, as it had been for so many years, interestingly on its last legs. But of course it wasn't on its last legs.

EDWARDS: We're all on our last legs, but, thank God, the legs last a long time.

MAC LIAMMÓIR: I remember a description of the Abbey in 1923. Somebody said it was like a wake with Lennox Robinson as its chief

Jack MacGowran with Roman Polanski (right) on location for Polanski's film *The Dance of the Vampires*

Anna Manahan who played Serafina in the controversial Dublin production of *The Rose Tattoo*.

Brendan Smith, director of the Dublin Theatre Festival.

F J McCormick during an Abbey Players' tour of the United States.

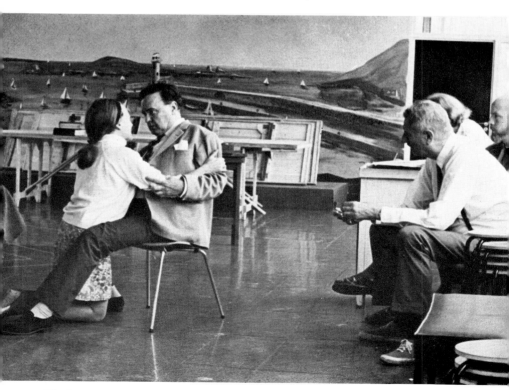

The late Tyrone Guthrie rehearsing Micheál MacLiammóir in Eugene McCabe's play *Swift* at the Abbey Theatre, Dublin. McCabe (with beard) is on the extreme right seated beside Guthrie.

keener. Until the discovery of O'Casey it did seem to be falling on evil ways. It had not attained the poetic, rhapsodic beauty that Yeats had hoped for, and the miracle of John Millington Synge was short-lived. I think the most important persons at the time were Lennox Robinson, T C Murray, and that much overlooked man who wrote *The Dandy Dolls* – what's his name, my God – George Fitzmaurice.

EDWARDS: A very fine playwright –.

MAC LIAMMÓIR: A sort of Douanier Rousseau of the Irish stage with a wonderfully primitive and inventive mind who at times seemed to have been overlooked. But there were the old plays, the old William Boyles and the old Lady Gregorys – those charming comedies and what one can only describe in English theatrical terms as Christmas plays, those very beautiful folk tales and fairy tales. I often used to wonder what people meant in the early twenties when they said the Abbey had gone to the dogs. Since 1903 or 1904 there had always been commercial plays at the Abbey.

EDWARDS: And we have put on lousy plays –

MAC LIAMMÓIR: – as well as great plays.

EDWARDS: In our first season, which was considered one of our best seasons, we put on magnificent plays and we also put on one of the worst plays ever written; but I'm not going to remind you of it. We have been fallible and made mistakes and, please God, always will.

MAC LIAMMÓIR: I have on various occasions played at the Abbey. In fact, I played there as a boy in 1917 in a completely forgotten play called *Blight* by Oliver St John Gogarty, which was the fore-runner of O'Casey's slum plays. I appeared as a crippled boy. I knew O'Casey, not intimately, but reasonably well. I regarded his so-called exile as the most comic thing in the history of the Irish theatre.

EDWARDS: His self-imposed exile.

MAC LIAMMÓIR: He wrote three fine plays which in many ways put the Abbey on its feet. He wrote a fourth play which the Abbey did not quite approve of. Yeats and Lady Gregory, who were extremely good friends and great admirers of his, wrote most courteously to him. As a result of having had a play turned down he flounced out, as you might say, and went to live in Devon. That was his lookout. If we were all to leave our country and go to live somewhere else and call ourselves exiles because we had been turned down, everybody would be an exile. By the thirties the Gate was going well.

EDWARDS: The Gate has never gone well.

MAC LIAMMÓIR: Well, it was developing. It was at its most creative in the thirties and forties, more so in the thirties because in the forties we had less rivalry. The forties, obsessed as they were by the Hitler war, had less rivalry from English or American touring companies visiting Dublin. By that time we had split with Lord Longford and formed two companies.

EDWARDS: We started without him, remember, and then after the first three years he joined us. He helped us out of a bad financial mess, which meant eventually that we were in debt to him.

MAC LIAMMÓIR: I may be wrong in my dates, but so far as I remember Lord Longford joined us in 1933 and I think we parted company in 1935 after our first Egyptian tour, when it was decided to have two companies.

EDWARDS: Because of our tour of Egypt we were able to subsidise our theatre in Dublin. We have never been able to make the theatre of itself pay here. For many years we were young and ignorant; we are still pretty ignorant, though not young any more. In those days we went on various foreign tours and the money we made was put back into our activities here, which enabled us to expand. The Longford split originally happened because Lord Longford was against our going abroad; but it was only through our foreign tours that we achieved our independence. I think the Abbey was subsidised long before any English theatre. The present Abbey Theatre has had an enormous injection of money, which is to a great measure responsible for its resurgence. Let us put it on record that we have been helped from time to time by the Arts Council, which got us out of a bad jam after the war and which from time to time has subsidised us to the best of its ability, for which we are very grateful. This has enabled us to continue, but, though it may sound ungrateful to say so, the money has been a drop in the ocean compared to the Abbey's annual subsidy of £90,000.

The Gate was intended to be a temporary theatre, just as the Peacock was a temporary theatre of ours. It has been temporary for forty years. Without Micheál's one-man shows we would have been in a financially perilous state. Of their very nature these one-man shows have taken Micheál all over the world, which means that we have not been together to make a concerted effort at the Gate. Micheál suffers from one extraordinary limitation: he cannot be in more than one place at once.

MAC LIAMMÓIR: There are certain places one loves more than others. For no reason on earth I adored South America, except that they were the best audiences I have played to in the world outside of Ireland, Oxford and Cambridge. On the other hand, there were marvellous audiences in Australia, but I didn't happen to like Australia. It is a wonderful country with a glorious climate, but there was something in the air that was alien to me.

EDWARDS: In America Micheál has had a much better Press for *Oscar* than even in England; but the show has always done better financially in England.

MAC LIAMMÓIR: There is nothing to distinguish us from the English. 'We're not English, we're not English, we're not English', we Irish tell every bored little waiter on the Paris-Calais Express, as if it interested him in the slightest. We have the same tastes. We demand bacon and eggs for breakfast and a newspaper and marmalade. We cannot understand why the traffic must travel on the right. We cannot understand the decimal system. We cannot understand anything that all other people in the world understand. So far as the Continental eye can see we are completely like the English. The one definite thing that any country struggling for its individuality has is its own language. I still believe passionately in the Irish language. I think Douglas Hyde was born a hundred years too late. That, as Yeats would say, is the fault of fate, time and change.

83

EDWARDS: You know, it might be a good idea to get a square Fáinne and start a movement for the revival of some Red Indian language in America.

MAC LIAMMÓIR: To quote America is absolute absurdity, because America did not begin as an ancient nation conquered by a stronger nation; it began as a colony of mainly English-speaking peoples who beat down the Red Indians. Naturally the language chosen by the majority of those people was English, but the moment America became a nation it began to develop a language of its own.

EDWARDS: But according to you we are not Irish here; we are more or less English.

MAC LIAMMÓIR: I have a strong logical argument if you want to talk seriously about the language.

EDWARDS: My interpolation was an English thing called a joke, which I'll explain to you later.

MAC LIAMMÓIR: You can have a three-cornered Fáinne if you like and give it to the Chinese. That's just blather to my mind. To me the Irish language is a beautiful patient in the hands of incompetent doctors and nurses. Somebody said to me recently: 'Until I realised that yours is a Cromwellian name in the Gaelic form, I used to think how extraordinary to find a man with a Gaelic name playing Shakespeare.' Well, it should not have been extraordinary. It shows the fantastically idiotic point of view the Irish have of their own language as an absolutely unique, apart, sacred little thing in a glass case. But it's a European language like any other and if you don't speak it you must speak the language of the stronger people who have conquered you and accept that you are part of their tradition. The Yeatsian movement must move back from its interesting side-track into the great broad highway of English literature. God knows, there's no shame in belonging to a language that includes Chaucer, Shakespeare, Shelley, Keats, Blake – you can go on for ever; but if you want to belong you must take off your hat and say, yes, we are conquered. If our language goes, then Synge's and Lady Gregory's plays, for example, become an impossibility, because they are

84

entirely founded on the Irish language. When the well dries up, plays in an Anglo-Irish dialect will no longer be possible. For obvious reasons the language of the people of Ballinasloe or Gort or Killaloe is far nearer today to the language of the newspaper than it was fifty years ago. If our Irish language dies, there will be no more Synge, no more Lady Gregory, no more of that beauty.

The revival of the language has failed because of the innate, idiotic inability in our national temperament to organise. We cannot see straight. If you want to revive the language, never mind if a man wears trousers or kilts, whether he dances this way or that, or what sort of games he plays. The language revival was turned into a crank movement and this put a lot of rational and reasonable people off.

EDWARDS: When I go to England now I no longer feel at home. I'm forty-five years in Ireland, but when people say, 'Oh, you live in Ireland,' I answer, 'Oh yes, I work there.' I don't feel Irish and I still carry a British passport. I'm an Englishman and will remain so. I must say, if it is not a patronising tribute, that during all the years I have been here I have met through Micheál every kind of Irishman, from West Britons to gunmen, yet I have never had one moment's inconvenience because of my nationality. I have always been met with the utmost courtesy, tolerance and understanding. I'm hardly aware any longer that I'm in a foreign country. One of the few authors I know who can write plays about Irish people in which Ireland is treated as just another country and not a special little preserve is Brian Friel. I had no contact with Friel until Oscar Lewenstein, a friend of ours, sent me the script of *Philadelphia, Here I Come!* and asked if I would like to produce it for the Dublin Theatre Festival.

I have now produced three of Friel's plays, *Philadelphia, The Loves of Cass McGuire* and *Lovers*, two of them in London and three on Broadway. Friel and I have had hard times together. He is a man of great sensitivity and has suffered inordinately from commercial rough-handling. I am not a critic, but I would say that his work displays, above all, humanity, a great sense of compassion, coupled with an irony which is astringent and prevents the compassion

85

turning into sentimentality. His plays are not chauvinistic, but have a general appeal, and this is what has enabled them to succeed abroad.

MAC LIAMMÓIR: What I love about Brian Friel is his attitude to his own country. I often think it would be much more interesting to love somebody else's country, as Byron loved Greece.

EDWARDS: This love affair of the Irish for the Irish is an incestuous relationship. They adore one another.

MAC LIAMMÓIR: My definition of a genuine Irishman is one who knows all about Ireland and still goes on loving her.

EDWARDS: To know all is to forgive all. Even alcoholism. We have a good deal of it in England and elsewhere, although it's an Irish *métier*.

MAC LIAMMÓIR: It's regarded as an achievement.

EDWARDS: A wonderful tolerance is a gorgeous thing in a nation. But I often think, if I may say so – and this is the one criticism I have about Ireland – that they have got the priorities of their tolerances wrong.

MAC LIAMMÓIR: If actors are given to drink, then I think you'll agree with me, Hilton, it's because of the great chasm that exists after the curtain falls. You must remember that every time the curtain falls at the end of a play we die a little. We die a little, and that chasm invites one to some form of *uisce beatha*. But the tragedy is that actors who don't drink heavily dislike those who do, because drink happens to be one of those vices which apparently cannot time itself. It happens at the wrong moment. Acting is not like writing or painting. Our art depends, as the soldier's art or the boxer's art, on instantaneous potency. If you cannot do it at that moment, you are out. And drink spoils it.

EDWARDS: Ireland in the last five years has changed tremendously. There are three reasons why its drama hasn't kept in step. The first is that there is an established tradition that Ireland is a great dramatic stronghold. This is open to question. The second reason is that there is a great levelling throughout the world in our field, so that there are fewer people of astute intelligence and concentrated talents and, on the other hand, fewer ignorant people. One must remember that the impact of television has been even greater than that of the cinema. The third is that television, with which I have had a little to do, has had a double-edged impact on the theatre. It has offered security to the actor and saved his existence financially and, in consequence, made it difficult for the theatre with its much smaller resources to compete with it and hold a company together. The other thing is that it has skimmed not necessarily the cream but certainly a measure of our audiences away from us. We never had sufficient audiences for the theatre. The only complaint I ever had against Ireland is the smallness of the population, something which, incidentally, I have never done anything to remedy. But I console myself by thinking that if I tried I could not have done more than fill the stage-box for one night. But, to be serious again, I have come to the awful conclusion that if you really want to fill the theatre in Ireland (though there are exceptions to this) you have got to have a play about Ireland with the usual internal situation. I said to some-one during the interval of a certain famous play that came to Dublin recently: 'This play won't do here. It doesn't mention Michael Collins once.' It was a joke; but as it happened I was right. We are in the position of the blind leading the blind. Most of the people who know a good deal about theatre cannot afford to stay here, so that all the youngsters here are learning acting and direction by trial and error. Now this is a splendid way of learning, but it's a fright-fully slow way.

MAC LIAMMÓIR: It's no use saying to Ireland, or any other country: Why are there no great playwrights now? I can only sum it up by saying that to me art is a bird that visits certain countries at certain times, and then, for no reason, vanishes. Otherwise how do you explain the great days of Greece, the glory of the Italian Renaissance, the almost equal glory of the English Elizabethan age of literature, the long drawn-out glory of French civilisation, the twenty years' glory of German music and, by comparison, the barren years that followed?

87

EDWARDS: I have a theory that may be of no value. But it does strike me that the debt owed by Ireland to England has never been fully appreciated. When the English thorn was in the Irish side it set up a feverish condition, which threw out a great deal of vitality, a great deal of genius. You will notice that the best writing and the best playwriting was nearly always done when the English thorn was in the Irish side. Now that the thorn has been removed the patient has settled into a kind of convalescence, which may only be temporary. But it also strikes me as curious that nearly all the vital plays nowadays are coming from the North.

I have never been a propagandist. I have never believed that the theatre should compete with the Church – it has remained for the Church in Ireland to compete with the theatre. When you go into the small towns your first nights are chosen by the local clergy for the local dance. But whereas the clergy step on the tail of the theatre, so far as I'm concerned the theatre has no desire to compete with the clergy. I don't think that preaching or drum-banging are necessarily the function of theatre. I know that fine plays have been written on this basis, but some of the finest plays I can think of have no direct political significance –.

MAC LIAMMÓIR: *Hamlet, Romeo and Juliet* –.

EDWARDS: Except that they may become raw material for the Russians to distort, as they distorted *Hamlet*, as a vehicle for propaganda.

MAC LIAMMÓIR: The dullest part of that very great play *Peer Gynt* is when Ibsen tries to become a political propagandist.

EDWARDS: Hear, hear!

MAC LIAMMÓIR: The petty Norwegian politics of his day have no interest for us whatsoever. Brecht may be a great twenties figure, but I have an instinctive dislike of almost all the great German artists except Wagner; of artists who take hours, as the Germans do in music and drama and everything else, to tell you that the summer is hot, the winter is cold, the rich are often wicked and the poor often hungry and that two and two make four and four and four make eight and isn't it all wonderful?

EDWARDS: I love Brecht in many ways, but I find his theme of alienation really a revival of the Elizabethan theatre. You know you are in a theatre and you are constantly aware of the audience. I find that Brecht as a director and a playwright is a most exciting person, but I am not impressed with what he says as a propagandist. I am impressed by the writing *per se*, but the propaganda around the writing I often find contradictory, puzzling and of no value.

MAC LIAMMÓIR: To me he's a drooling genius.

7

❧ ❧ ❧

O'Herlihy: 'You can't starve in California'

F J McCormick, Eileen Crowe, Denis O'Dea sampled Hollywood and returned to Ireland. But when Dan O'Herlihy left Ireland for the United States after the enclosed years of the forties it was not to work for the big Hollywood studios. He followed the mercurial trail of Orson Welles who, like himself, had acted at Dublin's Gate Theatre. It was O'Herlihy who was cast for the role Buñuel intended for Welles as Robinson Crusoe. It earned O'Herlihy an Oscar nomination, and he did not return to Ireland as an actor. He was later followed to the States by his younger brother, Michael, who became a television and film director.

Dan O'Herlihy made his home at Malibu, but in later years he bought himself a house near the old family home at Dalkey, a resort overlooking the sea near Dublin, where his neighbours include Seán Ó Faoláin, Milo O'Shea, Constantine Fitzgibbon and Liam Redmond. It is here that he lives with his wife and children when he is not working in films abroad. This interview took place in a house overlooking Regent's Park in London during a respite from O'Herlihy's filming in *Waterloo* in Russia, in which he played Marshal Ney to Rod Steiger's Napoleon. Earlier that day he had renewed acquaintance over lunch with Hilton Edwards, for whom he had acted at Dublin's Gate Theatre when he was a young student. Dan O'Herlihy speaks with scarcely a trace of American in his accent. A tall, powerfully-built man, he talks fluently, often histrionically, about his profession.

*   *   *

When I was an architectural student at University College in Dublin I remember Liam Redmond coming to speak to us about drama. He had been a member of the College Dramatic Society. I had joined with other students to keep the Society going and we had attracted some attention. Because of this quite a number of us were offered small parts in the Abbey or the Gate.

During the war years Dublin was a cultural ghetto without contact with the outside world; and the theatre flourished as it had not done for some time. This period saw the flowering of the Gate Theatre, and the Abbey flowered too, because the companies could not go on foreign tours and everything took place within the confines of the island.

During my holidays from the university I worked with Hilton Edwards and Micheál Mac Liammóir and with Lord Longford Productions and toured the small towns. I suppose I must have appeared in as many as a hundred plays during those years. I played in the Abbey, but did not join the company. I auditioned for a regular contract, but was rejected because my Irish wasn't good enough; actually, it wasn't bad; but I imagine Mr Blythe may have been in a rather tough mood that day. During my second year at college I knew that I was going to make acting my profession. Not wanting to leave something unfinished I took my architect's degree, but did not pursue architecture beyond that point.

None of my family had been actors. I had not been a theatregoer, nor had I any previous interest in the theatre. The first time I was ever in a professional theatre was when I stood on the Abbey stage to play a fairly large role at the age of nineteen.

Some years later my father wrote to congratulate me on my Hollywood Oscar nomination for my portrayal of Robinson Crusoe in Louis Buñuel's film. He congratulated me on my success, as he called it, and added: 'Is it not high time you settled down to your profession of architecture? You have had your fill of your hobby.' My father, who was manager of Gardiner Street Labour Exchange for the last ten years of his life, addressed the letter to 'Daniel P. O'Herlihy, B.Arch., M.R.I.A.I., Malibu, California'. My father had been a Principal Officer in the Department of Industry and Commerce in Wexford and my mother is a Hanton from Wexford; but I was brought to Dublin at the age of three, with my sister Marguerite and brother Michael.

At the end of the war I was offered, like many others, parts in *Odd Man Out* and *Hungry Hill*. After this I received an offer to work with Orson Welles's Mercury Theatre in America. I played Macduff in the Mercury production of *Macbeth* in Salt Lake City. Afterwards we went to Hollywood and put the production on to film.

I stayed on. Welles was very much in the pattern of Hilton Edwards and the Gate Theatre, where he had come from. At this time Buñuel was trying to cast *Robinson Crusoe* and looked at *Macbeth* with Orson vaguely in mind; but when he saw me as Macduff he decided I was right for the part. Jaime Fernandez played Friday, and there were hardly any other speaking roles.

I became preoccupied with babies' arrivals. My wife is Irish. A few years before going to America I had walked into the old Grand Central restaurant in Dublin and found her on the point of signing a contract to tour with a theatrical company of which I had some experience. I put my foot down and stopped her becoming an actress.

We have five children. My daughter Patricia played for a year in the television series *Peyton Place*. She had been acting in minor theatricals around Los Angeles when Fox asked her to play in *Peyton Place*. They wrote in a part for her and called the character Patricia, expanding it as the year went on. She was doing very well, although I had never seen the series nor been able to watch her act. I was in a play in New York at the time and called her to ask how she liked being a professional actress. I can remember her answer clearly: 'Daddy, it's a drag – at three hundred bucks a week.'

She waited until the series was finished to ask me if she could marry the boy she had known since she was fifteen. By this time I was filming *Waterloo* in Russia and could not get back to America. So she flew to Rome with her fiancé and his parents and the brides-maids, and we all went to the wedding in Santa Susanna.

I suppose I have appeared in some sixty films. Some of them I liked: *Home Before Dark, Fail Safe, The Cabinet of Dr Caligari*. But I could count these on the fingers of two hands. But what percentage of plays that go on in the West End or on Broadway are of value? Fifteen per cent? If you were to wait for one play in that fifteen per cent to come your way you might work once in the three years. The best you can do, no matter what your medium, is to say no to the dross and work the middle ground and then wait for the worthwhile part to come along.

I have always been drawn to theatre rather than films, because, although film actors are the best known in the world, the film is not the actor's medium. Film is the director's field and Welles, Buñuel, Leroy, Lumet and, of course, Reed, are among the best directors I have worked for. I have tried to keep my hand in with theatre, but it is not that easy in America where you have theatre mainly in New York and the amount of theatrical playing throughout a country of 200 million people is small. I am offered plays frequently, but most of them are worse than the movies I am offered.

Television can be very lucrative, depending on what you want out of your profession. I have done two television series, one bad, *The Troubles of Jamie McPheter*, and one that I liked, *The Long, Hot Summer*. You take a gamble when you begin a television series; it can look marvellous when you start until the commercial interests begin to exert pressure, and then it turns sour. I could have become rich from the series I was offered, but by the time I had finished them nobody would have taken me seriously as an actor; particularly if they were successful and ran for seven or ten years. I am already twenty-three years out of Ireland.

My early years in Hollywood were a struggle; early years always are for an actor. Recognition in America is pegged at a commercial level. You may receive fine reviews for your performance in a film, but if the film is not financially successful it does not count for much except within a small clique in the industry. Hollywood is a cruel place, but no crueller than London or Dublin. The theatre itself can be cruel.

I had my professional disappointments, but never went hungry. That's one of the advantages of California. It is warm enough that you don't feel cold. You need only a pair of shorts, so there are few clothing expenses for the children. The dole is sufficient to feed a good-sized family and pay the rent and fill the car with gasoline twice a week. I settled in California and I'm fond of it. Two of my children have grown up in America and are married there.

Films are such an international medium that it is difficult to say if the centre of film-making has shifted from Hollywood. In the great days of Hollywood you could easily have said that the atmosphere was European. Hollywood attracted European directors and players, but these can now make their films in Europe. But the financing of Hollywood's films, and London's films, comes from New York. Hollywood has been blamed for much of the dross in films, but I have seen producers frustrated because New York will not approve some worthwhile idea. It is in the film industry's equivalent of Madison Avenue that the power lies.

In the great days of comedy, nobody could match Keaton, Chaplin, Laurel and Hardy. Those were the creative days when film-makers were not weighed down with today's production costs and could afford to exploit the inventiveness of the moment when shooting a film. Today films must be planned so far in advance that spontaneity has become an expensive luxury.

I have not made many close friends in the film industry. My interests outside films have been in books and writers and in politics and politicians. I was an Adlai Stevenson man. I have always protected my privacy to some extent and have accepted publicity only when it seemed essential. Actors, I would say, generally resent intrusion in their private lives. Many of the older gossip-writers who

94

have lived in Hollywood for many years are not wicked, just childish. Their only interest has been in the wealthy members of the profession, and many of them were envious of the people they interviewed; envious of their notoriety or fame or the money they had made. I think this was emotional neuroticism on their part. The younger columnists are not like that; they are educated and rational people.

I knew Hedda Hopper quite well. My youngest son got his name because of her. I had just finished filming *A Terrible Beauty* in Dublin, and the baby's birth was sudden and unexpected there. The christening was six weeks away and we had not thought of a name for the boy. In America you must fill in a form with the baby's name at the time of birth. Being in Ireland we never thought of this. The telephone rang in the nursing home in Dublin. I picked up the receiver.

'Hello, dear. This is Hedda.'

'Oh, hello, Hedda.'

'You've had another? What's that – twelve?'

'No. Five.'

'What is it? Boy or girl?'

'A boy.'

'What's his name?'

I knew I must give an answer. The telephone directory was open in front of me and I looked down and saw 'Bourke, Lorcan P.' So I answered:

'– Lorcan P.'

That's how my son got his name. Now Lorcan and my other son have made their acting début in *Waterloo* as boy drummers in Napoleon's army.

When you have been out of Ireland for a few years you can romanticise about it; but I have kept coming back and it has stayed in perspective. The wealthy middle-class families of Dublin remind me of the families in the San Fernando Valley; the same urges are pushing them to keep up with the Joneses, and they have developed the same tensions that arise from this.

In the last few years Ireland has become a wealthy country in comparison to the Ireland I left. My generation had grown up in a

95

ghetto during the six years of the war, and the very fact of our confinement to one country was suffocating. That is why there was so much emigration after 1946. I was part of that, too. I think I would have emigrated, even if I had not been an actor.

To me the Irish in America contribute nothing culturally. For a hundred years they have been identified with the minority scramble to reach the top, and have had no time for cultural side issues. But with the emergence of the Kennedy syndrome the new generation may make some contribution. At one stage in my career I ran a theatre in Hollywood and put on plays with Irish backgrounds. Fifty per cent of my audience was Jewish and I was lucky if one per cent was Irish. On the other hand the Jews have had a tougher time, yet they have reclaimed and expanded their cultural interests. I think that when the Irish leave Ireland they are more materialistic than most peoples. They seem to be more interested in money than in anything else. Perhaps they see light at the end of the tunnel and it hypnotises them.

I have very strong feelings towards Ireland, although I consider nationalism one of the curses of the world. I have also strong feelings about America. America's is the only society I have come across that is so critical that when a generation rouses itself, as a generation did fifteen years ago, it can see what is wrong with society and tear it apart and reassemble it. I would say that as a society America has advanced sixty years in ten. That has been exciting to witness. When I first went to America it was conservative and self-satisfied. It has been anything but that for fifteen years.

I think the time is coming for great playwriting in America; any society in a state of extreme flux seems to produce such writing. Ireland is the obvious example.

8

❧ ❧ ❧

MacGowran : Waiting for Beckett

ON THE OCTOBER day in 1969 on which Samuel Beckett was awarded
the Nobel Prize for literature, actor Jack MacGowran was invited
to the BBC television studios in London to read from the writings of
his fellow-Irishman of whose works he had become the acknowledged
interpreter.

Twenty-five years earlier in Dublin, MacGowran had been a
young amateur actor invited to the Gaiety by Hilton Edwards to
play a small role in *Abraham Lincoln*. He soon decided to make acting
his life. In Dublin during the postwar years there were few opportunities for young actors of ambition, and a sense of frustration drove
him eventually to London where success came gradually.

Today MacGowran has established himself as an actor whose
versatility ranges in the theatre from O'Casey's Joxer Daly to
Shaw's Dauphin and in the cinema from Lester's comic soldier to
Polanski's vampire hunter.

Our meeting with MacGowran took place in the Marylebone
flat which he shares with his wife and young daughter. A slightly-
built man with dark eyes and expressive features, he perches rather
than sits in a rocking-chair.

*   *   *

97

Until my early twenties I had not considered the theatre as a place in which I had any right to be. The theatre was where I went to watch and wonder, but never for one second did I see myself on the other side of the footlights. During the days when I worked in a Dublin insurance office Brendan Smith was putting on plays, which he had written himself, in the Peacock Theatre. A fellow-clerk who was going to audition for a part in one of the plays asked me to go with him to lend moral support. So I went down to the Peacock, and whilst I was there Brendan Smith asked me if I had ever done any acting. I said I had played only in the chorus of Gilbert and Sullivan operas because my sister was a member of an amateur musical society. He asked me to read some lines, and the next thing I knew I was playing a leading role in a straight play. I appeared in other plays which Brendan Smith had written, and during this time Hilton Edwards and Micheál Mac Liammóir saw me at work and must have mentally noted that I might be useful in the theatre, because when I was still working in the insurance office they sent for me. I was to be an extra in John Drinkwater's play, *Abraham Lincoln*.

I was highly delighted that the Gate Theatre should want me and I joined the production with tremendous enthusiasm. This brought me into the semi-professional ranks because I was now being paid. During the run of *Abraham Lincoln* there was a 'flu epidemic and I took over five roles in succession. I think I played every character except Mrs Lincoln. From then on, Hilton Edwards sought me regularly for roles and I was beginning to think seriously of a life in the theatre. I knew there was no point in continuing as a part-time actor. Having watched F J McCormick and other great players of the golden age in the Abbey, my mind was set on joining the national theatre. I was taken on to play small parts in the Gaelic pantomime. Perhaps, after the praise I had received in my semi-professional days, I had an inflated notion of my own worth at the time, but I left the insurance company without having secured a permanent job in the Abbey. When Ernest Blythe said there was no room for me in the theatre because they had enough character actors, I became desperate. I was full of determination to get into the Abbey, and I thought the only way to do this was to wear the man down. I sat outside his door for three days until I forced him to employ me. That began my professional career. But I played very few parts of any consequence, because I think Ernest Blythe must have felt that I had almost blackmailed him to get myself into the theatre, and he was not inclined to use me in many parts. I found it was becoming almost impossible to live on my basic minimum salary of three pounds ten shillings a week. I decided I had to do something. I reopened the experimental theatre in the Peacock and began working there with younger members of the Abbey Company who were not playing in the parent theatre. It was then that I began to experience full creative enjoyment. I was able to act, direct and paint scenery and stage, not the kitchen comedies that the Abbey were doing, but Lorca and O'Neill and new plays like Jack B Yeats's *In Sand*. Then they closed the Peacock down. I could only think this was because we were receiving more attention than the Abbey. Otherwise there seemed to be no reason; actors were being employed in the Peacock when they were not working in the Abbey and it seemed a shame to deprive them of a chance to develop. Nothing was happening for me in the Abbey, except the occasional small part. A play would run for weeks on end and I wouldn't be in it. With the good wishes of the French Ambassador I took off for Paris. I wanted to learn body co-ordination and mime, and I knew that France was a base for classical mime.

I had free access to the Comédie Française and to the Atelier Marigny and to various theatre personages. I studied mime under Decroix, who was then a famous teacher. After much heckling I had got an advance on my salary from the Abbey for a period when I would not be wanted, but eventually the money ran out, and I had to come home. By this time I had been five years at the Abbey and had played in all the Gaelic pantomimes, but never a leading role in a straight play. I never played O'Casey in the Abbey. I suppose if Ernest Blythe were asked today he would say the best part I ever played was an Indian; but, as he said to me, you don't find many Indians in Irish plays. It seemed that I would have to wait until another Indian part came along, and this worried me greatly. I had written to Lord Longford, asking him to take me into his company, but instead Ria Mooney persuaded me to join the Radio Eireann Repertory Company. It was 1950. At the end of that year Paul Rotha was making a film in Ireland called *No Resting Place* and I found myself cast in one of the feature roles. The following year John Ford brought me out to Hollywood to film in *The Quiet Man*. The film turned out to be a great success, but it did not endear me to Hollywood. This was a turning point in my life. I stayed there for a time, considering what my future should be. Either I could stay in Hollywood and develop my career in films or I could come back to Ireland and do what I wanted to do in the theatre. I decided to come back. I felt I was not a fully-fledged actor by a long chalk and I did not want to be typecast in Hollywood as an Irish leprechaun. I came back and made two films at Ealing Studios, but then decided I had neglected the theatre for too long. I returned to Dublin and played the Dauphin in Hilton Edwards's production of *St Joan* with Siobhán McKenna. I directed *The Playboy of the Western World* with Cyril Cusack for the Paris Festival and then formed a company of my own called the Dublin Globe Theatre. The codirectors of the company disagreed with what I had set out to do, so I decided there was nothing left for me in Ireland. The Globe company continued for seven years after that and went on for as long as it could. Norman Rodway and Milo O'Shea joined after I had gone, but at the start there were Denis Brennan, Godfrey Quigley, Michael O'Herlihy and I.

I became a permanent exile in 1954. I arrived in London to play the Young Covey in *The Plough and the Stars* at the New Lindsay, and immediately thought of starting a new career there. But despite the good notices I received, a blank period followed and many a time I was tempted to go back to Dublin. After about a year I was offered some work on the BBC Third Programme and later appeared in a television series. This earned sufficient money for me to be able to put on *The Shadow of a Gunman* at the New Lindsay, which later transferred to the Lyric in Hammersmith. From then on the theatre began to take an interest in me. I was beginning to take steps which I could not have done in Dublin.

I cannot pinpoint the year exactly, but it was about this time that I began to take an interest in the world of Samuel Beckett. I had played the Pedlar in a broadcast of M J Molloy's one-act play, *The Paddy Pedlar*, for the BBC. By some chance Beckett heard the broadcast in Paris. He was curious to know who had played the Pedlar and wished the actor to be included in the broadcast of his play, *All That Fall*. Beckett was a name that conveyed nothing to me at the time, but after I played in *All That Fall* I was impressed with his work. I did not know he was Irish; I thought he was a French writer who had been translated into English. I then saw *Waiting for Godot*, which was badly done because the actors were not fully aware of what it was all about. I, myself, did not quite follow what it was about, but I was much impressed by the play which aroused something that had been long asleep in the recesses of my being. I proceeded to read all Beckett's work. The more I read the more involved in it I became. I found him a writer of such profundity and compassion, and with such a brilliant style, that I could not put him down. For the past ten years I have devoted time to studying Beckett. He has become a part of my life. I first met him when one of his plays was being performed at the Royal Court Theatre in London. At this time I had not appeared in his work on the stage, but I did so want to meet the man. Donald McWhinnie, who at that time was directing most of Beckett's plays for radio, arranged the meeting in the Royal Court Hotel before the performance. He introduced me to Beckett and then left the two of us alone together. I was terrified in the presence of the great writer. What could I say to him except that I had wanted to meet him? I did not realise that he was an equally shy man and must have felt just as awkward at meeting me. We had recourse to drinking several glasses of whiskey. We both communicated in some way; I don't quite know how. I never got to the Royal Court Theatre that evening; I spent the time in the hotel bar with Sam Beckett. I kept thinking what rubbish this brilliant man must think I'm talking. But, in fact, he is interested in everything one says to him. He enjoys horse-racing and shows prowess at golf and cricket. I like being with him, except when he drives his tiny Citroën too fast through Paris.

After that first meeting I felt I knew Beckett to some degree and that I was free to contact him whenever I went to Paris. Subsequently I played in much of his work and became more and more aware of what he was trying to say. So much so, that I felt he was gravely misunderstood by critics and public alike, largely because his work was not properly produced or was not being given the correct levels in production. This led me to think of adapting all his works into one single piece so that I could interpret him, as I thought, at every level. What people call his pessimism and despair hardly exist except in the situations of the characters. What does exist is hope, a high sense of comic imagery and, above all, a tremendous compassion for the human condition. After I had finished the adaptation I showed it to him, and he agreed with it in principle, but made minor alterations until he was happy with it. When I made a long-player of this adaptation he supervised the recording. Today I never really do anything of his without consulting him first. Our relationship has become so close that he has written two plays specifically for me, one a play for radio called *Embers*, which won the Prix Italia Prize, and the other a television play called *Eh, Joe*. I am fortunate to have a writer of his stature writing something specially for me. This has forged a link in our relationship and given me a deeper insight into his work. A certain amount of Beckett's writing is apparently ambiguous, and there are several avenues you can explore and get lost in. You usually throw away the simple solution to his work because you think it must be more complex than that; but when I go to Beckett himself for guidance I find the answer is the simple one which I have rejected.

Out of Beckett came my meeting with Roman Polanski. He had come to see me playing Lucky in *Waiting for Godot* at the Royal Court Theatre, and after the performance asked me to play in his film *Cul de Sac*. Until I began working with Polanski I had not enjoyed making films. I had never played anything worthwhile; my roles had been small and unsatisfying. But after I met Polanski my whole idea of the cinema changed. I began to see it as a very exciting medium and my career took a completely different turn. My relationship with Polanski deepened and I played the leading role in the next film he made, *The Dance of the Vampires*. This development in my career happened because I had looked further afield than Ireland. I remember Frank O'Connor saying that an Irishman's life begins at Liverpool. To me that speaks volumes. To me it means that one's development in the creative field takes place when you leave Ireland. Not that Ireland is lacking in culture; its cultural basis is very great. It has had its great literary years which surpassed those of other countries. But it cannot support the individual who is ambitious enough to want to develop his talents to the fullest.

I have asked myself over and over again if I would go back again to live in Dublin. They talk of *bás in Eirinn*. I am nostalgic enough to want to retire to Ireland but it would have to be to Kerry, the county where I spent the happiest days of my youth. I still consider myself very much a Dubliner, but I have in a small way what Joyce had, a love-hate relationship with the city. I love it because I know it so well. I hate it because I know it so well. If you want to join the pub set, the if-I-were-king-set, everybody is happy because you are no longer a threat to anybody. If you become a threat in your profession you arouse enmity and the city and its people turn on you. Dublin can be cruel to its people. I have found jealousy in pockets in London, but London has a very large population, whereas in Dublin, which is confined within one circular road, jealousies are obvious and rife. But I will never call myself anything but Irish. I am a nationalist to the degree that I believe that the Gaelic language is part of our heritage; I do not mean that the language should be used in a trading sense, but it would be disastrous to lose it because it is a part of our nature.

Nobody has influenced me so much as Beckett has, but others have influenced me very strongly. Happily I had the chance to know Jack Yeats, Sean O'Casey and Louis MacNeice. I love O'Casey's plays. I knew in my heart that I could interpret his characters, and this is why I went to see him in Torquay and had many, many talks with him about his plays, which I wanted to present in London. I have played O'Casey in New York, but only once in Dublin when I played in *Juno and the Paycock* at the Gaiety Theatre with Peter

103

O'Toole and Siobhán McKenna. O'Casey's pen was deceptive. From his writings many people thought him narrow and bitter, but he was the antithesis of these things. He wrote with rage about narrow institutions because he himself was broad in mind, and he wrote with an acid pen because he disagreed with so many establishments. But he was a wonderfully expansive man to talk to, full of good humour. Within half an hour of your meeting him, he would want to sing ballads. He wanted to create joy and be surrounded by joy. He used his plays as a platform for this belief and never gave up until the end of his days. Sadly, he lost touch with what was taking place in Ireland, and played out a situation that could not be altered. The Dublin of today is quite different from the Dublin of twenty years ago, and broader in its thinking. But O'Casey's plays will never become tired. His richness and colour of language and character will always keep them popular and successful.

Jack Yeats was a profound, wise and quiet man. We all know him as a great painter, but he had other strings to his bow. He wrote a couple of books and about three plays. They are not in the major class, but they have a value. His play, *In Sand*, was overwritten, and when we presented it for the first time at the Peacock in Dublin it had to be cut by a couple of hours; otherwise it would have taken four hours in playing. But it was a play with a lovely quality of gentle satire; I don't think it has been staged since then. It gave me an opportunity to know and listen to the wisdom of this marvellous man who spoke to me on many fronts and in many areas.

People like Sean Kenny and others who are Irish and have had large ambitions and achieved them here form the nucleus of a group in London with which I never lose contact. The identification is there all the time. When I left Ireland in the fifties the golden age of the Abbey Theatre had collapsed. There was no literary revival, only a terrible doldrums. But in recent years I think we Irish have begun to show our vitality in the arts again and there is a new thrust forward in Ireland by the younger generation. Maybe I'm a little too old to go back and join them.

9

∾ ∾ ∾

Guthrie : Voices from the Everywhere

JACK MACGOWRAN HAD gone into exile in 1954. During that year
Tyrone Guthrie arrived in Dublin to direct Sean O'Casey's new play,
The Bishop's Bonfire. Guthrie, whose reputation in theatre and opera
had been achieved outside Ireland, was an infrequent visitor to Dublin. To the towering figure with the clipped military moustache,
Belfast was more familiar territory. In his autobiography he
describes the occasion:

> The last O'Casey play to open in Dublin had been *The Plough and
> the Stars* at the Abbey some thirty years earlier. On that occasion
> there was a riot in the theatre . . . . Word had gone round that *The
> Bishop's Bonfire*, like *The Plough and the Stars*, was not just a bouquet
> laid at the silver feet of Cathleen Ni Houlihan, nor yet a penitent
> heretic's apologia to Mother Church. Dublin knew its own Sean
> O'Casey . . . . By lunchtime on the day of the performance you could
> not get into the street where the theatre stands. At three in the after-
> noon the mounted police were called to clear the crowd. When the
> doors opened the police had to be called again, because about a
> thousand people were storming into a gallery which holds less than
> three hundred . . . . The streets were ringing with boos and cheers

when the little lady who leads the theatre's orchestra – violin, 'cello and an exceedingly upright Ibach – struck up, for reasons which she and her God alone can have known, with a spirited rendering of 'The Bells of Aberdovey'. 'No,' yelled the gallery. 'Irish music. Make it Irish.' Programmes were folded into paper darts and hurled at the orchestra pit. The rest of the theatre took up the cry 'Make it Irish, Irish, Irish' . . . . The curtain was now up and the actors were finding the competition rather severe . . . . At first the audience played up. Supposedly anti-Irish or anti-Catholic lines were received with jeers and hisses or, by the minority, with exaggerated laughter and applause. But gradually it became apparent that the jokes were not of the finest vintage, the satire not very pointed, the plot a little 'hammy' and the performance, in spite of manful efforts by Eddie Byrne and Seamus Kavanagh, a little amateurish. By the end of the second act the excitement had fizzled away. The audience was like a wedding party after the departure of the bride; after the elation of the nuptials and the unwanted champagne comes the reaction: a melancholy, punctuated by hiccups. By the end of the last act torpor was turning to positive vexation. Cyril Cusack came forward at the curtain call and made a long, prepared speech in Irish. After thanking the audience for its wonderful reception, he gave a harangue on behalf of tolerance and liberty. Under this final douche of cold water, *The Bishop's Bonfire*, which had never quite blazed, fizzled finally into a heap of damp ashes.

Tyrone Guthrie and his wife lived in a secluded old mansion in County Monaghan. A winding, tree-lined drive suddenly reveals the great house poised above a lake. The unadorned front door opens on to a vista of lakeside and thickly-wooded hills beyond. It is to this house that Guthrie returned after his lengthy sojourns in the great theatres and opera houses of the world. A few miles away is the village of Newbliss, where Guthrie was one of the directors of a successful local jam-making factory.

Ensconced in a window seat at Annagh-ma-Carrig, looking out across the spring countryside, Guthrie talked to us about his life and his attitude to Ireland. It was in this house that he died in May, 1971.

* * *

Although I was born in England, where my father was a doctor, my parents brought me to Ireland at the age of three weeks. Thereafter we generally spent our summer holidays here at Annagh-ma-Carrig which may be a corruption of the Bog of Carrick, though I have never met anyone who can tell me. My great-great-grandfather, who was a doctor in Newbliss, bought the house about 1780 for his retirement, hoping to live off the proceeds of the turf bog, which indeed he did. Other parts of the house have been added down the years. There were big alterations made in 1870 by my grandfather, who joined the dwelling house to the farm buildings with a long wing and engaged a cousin of the family from Dublin to design it; and he brilliantly placed all the bedrooms facing northeast.

I have never actually lived the whole year round here, and this is the first time I have seen the spring in Ireland for four years. But this has been my true home. My mother retired here when her husband died in 1929; and we used to spend a good deal of time with her every year. During the past twenty years I have spent more than six months in every year out of the country, in Canada or America.

I was called Tyrone (after my mother's grandfather, Tyrone Power, the Irish actor) and educated in England – mistakenly, I think. My parents imagined that an English public school education would be a good idea, and I truly did not graduate to Ireland until I was able to choose for myself. I gave up the idea of becoming an actor at the age of eighteen, and finally learned my lesson at the age of twenty-three. Having made a poor showing in my finals at Oxford I had joined a repertory company. I was hired for the leading part as Captain Shotover in *Heartbreak House* and was dismissed after the first morning's rehearsals. I was taken aside at lunch and told that it had all been a great mistake, but that I might stay on if I wished and assist the stage management and do some of the lesser chores like cleaning the lavatory. Or I could go that minute.

So at twenty-three I returned to Ireland and soon found myself in charge of talks, plays and poetry readings at the BBC in Belfast. Two years later I was placed in charge of the Scottish National Players in Glasgow because of their difficulty in finding a director. After a period of ten years, during which I had moved from Glasgow to London and worked again for the BBC and for the Canadian National Railways – which, odd as it may seem, operated a radio station in Montreal – and in the Festival Theatre in Cambridge and the Westminster Theatre in London, I was summoned by Miss Baylis to the Old Vic. There was a vacancy at the Vic which I filled, because the salary was such that there were not many in the queue. I spent some eighteen years with the Vic, with an interim in the West End and on Broadway. These were the years of Laughton, Evans, Guinness, Robson, Richardson, Olivier. In 1936 I directed Olivier in *Hamlet*. His reputation at the time was promising rather than high. His Hamlet was extremely intelligent, very exciting to look at and listen to; very starry – but as a star Olivier's great part, I thought, would never be Hamlet. I don't think he was extra well cast. He was too extrovert, and his Prince had nothing of melancholy about him, though I don't think Hamlet's is necessarily a melancholic nature. I don't think either that it was quite good casting vocally, even though it was an extremely thrilling exhibition. As Olivier has said of himself, the voice has brass but the strings are weak. I think he is a marvellous speaker of verse because he is a musical man. He has such a vocal technique that he can stretch the voice from top to bottom as a singer does. He and I both rather dislike the voice beautiful; the plummy, elocutionary verse-speaking which the critics, I imagine, rather like. The critics prefer to recognise verse as opposed to prose. They like to hear:

> Di dum, di dum, di dum, di dum,
> Di diddly, umpty, umpty, um.

Guinness was only twenty-two years of age when he played *Hamlet*, and perhaps it was asking too much of him. It was a modern-dress *Hamlet*, and one of my own best productions I think. Guinness made a fascinating, subtle and clever Hamlet; but because of his age the audience had to reach out and take the character, rather than the actor's offering it as a star does. He had not then achieved either style or quality.

I was home in Ireland and sitting in this room on a summer's day in 1952 when a voice from the Everywhere came on the telephone and said he was a Tom Patterson from Toronto and would I come to Stratford, Ontario, to give advice about a Shakespeare Festival.

I said: 'When would you like me to start?'

He said: 'Tomorrow.'

I asked: 'Will you pay my expenses?'

He answered: 'Of course. And a small fee.'

And I said: 'Expect me the day after tomorrow.'

I looked up Stratford, Ontario, in an atlas and it didn't seem to be a metropolis. But, at least, two railway lines met there. And that was a good start.

Looking back on the successful experiment at Stratford, where the open stage allowed no illusionary scenery, I think I attempted an experiment on a more elaborate scale than anyone else in the theatrical field.

In my time I may have been called a harsh director. I don't believe a director need impose his personality on a cast, but he must impose discipline. In any cast there are likely to be some bores and some obstreperous people who must to some extent be suppressed without knowing it. A lot of actors like to be the centre of the rehearsals, as well as of the performance; so the director has got to prevent this, politely and imperceptibly. In the long term, directing is more demanding than acting. A director does not need the same technical preparation an actor needs, or anything like the same preparation a singer or musician needs; but he needs a wider range of preparation, a wider knowledge and the ability to hold a group of people together and make them like working under his direction. Which, I suppose, is what you call authority.

Despite my time abroad I have always regarded Ireland as one of the cornerstones of my existence. I don't think I can define what being Irish means, except that it is a feeling of belonging here, which is a very strengthening thing. There are a great many people in the world who don't feel they belong anywhere.

I think that eventually Ireland will be united because the forces that make for union, the economic-sociological community of in-terests and ideas, will draw us together more strongly than the religious and historical differences can force us apart. I don't think the Border will disappear in my lifetime, I think it is going to take longer than that; but I do feel that I have seen a great diminution in this part of the world in religious prejudice. I dislike bigotry and I dislike violence. I think we should have now progressed to the stage where we can handle our affairs by reasonable argument. I suppose violence can betoken vigour, which I admire; but I can distinguish between violence and vigour. Bigotry is stupidity and unkindness, and I have no use for it.

A tiny community like the Irish is doing jolly well if it produces every ten years in fifty one playwright who will last. I think we are fulfilling that average, and looking around the world such an average seems to be on the generous side.

I think language is very important to a nation, but then I don't think being a nation is very important. I would prefer to think that we were citizens of the world rather than citizens of the blue or the green or the yellow country. I can see why in 1922 it was important to try to establish the Irish language, but in my humble opinion the experiment has proved a complete failure. It would be braver and wiser to accept this failure than sentimentally maintain the experiment in the face of overwhelming evidence that it doesn't work. I don't suppose there are people writing in Irish who are mute, inglorious Miltons because of their loyalty to the Irish tongue. If they had it in them to say what Milton had to say they would have said it in a language that most people could understand. There may be people of genius who are devoted to the language; I cannot say. In the practical sense, young people who have left us to go to England have been compelled to take lowly positions on the ladder of employment. I think if Irish education could get this bee out of its bonnet it would be a more efficient instrument.

Over the years I have worked in Dublin only occasionally: *Hamlet* for Ronald Ibbs in 1950, *The Bishop's Bonfire* for Cyril Cusack in 1954 and recently *Macook's Corner* and *Swift* for the Abbey Theatre. If I had been asked to become artistic director of the Abbey I would have arranged my life to fit the salary. But I don't think the other directors and I would have seen eye to eye. There was a strong feeling that the Abbey must express what I regard as a narrowly nationalistic point of view, and with this I would not have agreed. I'm pretty sure that it would not have been a happy arrangement for anybody, and there would have been trouble. The Abbey lived for a good many years on its legend, but it's beginning to look up again, and I could not be more delighted. In the days of McCormick, Sinclair and the Allgood girls the Abbey Company was a marvellous ensemble.

I remember McCormick in a great variety of parts. What impressed me was his individuality; in each part he looked different and sounded different. He was a marvellous chameleon, but, though his range was very considerable, the Irish dialect plays did not stretch his capacity. Sydney Morgan I remember only in the O'Casey plays, but he always seemed to me to be the character he was playing. He was a very authentic, 'unactory' personality.

In its heyday the Abbey Company was never really tested. There was the repertory of Synge, Robinson and Lady Gregory's rather underestimated works, and some of the difficult and important Yeats plays. O'Casey was there with four tailormade plays which, whatever one may think of them now, were great shooting comets at that time. I knew Sean O'Casey and liked him very much. I don't think he was the most reasonable of people, but he had more than compensating qualities of heart and mind. I would not say that any of us is in a position to know yet whether he was a great playwright; I suspect not. I find that the so-called great plays seem to have dated very much; but I guess there is a period when the greatest plays seem to date. Pepys thought Shakespeare's plays overrated fancywork. Maybe Sean will come into his own again; but right now I don't think so. I cannot take his later plays. The English setting and the English characters seem to me to be a sort of pretence. O'Casey should never have abandoned his Dublin origins and it was a great pity that he felt he had to try. I think that some important part of him died when he went away.

My experiences in the Belfast theatre have been happier than those in Dublin. Culturally I don't find Dublin an exciting city. It has ideas above its true value. I always seem to be hearing self-satisfied talk about Dublin, with the implied assumption that Dublin is a great metropolitan city. I don't find this so. In general, Dublin's taste is about level with that of Bolton. Dublin has a marvellous art collection, both in Charlemont House and in the National Gallery, yet whenever I have been to either place the only visitors I have seen are elderly men who were obviously there to enjoy the hot pipes. Dublin would not be at all flattered to be compared to Birmingham or Manchester; Dublin wants to be compared to London and Paris. It is not in that league.

The most stimulating theatrical production I ever saw was not in Dublin or London or Paris but in Tel Aviv. This was the Habimah production of *The Dybbuk*, a play by Ansky translated into Hebrew from a Polish story by Vialek. It had first been produced in Moscow in the early twenties by Vakhtangov, who was a kind of righthand man to Stanislavsky at the Arts Theatre. I saw the twenty-fifth anniversary performance in Israel. I had seen it years before in London, but it still seemed to me an *avant-garde* production. News of the performance had been the main topic in the newspapers for a week or two beforehand, and the first night was like an all-Ireland football final. Most of the original cast were still playing the same roles. The young girl was played by a sixty-year-old actress. They were all much too old; but they had been living this play for twenty-five years and it was marvellous and touching. Even in the Diaspora the Jews remained a highly educated people in the Hebrew tradition. Their mythology made for a commonweal of knowledge to be drawn upon. You arrive by bus at a very undistinguished village in Israel which hasn't changed in two thousand years, and the conductor asks: 'Anybody for Cana?' I defy you not to be thrilled by that. I suppose I'm probably too pro-Jewish and not enough pro-Arab, but as an example of human effort the assimilation by Israel of two million people from all over the world, many of them extremely old and practically all of them totally indigent and unable to contribute anything physical, is one of the miracles of the age.

I'm a churchgoer, but more because I want to be neighbourly and sociable than because I believe all that's going on. I cannot say that I believe strongly any longer in the things that one stands up to recite in the Creed; but for this reason I don't think you could say I was irreligious. I think a good deal about why we are here, and if the conclusions I reach are pretty childish it is not for want of trying. I know that I have missed the bus in many directions. A lot of things have simply passed me by. But this is the human condition, and I don't think I am different from anybody else.

If I were asked if I would have my life over again, I would say no. I am convinced that I would make just the same mistakes. I absolutely disagree with the notion that one's happiest time is childhood or schooldays. Life didn't begin to open up for me until I was at least twenty-five. I am realistic enough to know that every year one grows a little more old-fashioned. Young people already regard me as Methuselah, and they must think that many of the things I say to them are the utterances of a very old and out-of-date teacher, but there is always a gap between the generations. Older people who accept that they are old and don't try to rouge their ideas up can establish with younger people a satisfactory relationship.

10

❧ ❧ ❧

McClory : At the gates of Ealing

KEVIN McCLORY MADE his first stage appearance in Ireland as the baby in Maria Marten's arms. But, like Tyrone Guthrie's, McClory's career in acting was shortlived and his eventual success was achieved away from Ireland in other capacities. He collaborated with John Huston, Mike Todd, Harry Saltzman and Albert 'Cubby' Broccoli in film-making. From the proceeds of *Thunderball*, which he produced, he bought himself a mansion at Straffan in the County Kildare and returned to Ireland to live there with his wife and four children.

Tall and debonair, McClory is regularly seen in Dublin at theatrical first nights. Observing the new Ireland at close quarters, he champions the cause of the patriot leader of the twenties, Michael Collins. He has called his youngest daughter Saoirse, the Gaelic word for 'freedom', because, he says, 'I believe in freedom of speech and civil rights, and every kind of equality.'

*   *   *

My father had said that no son of his would be born on English soil. He came from Banbridge in County Down and my mother from

Wexford. My father was very nationalistic and had taken part in the Rising of 1916. He was furious, having played a reasonably active part in that revolution, at the drawing of the Boundary, by which the place of his birth remained under British domination. My father and mother ran fit-ups. They had met in England, where my mother was in a play called *Paddy, the Next Best Thing*, and my father had been playing Christy Mahon in *The Playboy of the Western World*. Together they travelled round Ireland with a truck and scenery, presenting plays like *Todd Slaughter, Murder in the Red Barn* and *Maria Marten*. My father used the stage name Desmond O'Donovan, which is the name of my brother.

I was born in Dun Laoghaire, near Dublin, in 1924. My brother and I travelled with our parents and made our first theatrical appearances. I was the child born to Maria Marten, although they could easily have used a doll as a prop. But I think my parents believed that we should start early. I think my father found it a little difficult to make a living in Ireland, and not wishing particularly to live in England he decided to emigrate to America. His timing was remarkable. We emigrated in 1928 and the depression followed us. There was less employment in America than in Ireland and no employment in the theatre. Times were pretty harsh. My father died when quite young, and Desmond and I, who had gone to school in New York, were brought to England for a few years and educated there. I was not too happy at school, so at fifteen I went to sea. The war was on when I joined the Merchant Navy and my return to Ireland in 1943 was dramatic.

I was one of the crew of a Norwegian oiltanker on its way to America when we were attacked. Our ship was sunk. It was Sunday 21st February, 1943. We were in the lifeboats for quite some time. We had no navigation instruments and were not sure of our position. We suffered from frostbite and a number of men in our boat died through lack of water. We had sailed about six hundred and thirty miles when we reckoned ourselves to be some fifty miles from land. The Norwegians were perturbed that we might be near France, and believed that if we made the coast they would be interned. On 8th March we were picked up by a trawler and landed, to our great relief, at Valentia in County Kerry the next day. That was my first return to Ireland; I remember it was a Monday.

I spent some time in hospital after my rescue and then went back to sea again. This has little to do with the theatre, and the only reason I mention it is that after this period the only profession I sought was acting, which had been bred in me. But one result of my shipwreck was a speech impediment. For some time it was pretty bad, and it put paid to any real possibility of my becoming an actor. Yet my interest in the theatre was very evident and I decided to try for the film industry. I entered the industry about 1948 through perseverance. It is not an easy industry to enter. For a time I worked on a building site in Lewisham and in a brewery near London Bridge. My impediment was so severe that it wasn't easy for me to find any other kind of work. But all the time I was trying to find a way to enter films. I would go to one studio after another and on being asked whether I was a member of a union I would traipse back to Two Soho Square where the union has its headquarters. One day I went down to Ealing; I had been turned away from the main gates of most of the studios, but now I was back at Ealing again. There was a man on the gate whom I had not seen before. He asked me my business. I saw a list of names on a board and at the top of the list was 'Harry Watts'; so I said: 'I have an appointment with Mr Watts.' It took me a long while to say Watts. At that moment an enormous car drew up at the gate and the gateman said: 'There's Mr Watts now.' He walked over to the car and said: 'Mr Watts, there's someone here to see you.' 'Jump in,' said Watts. I got into the car and he introduced me to a very tall man who was Chips Rafferty, the actor.

The car drew up at a block of offices. Watts got out and went in. I followed him into an office in which there was a secretary and a couch. I sat on the couch. Rafferty disappeared, and Watts picked up some papers and started to do some work. His secretary said: 'Mr Watts, they are ready for the meeting.' Without looking at me Watts walked out of the office into another room. Through the open door I could see a long table with chairs around it. I got up and went in. There were people sitting at the table with notepads in

116

front of them. So I sat down, and there was a pad and a pencil in front of me. I was surprised that nobody asked who I was or why I was there. But now I know the reason. This was a preproduction conference; and very often at these conferences they have the cameraman, the head of the sound department, the chief gaffer, the chief construction man, the art director and so on, and it's conceivable that these people may not have worked together previously. So a strange face would not seem out of place. Any word like 'postsynch' that I had not heard before I wrote on the pad. I must have looked very industrious.

After the meeting everybody went out, so I got off my backside and followed Harry Watts into his office. Watts, who is now in Australia, had been one of the best documentary directors for many years, and he was about to make his first feature film, *The Overlanders*. I sat there whilst he got on with his work, but when he stood up and put on his coat to leave I thought I had better say something.

'Excuse me,' I said. 'May I have a word with you?'

'What department are you in?' he asked me.

'I'm not in any department.'

'But you were at the meeting?'

'Yes, but I came to see you.'

'About what?'

'I'm looking for a job.'

I told him I was interested in the film industry and explained my predicament about the union. I was determined to get into films, I told him.

'I want to be a director like you, sir,' I said.

'How are you going to go about that?' he asked me.

I told him: 'If you give me a job as a fourth or fifth assistant director, then perhaps I can work my way up. I could bring you tea, make out call sheets, do any chore you ask.' He told me to come back after lunch. Outside the studio was a grass verge where I sat on a bench and waited until it was time to return. When I went back to his office a girl came out and said: 'I'm sorry to disappoint you, but we won't be able to take you on the picture. However, Mr

Watts has written this letter for you to take to Mr Elvin.' George
Elvin was the head of the union, in which it turned out that Watts
was very active. On the way up to town in the Tube I took a peep
at the letter which said I was the sort of man who should be in the
industry and that the union should help me find a job as an assistant
director.

I took the letter to Soho Square, but when I tried to see Elvin I
did not succeed. But next day the union rang to say that assistant
directors were needed at Shepperton. I went to see the studio manager
who looked at me quizzically and asked if I could answer a telephone.
When I said 'Y-y-y-yes,' he remarked: 'I can see you can.' Against
my wishes he sent me to John Cox, the head of the sound department, who told me I could start in his department on Monday at
four pounds a week, and that once I was in the union he would talk
to friends at Pinewood and get me a job as an assistant director.
That's how I began.

I worked in the sound workshop, but pestered John Cox to be
allowed on the floor because I was interested in production. I
became an assistant boom-operator – the man who pushes the man
on the boom around and plugs in the cables. I practised operating
the boom until I was able to work on one or two films in that
capacity. I found that this was a most advantageous position. You
have a pair of earphones and a long arm on the boom, which is very
mobile, and on the end of the boom is a microphone. I would
pretend to be reading a magazine whilst I pushed the mike across
to eavesdrop on the director and cameraman. I would listen to the
conversation if the director was talking to an actor or technician. I
had a remarkable perspective from my elevated platform.

When I joined the unit on *The African Queen* I got to know John
Huston. He asked me: 'Why are you in the sound department?' In
the evening I used to sit with him and we would talk about scripts
and storylines. He then invited me to become his assistant. This was
some five years after I had been in the industry, so when I went to
John Cox and told him not to bother talking to his friends at Pinewood he confessed he had forgotten my earlier request. We have
been great friends since then.

I worked with John Huston for some six years. I first met Mike Todd when he turned up on the location of *Moby Dick*. Todd had not made a motion picture at that time, but had been instrumental in bringing about the new widescreen process which had been developed at the American Optical Company – the AO in Todd AO. We had been working for about three or four months on *Moby Dick* when Todd asked Huston to stop work on the production and begin again in Todd AO, for which he would pick up the tab. But it wasn't practical. Later, when he came to make *Around the World in Eighty Days*, he asked me to work with him. I started on that picture and eventually became associate producer. Todd was incredibly energetic and restless, but he was able to channel his energy and his restlessness into constructive work. He was the greatest showman I have known. He would not accept that there was a word 'no' for anything that was materially obtainable, and basically my job with him was to see that material things were obtainable. He lived above his means. When I was with him he didn't really have any money. The picture was being made from hand to mouth whilst he went around raising finance wherever he could. At one stage he gave me an air travel card and told me to collect a crew. I gathered an English camera crew together and took them to Kuwait in the Persian Gulf. From there we went to Karachi in West Pakistan. When we got to Dacca in East Pakistan the mail had caught up with us and none of the crew had been paid. I knew that I hadn't been paid either, but it was a big responsibility for the others as they had wives and I had no wife. I had tied up the East Pakistan Railway with promises of lots of rupees, because when I arrived in Dacca I expected to find lots of money, and I certainly hadn't any money. We worked on for a few weeks until the man who ran our hotel and had been feeding us said he would like to be paid. I had been cabling Todd and had received no replies. I was somewhat desperate. So I gave all our camera equipment to the man in the hotel. 'Keep this,' I said. 'It's worth a lot. And when I come back I'll have some money.'

Fortunately I had my air travel card, so I bought a ticket to California and cabled Ernie Anderson to meet me at the airport. Ernie said: 'Todd's thrilled with your work and he wants to see you in the morning.' 'I'm not thrilled with Todd,' I told him 'I want to see him tonight.' Ernie said that Todd was having dinner at Chasen's and that he would take me first to my hotel in Hollywood. I was wearing an old bush jacket and hat and a beard, but I insisted on going over to Chasen's at once. Todd was having dinner with some people.

He said, 'How are you, Kevin? I didn't know you were coming back.'

I said: 'You probably didn't get my cable, sir.'

'Well, see you in the morning,' said Todd.

I answered: 'I'll see you right now.'

He asked: 'Well, what is it?' I told him I didn't want to talk in the restaurant, so we went outside and at the end of three minutes he had fired me. He had taken off his coat and thrown his cigar away. I thought we were going to have a real slogging match on the pavement. I told him: 'You can't fire me because you haven't paid me; but I'm quitting anyway.' He said: 'Be at the studio at eight o'clock in the morning.' He didn't go back into the restaurant, but drove off in high dudgeon in a great white Cadillac with the numbers 4444 – his lucky numbers.

I decided to get to the studio by seven-thirty in the morning to be ready for him. But as I drove through the gates they said: 'Mr Todd is waiting for you in his office.' You could never be ahead of that man. He had already been on the telephone to New York and was all charm and smiles, telling me there had been a terrible mistake and that he had been horrified to discover that nobody had been paid. None the less I had to stay in Hollywood for six weeks before I could return to Pakistan, and in the meantime the film crew were there doing nothing. When he had raised some more money, we went on to Bangkok, Hong Kong and Japan. By then Shirley MacLaine and Cantinflas were in the film, I had a Japanese crew and it had become a big production.

When I came back to California I found that the production had been moved out of MGM studios and out of RKO because we couldn't pay the rent. We were in a studio called King at the corner of Sunset and La Verne; and this is where we completed *Around the*

World, the film which won six Oscars and revolutionised the industry in terms of wide screen. In the cutting-room Gene Ruggiero and his assistants were working under unusual conditions. Sitting in a chair was a sheriff armed with a revolver. I saw him there in the morning and when I came back to the cutting-rooms after lunch he was still there. Apparently it was believed that we would try to remove the film from California, where money was owed, to New York. So we worked on one reel at a time, and after each reel was completed it was locked in a vault to which only the sheriff had the keys. That was how *Eighty Days* was finished.

One of the great tragedies of the film industry was the untimely death of Mike Todd in an air accident. He was on his way to have dinner with a friend in New York. Although the weather reports were bad, he persuaded the pilot to take off. No one ever refused him.

When I met Todd again after *Around the World in Eighty Days* he asked me if I would work on *Don Quixote*, which was going to be his next picture. But by then I had decided that I wanted to make a film of my own. After *Eighty Days* I had gone to the Bahamas and found myself enthralled with the life there; completely enthralled with the underwater life. I toyed with the idea of making an underwater film and began to develop a story.

A producer named Martin Ransohoff had a commercial film company in New York, but had not at that time made a feature film. He and I teamed up and I became the leader of an expedition in which we drove six cars around the world. The idea had been to take a Ford around the world in eighty days; but eventually it developed into a caravan of two camera units and a lot of people, not to mention big trucks with spares. We had become involved with an advertising agency and they wanted to make a commercial in every country we passed through. We started in New York, drove across Europe and then through Iran, Afghanistan, India, the Malay Peninsula, on to Thailand and down through Cambodia into Saigon. We completed the schedule in one hundred and four days.

I was returning to California via Honolulu when I ran into Todd at Honolulu Airport. He asked me again if I would work on *Don Quixote*, and again I said no. I was still thinking of my own film. In

Cambodia I had read a short story called *The Boy and the Bridge*. It was about an American boy in San Francisco, but I intended to change the character and the setting to a Cockney boy on Tower Bridge. When Todd asked me what my plans were I told him I had two pictures in mind: one of them an underwater picture and the other, an alternative, the picture about the boy on Tower Bridge. After listening to me, he spoke the most prophetic words: 'I know you very well, Kevin. If you make this film about the boy on the bridge, you may have an artistic success, but you can't eat awards. Take my advice and make the underwater picture.'

I ignored his advice. I made *The Boy and the Bridge*, which had a modicum of artistic success but was a disaster financially. I raised £100,000 privately and directed and produced the picture, which was probably too much work for me to undertake. I don't think I had the capacity to do both jobs; one should confine oneself to one or the other. The subject required total concentration on the part of the director. On the production end we had no distributor. I simply got a unit together and we worked from a house in London. The picture took about five months to complete and when I realised what had happened it was too late. When I re-run the film today I can see the snags. I had tried to make a feature out of a short story and there was too much padding.

We negotiated a contract with Columbia and they agreed to distribute the film in Britain, largely because it had been chosen to represent Britain at the Venice Film Festival, so they probably thought it had some monetary value. It didn't do badly in Britain, but Columbia did not pick up the option to distribute the film in America.

I decided after this to throw over my artistic notions temporarily and make films purely in terms of box-office. It was then that I returned to the Bahamas, quite convinced that an underwater picture, using wide screen and colour, would be successful. And this, of course, was *Thunderball*. I visualised an underwater Western, but my backer wasn't enthusiastic. I considered that sequences involving underwater battles would be a very important ingredient, and this is how it eventually turned out. But my backer asked me to read the Ian Fleming's novels, *Diamonds are Forever* and *Live And Let Die*. I read them, but reiterated my idea for an underwater film. We eventually agreed on a storyline in which an atomic aircraft would be hijacked and hidden underwater in the Bahamas, with James Bond coming to save the world. I engaged a writer called Jack Whittingham, and he and I worked on the script.

When I was first introduced to Ian Fleming he had already written seven James Bond books, but not one of them had been sold to a film producer, except *Casino Royale*, which had been bought by Gregory Ratoff. Ratoff was unable to interest any distributor. Nobody saw the potential of James Bond at the time. But to me the potential of Bond was all too apparent. I was not too enthusiastic about the stories as they were written; Fleming had written them for a reading public, but to me they were not sufficiently visual. The books would have to be re-written, so I thought how much better it would be to start from the beginning and write a story specially for the screen using the character of Bond. I told Ian Fleming what my views were: that I was interested in filming an underwater story set in the Bahamas, that the character of Bond would be a box-office attraction and that the setting of the islands would be totally right for him.

Jack Whittingham worked at his house down in Esher, but every week he would come up to London and he and I would go over the storyline together. By now we had practically completed the first draft of the screenplay. Ian had not done a great deal of work, and we didn't see too much of him. At this time I think Ian got himself agents in MCA and someone may have said to him: 'This is a great story, but why do you have to do it with McClory? You know *The Boy and the Bridge* was not a success.' Somehow or other I think he got into this frame of mind and problems arose. He went off to Gold-eneye in Jamaica and wrote a novel based on the screenplay. This led to the court action which I eventually had to take against Ian Fleming, in the first instance to try for an injunction against the publishers of the book. But by that time Jonathan Cape had already printed I don't know how many thousand copies. The judge said that because there might be more to the case than met the eye he could not penalise the publishers at this stage and that we would have to resort to further action. And so the book was published without any credit to Jack Whittingham or myself. The storyline was ours, but the title and central character were Ian's, and the film project ought to have gone through successfully. In fact, our company should have had all the Bond pictures. We had an agreement with Ian to make the first Bond film, the idea being that we would choose the actor to play Bond and if the film was successful we would go on to make others. Although I was legally bogged down I was determined not to give up. I had put too much of myself into the venture, and I was determined to fight no matter how long it took me. It took a long time. I didn't have the resources that other people might have had to fight, and unhappily the case had to go to court. After ten days the other side capitulated. They had to pay the costs, which were enormous, and they had to assign the screen rights to me and admit that *Thunderball* was a joint work and that it was improper for Ian Fleming to have published it as his own.

I now found myself the sole owner of the screen rights of *Thunderball*, leaving Ian with the rights of the novel. I joined in partnership with Cubby Broccoli, for whom I had worked for some time, and Harry Saltzman, and we agreed that I should produce the film in the Bahamas with them as partners. Whilst I had been battling away with Ian he had made a deal with them and sold them the rights of all the books that he could, including *Thunderball*. They had made *Dr No*, which was a highly successful film, and then *From Russia with Love*, which was even more successful. With *Goldfinger* James Bond had really caught on. So although those years had been spent in what seemed futile and frustrating legal battles, by the time *Thunderball* had reverted to what I can truthfully call its rightful ownership, the public was ready for it and the distributors were ready to put up the kind of money required to make it. Had the previous Bond pictures not been made, commercially it might not have been easy for me after *The Boy and the Bridge* to raise six million dollars to make *Thunderball*. As it turned out, the investment was fully justified and *Thunderball* was the most successful James Bond picture.

Before making *Thunderball* I decided to make a home in the

Bahamas and bought a house there. The Bahamas are the base for the various companies I control. The most important part of one's existence is not the creation of a motion picture or the writing of a story, but the obligation of bringing up a family. I don't think the Bahamas are a good background for a child; the life is indolent and the educational facilities are not as good as they are here. A camera crew is a camera crew, a location is a location, and a subject is a subject. I had been used to making films anywhere, but my decision to return to Ireland was made for me by my children. I wanted them brought up in Ireland just as my father had wanted the same upbringing for me.

Twenty-five years ago I was more concerned with developing myself, and although I wanted to return here I had to go where the work was offered. The more time I spend in Ireland the more interested I become in the facilities for making motion pictures; and almost everyone I meet is a born actor. When you make a film like *Thunderball* you get together with another writer and dream up ideas of characters being eaten by sharks and find new ways for them to fall through holes in the floor. But in the film I plan to make in Ireland I shall deal with a very sensitive period of history, the unfortunate period of the Civil War. Men still refuse to forgive and forget, and yet I think they should and that Ireland would benefit by it. There are people who don't want to see me make a film about Michael Collins lest he may become a national hero. If Collins deserves to be a national hero, he will be one whether or not my film is made. Five years ago a friend of mine gave me two volumes on Collins written by Piaras Beaslai in 1926. When I read the books it occurred to me that this was a man about whom I didn't know very much, and when I talked to other people they didn't seem to know much about him either. I felt that a knowledge of Collins was being denied to young people, and I was interested in knowing why. The man had played a significant part in the movements necessary to bring about the Republic of Ireland, and I think it a tragedy that the Irish people are not able to give recognition to him without worrying what their neighbours will think or what the Government will say. Either Collins was a talented, resourceful, energetic, magnificent organiser who believed totally in a free Ireland, or he wasn't. That is how the dreadful split came about. To say that the man was a myth is to create a legend.

Shaw's letter to Michael Collins's sister suggested that if Collins had lived he might have been a disappointed man. Shaw wrote with the knowledge he had of other political figures, and he was talking about a Collins who was thirty-two years of age and had achieved a great deal in the six years before his death. I think Shaw had a pretty good knowledge of politics and could see that it was more than possible that Collins, like any other man, could become totally disillusioned. Had he lived – and he would be over eighty years of age now – he might be in power today, or he might have been thrown out of office years ago and be living on a farm. He might have done something worthwhile with this country and on the other hand power might have gone to his head. The information I have researched on Collins has never been published. Maybe those authors of the Collins biographies have undertaken more thorough research than I have, but they may have chosen not to write everything they knew. For that reason I suspect that some of these writers have been more interested in a romantic than a factual figure. I find the man too realistic to be a romantic figure. I don't think he looked on himself as romantic, although many of his enemies say he did; they point to a photograph of him in uniform with his chin held high. Maybe it was his proud bearing; on the other hand he could have looked up at the moment the camera clicked. But the photograph gives his enemies ammunition. Collins was a total realist, I think, in comparison to the majority of the others, who were idealistic. But he was running from house to house and climbing in and out of skylights and he had no time to study politics. This basically was his undoing.

Let me finish with a story. Once upon a time in Banbridge in the County Down there was a farmer who had a daughter who was the belle of the village. Her name was Alice McClory. The McClorys were a very Catholic family, but Alice met a Protestant named Hugh Prunt, or Prunty as it was sometimes called. Now Alice's father, Red Paddy McClory, was a formidable, heavy-drinking man who wielded a large club and chased anyone who came near his daughter. When he learned that Prunt was a Protestant he invited him to his house and offered him drink. But Prunt didn't risk drinking, so McClory and some of his relatives beat him up and Prunt fled.

Paddy now decided it was time Alice was married. After some persuasion she agreed to marry a Catholic farmer named Byrne, who lived in Banbridge. The banns were called and the wedding arranged. It was the custom in those days for the bridegroom to ride with his friends to collect the bride at her house. Drinks would be waiting and the man who got the first cup would become the bridegroom. So his friends would allow him to reach the house first. But when Byrne arrived at the McClory house, Alice had gone. She had last been seen in her wedding dress, riding over the moors with a stranger on a black horse.

The wedding party set off in pursuit, but they never found her. When they returned to the house they found a message inviting them to drink the health of the bride who had married Prunt; which indeed she had.

Prunt changed his name to Brontë and had twelve children by Alice McClory, who was my great-great-great-aunt. Although she' was a Catholic, they became a Protestant family and moved to Yorkshire. One of those twelve children was the Reverend Patrick Brontë, the father of Emily, Charlotte, Anne and Branwell. Branwell died at thirty, having drugged himself on laudanum and drink and God knows what else. I think he was a much maligned man and had a great deal to do with aiding the imaginative and creative powers of his sisters. Out of a sense of family history my wife and I have called our son Branwell.

11

ᘓ ᘓ ᘓ

The Rose Tattoo : Arrest and Trial

ON THE MORNING of Friday, 24th May, 1957, the following report appeared on the front page of the *Irish Times*:

DUBLIN THEATRE DIRECTOR ARRESTED

Four detectives arrived in a squad car at the Pike Theatre Club in Herbert Lane, Dublin, last night, and took Mr Alan Simpson, co-director of the theatre, to the Bridewell. While Mr Simpson was being taken away a capacity audience in the theatre was watching the first English-language production in Europe of *The Rose Tattoo*, by Tennessee Williams. The theatre was given a guarantee by the Dublin Tóstal Council in connexion with the presentation.

Before the police arrived to take him away Mr Simpson told reporters that last Tuesday Inspector Ward of the Civic Guard informed him that if *The Rose Tattoo* was presented that night he would be arrested. Mr Simpson said that Inspector Ward told him that his instructions came from Deputy Commissioner Garrett Brennan.

The squad car carrying the four detectives arrived at Herbert Street and was parked at a corner of Herbert Lane. A number of photographers were present outside the theatre and the detectives remained in the car for some time. Eventually, two detectives left

Milo O'Shea as Leopold Bloom in the film *Ulysses*.

Sean O'Casey, who withdrew his Festival play, *The Drums of Father Ned*.

[*To face page 128*

Dan O'Herlihy as Marshal Ney and Rod Steiger (right) as Napoleon in the film *Waterloo*.

Micheál MacLiammóir at lunch in the garden of his Dublin home.

the car and walked towards the theatre. One stopped half-way to the theatre and the other continued on. At the entrance to the theatre he approached the photographer and said he objected to having his photograph taken and the photographer replied that nobody had taken his photograph. The detective then walked over to Mr Simpson, who stood with his wife (Miss Carolyn Swift, co-director with him of the theatre), and spoke to him for some minutes. As this conversation was proceeding, photographers took pictures and the detective ushered Mr Simpson and his wife through the door into the entrance of the theatre, where the conversation was continued. The detective left shortly afterwards and returned to the squad car in Herbert Street.

Mr Simpson reappeared almost immediately and said that he had been asked by the detective to go round to the squad car to have a chat with Inspector Scanlon as they wanted to avoid publicity. Mr Simpson said that he declined to do so. The squad car was driven off. Twenty minutes later it reappeared and was driven into the lane. Three detectives spoke to Mr Simpson and escorted him to the door leading to the booking-office. They stood just inside the door, talking, and as photographers levelled their cameras, the detectives put their shoulders to the door while Mr Aidan C Maguire, manager of the theatre, attempted to hold the door open to allow the photographs to be taken. Five minutes later Mrs Simpson went to the door, which had been opened, and had a brief conversation with her husband, who was then led to the waiting car, a detective holding his arm. After the car had been driven away, Mrs Simpson said that her husband had been taken to the Bridewell.

On the following morning Simpson, described on the charge sheets as 'an Army officer', was charged in the Dublin District Court with 'producing and showing for gain a performance which was indecent and profane'. The court was filled, according to one newspaper, 'principally by members of the theatrical profession' and some members of the Press could not find seats. The case was adjourned until 4th July and Alan Simpson released on bail.

On the stage of the Pike Theatre on the night of Simpson's arrest was Dublin actress Anna Manahan playing Serafina in *The Rose Tattoo*, her first important role.

* * *

It was just before the first Dublin Theatre Festival that Alan Simpson asked me to play in *The Rose Tattoo*. I had first met him in the summer of 1949 when I was with a company called the 37 Theatre with Barry Cassin and Nora Lever. I was only a girl, but I was playing character parts for which I was far too young. Alan saw me playing in Limerick one weekend and said: 'Some day I will find a wonderful part for you.' In the following years I worked at the Gate with Hilton Edwards and Micheál Mac Liammóir. In 1956 we went on a tour of Egypt, where my husband, whom I had married the previous year, died from polio and was buried in Alexandria. When I came back to Ireland the Gate ceased to function as a nine-months-a-year company. The roles for actresses in the Dublin theatre were few. I made my way slowly and earned just enough money to get by. Managements couldn't afford to pay you much, and when I played in the basement theatres I earned from two pounds ten to four pounds ten a week. By 1957 I had begun to play more or less permanently with the Globe Theatre. They were very good to me and gave me constant employment. Norman Rodway, Milo O'Shea and all of us were earning the princely sum of six pounds a week, but we also played small parts in radio shows for thirty shillings. We were happy, but you could not build a life on such earnings. That year I had played in several shows at the Pike when Alan said: 'Anna, I've found the part for you.' I had never undertaken such an enormous role as that of Serafina, one of the longest parts written for a woman and very taxing both physically and emotionally. I was scared of it and told him I did not think I could do it. But Alan had a gift of picking the right people for parts. Actors like Milo O'Shea blossomed in the Pike. Godfrey Quigley said to me: 'If I were directing this play I would put you in it.' So I went, with Godfrey's blessing, from the Globe and began to rehearse *The Rose Tattoo* without pay. It was to change my whole career.

We have no censorship in the theatre in Ireland, but if somebody complains to the police they must act on that complaint. It was on the fourth night, I think, that Alan Simpson was taken to the Bridewell. We finished our seven nights' run. The police allowed us to go on every night but warned us that we were likely to be prosecuted, but we continued to the end because we believed in the play. The bone of contention was that the truck driver drops a contraceptive on the stage. What in fact was dropped on the stage was an envelope which, it was intimated, contained a contraceptive; but there was no actual contraceptive in that envelope. In the play Serafina rejects him because of this action and throws him out of her house. She could not possibly love any man except as her religion ordained her, which makes the play entirely acceptable from a Catholic point of view. Much of the dialogue was in Italian at that point and it was left to the audience to deduce what had happened. I think the police were privately disgusted with the whole affair. People said that a friend of somebody who was powerful in high places had brought pressure to bear, but the true story has never come out. I will always remember the dramatic moment when the judge acquitted Alan after all those weeks. He got his books and banged them together and said that the play was tragic, sad and compassionate. He strode out of the courtroom in a magnificent final exit, as though to suggest that people who bring such charges should not be tolerated. The case finished the Pike Theatre financially, but it made that little theatre known throughout the world. The Pike had evolved a marvellous style of its own and I was very sad to see it go. I remember my landlady being asked at the time what she was doing with an immoral woman in her house, and some of the semi-pros would cross the road when they saw me. This was something I had not encountered before, but the people who did it were few and when we were cleared in court I was acceptable again.

When I left school in Waterford, where my family for generations had been connected with the amateur theatre, I went to Dublin and studied under Ria Mooney who had formed the Gaiety School of Acting. Among my fellow students were Milo O'Shea and Eamonn Andrews. There were six of us in our family, so I went on tour with a company called Equity Productions to help pay my school fees. Wilfred Brambell was in that group. One of the people running the company suggested that I send my photograph to Gabriel Pascal who was about to form an Irish film company to be backed by the Government. But there was a change of Government, and with that the plans for the Irish film industry changed. But during the run of *The Rose Tattoo* Cyril Frankel and Bob Lennard, the casting director, came to see the play and offered me a featured role in my first film away from Ireland. It was called *She Didn't Say No* and written by Una Troy, a clergyman's daughter, and was a sympathetic story of a woman with six illegitimate children who eventually marries. We made the film at Elstree and it was banned in Ireland.

My first appearance on the London stage was in 1958 in John Arden's play *Live Like Pigs* at the Royal Court. On the morning I auditioned I took off my shoes to do a piece from *The Rose Tattoo*. I am shortsighted and when I took a step too far I fell into the stalls and ended up in St George's Hospital. I flew back to Dublin that evening and arrived on the stage of the Globe in Dun Laoghaire for my part in *A Lady Mislaid*, on crutches and with one foot in plaster.

I remember after *Live Like Pigs* George Devine saying to me in Sloane Square: 'Anna, you made a fine impression. Why don't you stay in London?' But as soon as I had made an impression I would always get up and go. I always went home. I spent a year away from Dublin when I played *Lovers*, Brian Friel's play, on Broadway, and I wasn't happy about signing a year of my life away. But in order to afford to live in Ireland I have to work abroad. Playing on Broadway is like being a horse in a high prize race in which your backer stands to lose one hundred and fifty thousand dollars. In London they will nurse a play, but on Broadway plays were folding all around us. The lights on other canopies would go out, but our lights would still be glowing. The critics said that Art Carney and I had a perfect stage marriage. Art is a supreme artist, but in no way does he diminish another's performance. But I have played Hannah throughout America and in Dublin and London to so many Andys, including Art Carney, Niall Toibín, Peter Lynn Hayes and Joe Lynch, that with each new performer it has been like beginning a new part.

The theatre is international and players must work from time to time in other countries. But I don't see why this should entail taking up your bag and leaving your own country for ever. I don't see why

Ireland should be just a country where people learn their trade. Ireland is a country of talented playwrights and actors and Dublin has an international name as a centre for theatre. But there are too few subsidies. One of the most important assets Ireland can lay claim to, apart from its archbishops and priests and handcrafts and bacon, is its theatre, which has a standing in the outside world. I have been more closely associated with Phyllis Ryan than with any other theatre manager in Ireland. Since 1958 she has struggled against tremendous odds. She has scraped money together for play after play and by staging plays like *Stephen D* and *The Poker Session* has brought recognition to the Irish theatre. In the sixties she championed the plays of John B Keane, who wrote his *Big Maggie* especially for me, and she revived *The Rose Tattoo*. But she has never been free from worry. Time and again she has come to me and said: 'Anna, I shan't be able to make it for next season,' but the next thing is she has found the money somewhere and she struggles on again. Unlike the London angels, most people in Dublin who put money into a play want it back. They are bankers, and when the play loses they cry.

12

❧ ❧ ❧

The Drums of Father Ned: O'Casey and the Archbishop

THE SORDID AFFAIR of *The Rose Tattoo* in 1957 was outdone in the following year during Ireland's Tóstal (the Gaelic word for 'a hosting'). Tennessee Williams's play had been presented on the stage of the tiny Pike Theatre, but in 1958 plays by O'Casey and Beckett and an adaptation of Joyce were withdrawn before they reached rehearsal.

In September, 1957, Brendan Smith, the Director of the proposed Theatre Festival, submitted a list of twenty-five productions to the Irish Tourist Board, which was to make a guarantee of £15,000 available to the Festival. The Board agreed that the basis of the Festival programme, part of the overall annual Tóstal, should be the new O'Casey play, *The Drums of Father Ned*, and a dramatisation by Alan McClelland of Joyce's *Ulysses*. Both plays were likely to induce tourists to visit Ireland. Three mime plays by Samuel Beckett were also to be included in the programme.

The Festival, as in the previous year, was to be part of the Tóstal, which included other events. When the Catholic Archbishop of Dublin, John Charles McQuaid, refused to celebrate a Votive Mass to open the proceedings, Sean O'Casey, believing that the

134

Archbishop had tried to censor his play, withdrew *The Drums of Father Ned*. The Tourist Board told the Council to drop the Joyce adaptation, *Bloomsday*, because of the danger of public controversy. Then Beckett withdrew his plays. The Theatre Festival was abandoned, but the Tóstal went on with a military tattoo, athletics and folk dancing.

One hundred and fifty members of Irish Actors' Equity, the actors' trade union, condemned the abandonment of the Theatre Festival. Alan McClelland told the *Irish Times*:

> My play is a merry play. It is a play of life filled with sparkling language, all Joyce's. I refused to let the Tóstal authorities do it last year, even consider it, because I imagined there would ge a lot of squabbling over it. I was persuaded by Brendan Smith to give them the opportunity this year. I thought that this year they had grown up. But apparently they haven't. I am completely stunned by the decision. One thing I am certain of is that the Archbishop has not read the script. I know that, because I had the play vetted by an authority on moral dogma and I am advised on any blasphemous passages, which I naturally agreed to leave out. I did not harm the play in any way by taking out such passages. In actual fact Joyce never intended them as actual blasphemy. They highlight the effect of the book, but were not intended as blasphemy. No serious reader would ever look upon them as such.

Hilton Edwards, who was to have produced *Bloomsday*, remarked: 'Everyone will feel very smug and very pure here; and they will be wrong as usual.'

A member of the Guild of St Francis de Sales, an organisation of Catholic journalists, was reported to have said:

> When the Archbishop of Dublin expressed his displeasure with the plan of the Tóstal Council to stage in Dublin, for visitors, plays of doubtful morality, and when he stresses his displeasure by cancelling the Votive Mass, it is a signal to all Catholics in the diocese to express their own disapproval. They can do this effectively in one way – boycott the Festival.

The Dean of Christ Church, the Church of Ireland Cathedral, said: 'We were to hold services, but we will have to discuss the situation.'

135

The *Irish Times* published an editorial comment, which concluded: 'Next year's Tóstal Council will be well advised to submit its programme to the Archbishop of Dublin in advance of publication if it is to avoid a similar wastage of money and effort.'

Whilst members of the Dublin Corporation threatened to withdraw their £3,000 grant for street decorations if the plays were presented, O'Casey wrote a letter from his home in Devon to the *Irish Times*. According to the dramatist Dublin took fright when the 'Face appeared at the window and the Voice spoke from the air.'

As O'Casey saw it:

> There we go; the streets of Dublin echo with the drum-beats of footsteps running away. The Archbishop in his Palace and the Customs Officer on the quay viva watch out to guard virtue and Eire; the other Archbishop draws the curtains and sits close to his study fire, saying nothing; and so the Hidden Ireland becomes the Bidden Ireland, and all is swell.

In the centre of the bitter dispute was a small man who came to be described as the Czar of the Irish theatre, Dubliner Brendan Smith, one-time actor with Hilton Edwards and Micheál Mac Liammóir at the Gate Theatre and now the head of an acting academy. His fee as the Director of the Festival which was to weather these storms is £1,200 with expenses totalling £500, of which £200 must be vouched for: money which he describes as 'idiotically low in relation to the responsibility which the job carries'. In his office above the acting academy, surrounded by scripts submitted from all over the world to the Dublin Theatre Festival, he talked without a trace of the bitterness he says he felt in 1958.

* * *

My contention was that Dublin was a city ideally suited to a theatre festival because of its unique traditions. The blueprint was submitted to the Tourist Board in 1956 and the Festival became a reality in 1957. From the word go, the Board had expressed extreme enthusiasm. The first Festival was as diversified as we could afford. I was able to arrange at the Theatre Royal for the first visit of the Royal Ballet and Margot Fonteyn, which placed a false emphasis on ballet in the Festival. We later lost the Theatre Royal when it became an office block; I was not sorry because it was in a way a botch of a building.

It was not the first time a festival had been mooted for Dublin, but I was the first to put the idea on paper and channel it in the right direction so that it might become a reality. With the approach of our second year we had a fine programme building up. The three main items were a new play by Sean O'Casey, an adaptation of *Ulysses* by Alan McClelland, and three mime plays and a radio play by Samuel Beckett. These were to be the core of the Festival; but in 1958 the Theatre Festival committee were wedded to a heterogeneous body called the Dublin Tóstal Council, which was set up to organise a spring Festival season not alone involving theatre but everything ranging from band parades to window-box displays and including a number of sporting events.

Because of the interests involved we had a great deal of trouble and this led to jealousy. Some members of the Council thought that the theatre end was receiving more support than the other activities. It was the custom of the secretary of the Dublin Tóstal Council to write to the Archbishop of Dublin for permission to hold a Votive Mass to celebrate the opening of the Tóstal. Before the 1958 Tóstal he wrote again, without regard to the fact that there was now a theatre festival included in the Tóstal and that it would contain controversial works. He applied for permission for the Mass, which was granted, but this permission was followed by a letter from the Archbishop's secretary asking if certain plays were included in the programme; to which the only answer was yes. After a lapse of some weeks a further note came from the Archbishop's Palace stating that, in view of the fact that these plays were included, permission to hold the Mass was withdrawn.

The matter could have ended there. But certain members of the Tóstal Council at that time made it their business to circulate among the Irish and the British Press the fact that there had been an exchange of correspondence with the Archbishop. As a result the news leaked first through the British Press, and Sean O'Casey was the first to react. He immediately assumed that his play had been censored by the Archbishop, which was quite incorrect; neither the Archbishop nor any of his representatives had seen a script of *The Drums of Father Ned*. Nevertheless, this was the attitude O'Casey took, and he withdrew his play.

It was then out in the open. The whole issue became disorientated. The Lord Mayor, who was automatically chairman of the Tóstal Council, was very uneasy. There was much discussion among the Lord Mayor, his chaplain, the Council members and the interests who were financing and supporting the Festival as to what should be done. There was a divided Tóstal Council, but not a divided Theatre Festival committee: they were of one mind that we should go ahead, even without O'Casey. But the Tóstal Council, through which all monies were channelled, reached the stage of debating whether the other plays should be also withdrawn.

Before they had arrived at a decision, Samuel Beckett withdrew his plays. There was unbelievable confusion. The Lord Mayor assured us that his chaplain had told him that there was nothing wrong about presenting an O'Casey play. Nobody, at any rate, knew what the play was about or whether it would be of interest. He suggested that there was no reason to feel so uneasy about the play as to encourage its withdrawal; however, the withdrawal had already taken place. Further confusion entered into the issue when the chaplain informed the Lord Mayor that there was no harm whatsoever in presenting *Ulysses*, which was a story known to everybody; but it didn't become clear until much later that he was confusing Homer's *Ulysses* with that of Joyce. As a result, an entirely artificial atmosphere was created. At no time did the Archbishop ask to see the script of *Father Ned* and the chain of errors began with the mistake of asking him to hold a Votive Mass. O'Casey was very sympathetic about our position, but he was convinced in his own mind that the play had been censored by the Archbishop, and nothing could dislodge this conviction. I did not go to Devon, but Jim Fitzgerald, the proposed director of the play, went to dispel

O'Casey's impression of what had happened and also to suggest certain changes in the script. He found a Sean O'Casey who was convinced that Fitzgerald was there as the Archbishop's emissary.

I had correspondence with O'Casey at the time, and he was genuinely upset, but for all the wrong reasons.

> Flat 3, 40 Trumlands Road,
> St Marychurch, Torquay, Devon.
> Tel. Torquay 87766.
> 19th July, 1957.

Brendan Smith, Esq.,
Festival of Dublin.

Dear Mr. Brendan Smith,

Of course there's a chance of a reply to your kind and courteous letter. I had a painful infection of the eyes, and had to limit my letter-writing, and keep only to the play. Well, here is the answer: There's a lot to be considered. I am on the fourth draft, and when this is done, it must be sent to a professional Typist to get fair clean copies. This will take a month at least. I havent any objection to your reading it (when it's ready), if you promise to keep its contents to yourself. First, though, to prevent unnecessary trouble to me and to you, I'd like to hear from you about your ideas for its production (provided that the play be acceptable – which is unlikely); the possible Caste, the probable theater, and the probable Director (Producer); as well as what you would be likely to offer financially for a licence to last only for the run of the play.

Another consideration: I amnt in any way eager for an Irish production, not being willing to provoke the Irish drama critics into another frenzy of making fools of themselves. Indeed, I have thought of refusing to allow a performance of any of my plays in the Republic. Another thing, too: I don't want to be one standing in the way of the younger or newer playwrights, who may have a play in hands for the Tostal. I've written to the Abbey already of how worried I was at them putting on JUNO for the last Tostal Week, instead of some play by a less known dramatist.

As for the play of mine, it is a little curious, a frolic, more or less, with an odd serious line here and there, and the Tostal as the background. I am of the opinion that this Festival could be a Bringer of new life and activity to Ireland, replacing the lost enthusiasm of the old National Movement, which, in many ways, is now old-fashioned, and outworn. Ireland, if she is to live, must create a new Ireland from the old one, and, I think, that this is the spirit of the play I have tried to write. Well, there's your answer, and, though it may not please you, be heavens, it's better than none.

With all good wishes and a dark blessing on the work you are trying to do.

Yours sincerely,

Sean Ó Casey.

———————

Flat 3, 40 Trumlands Road,
St. Marychurch, Torquay, Devon.
Tel. Torquay 87766.
9th September 1957.

Brendan Smith, Esq.,
i gceannais Festival of Dublin.

Dear Mr. Brendan Smith,

I am sending the MS of my play to Mr. J. J. Ó Leary, having completed it to my entire dissatisfaction.

He will give it to you after a preliminary reading of it – if he can find the time, and survives the reading.

I have changed the Name to THE DRUMS OF FATHER NED. I am sending it now because I assume that you will be anxious to arrange your program for the coming Festival as soon as you can; to make as many things as definite as you can as soon as possible. Of course, you will understand that the sending of the MS by me to you doesnt in any way commit me to finally deciding that the Festival can have it – provided of course that you might think it interesting enough. Now for a few remarks about what you say in your letter of the 10th of August last:

I am hesitant about giving the play, preferring that a newer Irish playwright should have all the chances of whatever honor and glory may be attached to the production of a play during the Festival; I am anxious to avoid anything that might arouse a natural envy, or a sense of frustration around any favor given to an older and, more or less, established dramatist; and I cannot – whatever you may say – forget the savage and ignorant reviews appearing when my last play was done by Cyril Cusack, from the lordly lad Dunno O Donnell Rory O Moore Cruise O Brien to the laddo writing in the English PLAYS AND PLAYERS: it was all an attack on Ó Casey rather than criticism of a play. I am human, my dear Brendan, and, like Yeats, don't like to give a chance to ignorance and venom to provide publicity for themselves.

I don't wish to have to do with the Abbey–Theater or Players. The first have never bothered to ask me for anything since Fred Ó Higgins died, so, since they're not interested in me, I am not interested in them. . . . For a Theater, I prefer by far the Gaiety, because, one, they did THE BONFIRE; and, more important, Mr. Elliman paid me the courtesy, when he heard I was writing another play, asked me to let him consider it; wrote again when he read that I had almost finished it; and, far as I can remember, I promised. So, when you have read it, maybe you'd let him read it, too, under the proviso that no one may be told of what the play is about. As for actors, there are in my mind C. Cusack, Eddie Byrne, S. Kavanagh, a chap named Quigley, I think, who played in the BONFIRE, Mairin Cusack, et al. The Producer? That's a question! I dont want to have - - - - - - - - - - - -, between ourselves; - - - - - - - - - - has had little experience, and has been confined to the usual naturalistic efforts, plus plays in the Gaelic, which, unfortunately, arent much to talk about. I have never heard of - - - - - - - - - - -, who, I assume, has no more experience than the others. You see, my play has something within it besides its 'realism', and it is this odd breeze within a wind that worries me in direction. However, we can discuss this later, if you should think after reading the play that it is worthwhile considering. Of course, all this in confidence, for I dont want to read angry letters in the Press, or have any floating in on top of me here.

Royalties: I don't want any GUARANTEE. The royalties paid for the BONFIRE, a sliding scale on the gross receipts (Cusack could let you know what they were; I haven't the energy to look up the contract), and an advance, say of £20 or £25 would be allright by me.

You say that 'exciting new material is just not coming up at present'; I cant say that my play will be 'exciting'; all I am personally sure of (and I may be wrong) is that if played and produced well, it will at least be exciting, with a lot of humor (I hope) and an overtone of seriousness threading it all together, touched by a fanciful imagination along the work's way.

By the way, I changed the name because I think the new one to be sturdier, and the play is, I believe, a sturdy one; and because I happened to remember that Mr. Molloy had written a play entitled THE WOOD OF WHISPERING – is that the right title? – and didn't want to confuse his with mine, a thing he might (rightly) resent. I hope your very fine program will come to pass, though I have doubts about a play on Casement. But beware! If Noyes hears you are doing ULYSSES, he wont set a foot on Ireland's pleasant strand. I wont say a word, of course, about the potential program. And by the way again, I think, if you do all you hope to do, I can hear Pangur Ban doing more than giving a purr! The cat in a rage! Well, no more for the present; I'll pack up the play and send it off to J. J. Now, I just want to thank you very much for your interest in my play, and for asking me to let you read it; this is, believe me, an encouragement, coaxing me away from some bitter feelings evoked by the abuse I have so often received for Play and Biography from my fellow-countrymen. See what was said in I. Press and I. Times about my New York Product of PURPLE DUST last year by an I. Crit. of the Irish News Agency, and never a word since, because, of course, the play was a great success, going on as strong as ever, and now in its tenth month. All good wishes to what you are doing for Ireland, and for the Tostal of the coming year. Amen.

Sean Ó Casey.

Flat 3, 40 Trumlands Road,
St. Marychurch, Torquay, Devon.
Tel. Torquay 87766.
11th October 1957.

Brendan Smith, Esq.,
Chairman, Irish Festival.

Dear Mr. Brendan Smith,

Very well, I give my approval that THE DRUMS OF FATHER NED be given its World-premiere in the Gaiety Theater, Dublin, during the Tostal Festival, and may God be with the work.

I am a bit uneasy still about the actors and the Director, but we shall have to leave this to God and to the best that all of us can do about it.

I am a bit troubled about the play being 'a full-scale National Production'. I don't want the play or the production to sound too big; so please try to modify this implication (Nat. Product.) as much as you reasonably can, so as to avoid any envy or sense of favor of choice by the other older or younger playwrights, who, indeed, may be working on a newer and a more original way.

One last thing is this proviso – the Agreement ends with the end of the run at the Gaiety Theater, unless additional arrangements be made by written consent of both parties to the understanding now agreed upon.

No more, now; I am struggling out of a heavy cold, influenza, lumbago, bad eye, and heaven knows what else or what others; and I'm busy starting on another possible book; so all I can add, have time to add is my best wishes to you and to all that you are doing.

By the way, our pal, J. J. had some criticisms to make, and, if he hasn't mentioned them to you, you should ask him about them, and see what you think of what he thinks too.

All the best to J. J. and to you again.

Yours very sincerley,
Sean Ó Casey.

143

Flat 3, 40 Trumlands Road,
St. Marychurch, Torquay, Devon.
Tel. Torquay 87766.
October 1957.

Brendan Smith, Esq.

Dear Mr. Brendan Smith,

Some time ago, Eileen [Mrs. Ó Casey] read THE DRUMS OF FATHER NED, and, talking about it a little, later on, said she didnt like the taking of the money episode between Skerighan and Bernadette. She thought that an Irish girl could be hardly so sophisticated (big word), so ready to seize a chance. Thinking over it, I think she is right. Irish girls (or Irishmen) arent clever at taking advantage of a condition of things which would mean money if they were a bit more brassy. They find it hard to make a bargain – bar at cattle fairs, where everyone is doing it. Alone, they are pretty hopeless; or dealing with one whom they know. They refuse what they are longing to take. Even the occasional lass on Leicester Sqr. isnt in it with her other-race competitors. We arent good for standing up for our rights, unless they are political ones, and when dealing with these, too, we lose sense, and become frenzied.

So I send you herewith the amended part of the play, and shall be glad if you would give it to the Director chosen to set the play out on the stage.

With all good wishes.

Yours sincerely,
Sean Ó Casey.

PS See additional change in second sheet. Some friends of mine discussing a Director have advised me to relinquish my prejudice against Hilton Edwards; so if you decide he might be best, go ahead.

Sean.

144

Denis Johnston, playwright turned war correspondent.

The late Padraic Colum, an early figure in the Irish literary renaissance.

Brendan Behan on a milk diet in New York for the opening of *The Hostage*.

Cyril Cusack as Pope Hadrian in *Hadrian the Seventh* at the Abbey Theatre, Dublin.

Flat 3, 40 Trumlands Road,
St. Marychurch, Torquay, Devon.
Tel. Torquay 87766.
16th December, 1957.

Brendan Smith, Esq.,
Tostal Committee, Dublin.

Dear Brendan Smith,

Thanks for your letter of the 9th of this month.

About Jim Fitzgerald: I'm neither convinced nor happy, for I know nothing about the lad. I'll have to wait to see how he does it. However, I have confidence in your judgement, for you have had a lot of varying experiences, and should know your left hand from your right by now. So, in that respect, I'm satisfied, with the proviso that I have permission to pray that Jim will do himself and the play proud. About the choice of actors – all I know is that S. Kavanagh, C. Cusack, Eddie Byrne and Maureen Cusack, are good. Maureen, for instance, I imagine, would make a good Bernadette; but Jim Fitzgerald already knows all this, and I leave it to him to make the best choice possible.

Regarding transfers to Liverpool, Belfast, and the London Court Theater: Take notice that in a previous letter I laid it down that your licence for production of the play would end with the ending of the production in the Gaiety Theater, Dublin; so no transfer can be arranged without my written permission. I should like the play to be done in Belfast, of course. When Cyril wanted the Court Theater for the BISHOP'S BONFIRE, he couldnt get it; and I'm in no way eager to let this play go there. I assume that Liverpool is the Theater under Sam Wanamaker – a very dear friend of mine – but I doubt that the play would suit Liverpool, and I don't want to hurt the great effort Sam is making there to bring the Drama to that part of England. (I assume that Jim F. has read the play, and that he is willing to take on the production. If he didn't like it, or is anyway reluctant, of course, I shouldn't like to press him into the work.)

Finally, regarding Advance Royalty: A sum of £20 to be paid as advance royalty; which isnt to be taken as any precedent. I am just willing to help the Tostal all I can; and wouldn't give the same terms to London or New York.

Now, to end the homily, all good wishes to all the work you are doing to try to jerk or coax Ireland out of her apathy, and produce more of the Smiles na gCopaleení.

Go mbuanaidh Dia an Tostal.

Sean Ó Casey.

Flat 3, Trumlands Road,
St. Marychurch, Torquay, Devon.
Tel. Torquay 87766.
29th January, 1958.

Brendan Smith, Esq.,
Tostal Council, Dublin, Eire.

Dear Mr. Brendan Smith,

This morning I received a letter from The Globe Theater signed by Messrs Norman Rodway and Godfrey Quigley, which assumes that I have submitted my play to that Theater for consideration. You know this isnt so. I wouldnt give a play of mine under any circumstances to them. I give you just one quotation – after a number of comments they make on the construction of the play, etc., – Here it is:

'It is for this reason that we are writing to ask you to give Jim Fitzgerald the necessary authority to make such alterations as he requires, before committing ourselves to any definite action with the Tostal authorities.' It is but necessary for me to say that it was I, and not Fitzgerald, who wrote the play; and it is I who shall stand or fall by the writing. The demand to sign over to Mr. Fitzgerald the right to make changes to Mr. Fitzgerald's 'requirements' is, as far as I know, an unprecedented one; and certainly one to which I would never agree – to Mr. Fitzgerald or anyone else.

It is plain to me now that there is no theater into which Ó Casey can be allowed to fit, which is all OK by me; and that Mr. Fitzgerald doesnt understand what I am aiming at in the theater, and, also, that the manner of my playmaking frightens him. Indeed, this demand left me with little to say: there is no answer to it, save silence.

I feared that Mr. F. would be timid about it from the talk I had with him; but tried to encourage him by pointing out that a play presenting no difficulty in production isn't much use to a living theater; but in my heart of hearts, I felt that this wasnt the man to make any attempt to do the play. Well, to end, I have come to the conclusion that there isnt a Director in Ireland today competent to do first-class drama, bar, probably, H. Edwards, so I have fashioned the decision to withdraw the play from any production in the Republic of Ireland during the Tostal, or after the Tostal is done.

I shall be very much obliged, therefore, if you would return the Manuscripts to me – the copy I sent to you and the one given to Mr. Fitzgerald in the hope that a more familiar knowledge of it would prompt to a fuller courage in play production.

With all good wishes, and thanks for requesting the play in the first place.

Yours sincerely,
Sean Ó Casey.

Flat 3, 40 Trumlands Road,
St. Marychurch, Torquay, Devon.
5th February, 1958.

Dear Brendan Smith,

No, there is no change in my mind, nor will there be one. My letter to you concerning the one that came from the Globe Theatre Directors holds my refusal to permit the play to be done by the Tostal Committee; a decision I very much regret, but I am not prepared to have my play manhandled either by negotiations or without them. Your letter of the 4th but repeats the demands already made by the Globe Directors (why from them is a puzzle), but be it from these gentlemen or from the Members of the Dublin Tostal Committee, they cannot be accepted by me.

It is plain to me now that the Irish Producers, quite as strongly as the Critics, have neither sympathy nor understanding of my mode of playwriting; that they have no desire to even tolerate experiments; that their blather about technique – which they do not understand – embraces, not technique as such, but embraces, with a view to destroy, the spirit and the structure of the play. If they are determined to defend that boxed-in mind, well and good; that is for them to do; it is a very safe attitude to take up; but it is not for me. Since that is so, another Producer (you mention Guthrie) would have a bad time of it; and I am not willing that he should suffer for my sake. Besides, there's the Bishop's blast which Jim Fitzgerald seemed doubtful about: any outside Producer would have to contend with a lot, leaving aside the determination of the Council members and the G. Directors telling how the play would have been made. It is comic, all this demand for 'requirements, arbitration, negotiations, technical discussions', making the acceptance of the play like a conference between international foreign ministers.

Jim Fitz. has MS of the play, given to him (as I told you) when he was here, after telling me that you frequently borrowed the original script, and he badly needed one for himself so that he could study the play. He left one copy behind him in the hotel where he stayed, and Mrs. Ó C. searched for it in his bedroom but failed to find it. We looked through his bag again, but it wasn't there; then Mrs. Ó C. went back to the hotel, searched again, and found it beside the telephone. So both of the MS were given to him, the search and the finding of a lost copy fixing it all conclusively in our memory.

It isnt just true to say he left it here. There isn't a shadow of a doubt that he had it safe when he left us, both copies in his bag. I shall be greatly obliged to you if you see that this copy is returned to me. I thought the giving of a second copy would help him, give him courage, and prompt him to throw himself into the play; but, alas, it would seem that he threw himself out of it!

By the way, again, the Globe's letter was sent to an address of Totnes, Devon, with name of neither street nor house; and only the kindness of Totnes P. Master brought it to me. I haven't lived in Totnes for years. You knew my address, so did Fitz. It is known in Paris, Holland, all over the U.S.A., in Warsaw, Buenos Aires, India, Bulgaria, Moscow, Peru, Leningrad, Yugoslavia, Israel, Scandinavia, Berlin, etc., but, evidently, still unknown in Dublin. Anyway, they didnt even pay me the courtesy of finding out my correct address before they sent the letter, which a phone call to you would have found for them. Yet they evidently think they can tell me how I am to make my plays. Surely, they should know by now that O'Casey, rightly or wrongly, is determined to remain himself.

I am deeply sorry that you have wasted so much time over the play, for you have enough to do; but, to make some amends, I have wasted a lot of time, too.

I most earnestly hope that all the other adventures you have in hand to do may be highly successful.

With all good wishes,

Yours very sincerely,

Sean Ó Casey.

As a result of artificially-activated controversy and nastiness the Theatre Festival was postponed. The Tóstal went on in the spring, but the Festival was finally cancelled and everybody thought that was that. I never considered resigning, although efforts were made to use me as a scapegoat. When attempts were made to refloat the Theatre Festival in 1959, certain parties to the resuscitation, not my own colleagues in the theatre business, suggested that my continuance in the post of Director might be an embarrassment. But at a general meeting I was unanimously reappointed in an honorary capacity and the Dublin Theatre Festival was set up on its own, which it should have been from the beginning.

In one sense I think the Archbishop had been placed in a very awkward position in having an application made to him to have the Festival opened with a Mass. When he discovered that the Tóstal included a Theatre Festival and that this Festival contained plays with which, according to his reasoning, a Votive Mass could not be associated, he had no alternative but to withdraw permission for the Mass. The Mass, of course, should never have been asked for, and would not have been asked for if we had been an independent body at the time. On another level, I think that the Archbishop's advisers were somewhat culpable in contributing to the situation in not ensuring that the application was quietly withdrawn.

It was an agonising period to live through and to work through. But the public had its opinions about the manner in which the Festival had been jettisoned, and it is quite significant that from 1959 onwards we have had little or no trouble from minority nuisance groups trying in any way to impose censorship on the stage.

But I had been very uneasy for a few months in 1958 about the future of the Festival. I did not go to see the Archbishop during the controversy, nor did I seek an interview, nor was I asked to go for an interview. I think that the Archbishop realised the situation and that he was in no position to demand sight of the script. All he was concerned with was one author, James Joyce; it was not O'Casey. As a matter of fact, we sought a lot of opinion at the time and one well-known Jesuit gave me a written report on the play and told me it was time Joyce was seen on the stage and made available to a wider area of the public which had only heard of him but not read his books.

O'Casey was elderly at the time, and living outside Ireland for so long he had acquired an unbalanced view of what was happening; he was living in an Ireland of memory rather than an Ireland of present-day change. He had written the play specially for the Festival and in his letters the tone was not so much one of anger as of great disappointment; and, though this may contradict what I am saying, one of his intentions in the play was to show that Ireland was maturing. In the end he conveyed the impression that he was suspicious of everybody's intentions over here, including mine. It was an unfortunate business. As a result, O'Casey put a ban on the performance in Ireland of any of his plays during his lifetime.

I never met O'Casey, but I spoke to him on the telephone before the controversy, when things were progressing well. I had asked him for the play and he had written it with the Tóstal as a background. He was always, like Joyce, very clergy-conscious, but in a different way. Part of his play was devoted to the clash of ideas between a reactionary parish priest and a radical curate. I am convinced to this day that the situation developed as it did because members of the Tóstal Council representing non-theatrical interests provoked a public row quite unnecessarily. They did this deliberately as a means of sabotaging the Theatre Festival. They had an idea that *Ulysses* was dirty and that O'Casey might be anti-clerical.

The Drums of Father Ned was later presented in Dublin in the sixties at the Olympia Theatre, where it ran for three or four weeks. It was O'Casey's last play, and O'Casey, in all humility, acknowledged that it was not a great play. I remember his writing to me for an assurance that when it was presented he would not be keeping some young Irish playwright off the boards. He was a very bighearted man in some ways. I'm no Communist – I'm a dedicated capitalist, but I'm quite convinced that O'Casey's brand of Communism was tongue-in-cheek.

13

❧ ❧ ❧

Harris : The Ginger Man

THE FIFTIES, THE most controversial decade in the Irish theatre since
the twenties, ended with a call to the Government to introduce
theatre censorship. This unsuccessful resolution was prompted by
the last play of the decade to outrage certain playgoers and critics,
the presentation at the Gaiety Theatre, Dublin, in October, 1959, of
J P Donleavy's adaptation of his own novel, *The Ginger Man*, by Spur
Productions London and the Dublin Globe Theatre. In a three-
paragraph notice the theatre critic of the *Irish Independent* described
The Ginger Man 'as one of the most nauseating plays ever to appear
on the Dublin stage'. He concluded: 'It is an insult to religion and
an outrage to moral feelings of decency. Now that it has shocked
everyone with an average sense of values who has seen it, the best
course open to all concerned is to withdraw it with the greatest
possible speed.'

After the third performance the play was taken off. The management of the theatre stated that the play's run was being discontinued
because of the refusal by Spur Productions to make cuts which the
management had demanded. On the last night the theatre was half
filled and after the second act some people left. But the audience

applauded certain passages of the play. 'Tonight,' the management announced, 'the theatre will be dark, and Friday, well, we have nothing yet for Friday. On Monday we have the Rathmines and Rathgar Musical Society in *Iolanthe*.' That same week the curtain was rung down at the Theatre Royal in Dublin on the pop singer, Billy Fury who had refused to abandon his performance with a microphone. The writers of letters to the newspapers praised the theatre managers. 'A lewd play will destroy the moral fibre of a nation,' said one; another insisted that a fair criterion for a play was: 'Can you bring your wife and children to it?'

The producer of *The Ginger Man* was Philip Wiseman, who told one Dublin editor that his critic's notice was 'a deliberate attempt to incite a breach of the peace'. The four members of the cast in Dublin were Richard Harris, Godfrey Quigley, Genevieve Lyons and Rosaleen Westwater. Harris, a ginger-haired Limerick actor with a reputation for engendering controversy, had already appeared in the London production of the play, which had police protection on its first night at the Fortune Theatre because the management decided that it contained controversial matter concerning Ireland and the Irish. The London critics acclaimed the play and Harris went on to make films for celebrated directors from Anderson to Antonioni. But after *The Ginger Man* in Dublin he went into a Cornish nursing-home. 'The aftermath of this is terrible,' he told the *Irish Times*. Ten years later, with the novel of *The Ginger Man* again banned after three months' liberty in Ireland, Harris looked back on that episode in Dublin.

* * *

When I was making a movie called *A Terrible Beauty* in Ireland I was offered a part in the stage version of *The Ginger Man* which was to be presented in London. Jason Robards was to play the Ginger Man and I was offered the part of O'Keeffe. 'That's impossible,' I told them. 'I should play the Ginger Man. It's me. It's my life.' So I read for the part and I got it. They even postponed the opening until

153

I had finished my movie. We took seventeen curtains on the opening night in London and received incredible notices; but it didn't do well. We had opened during a General Election and a heat wave, so everything was against our succeeding. I can't quite remember why we brought the play to Dublin; somebody asked us to come, but the cast refused. Because of the play's nature they would not risk appearing in Dublin. I was willing to take the chance. Except for myself, we recast the entire play.

From what I had heard about the Dublin theatre I suppose I thought there might be some fun. But the uproar was not as extraordinary as I had expected. On the first night there were jeers and boos, and people shouted from the gallery: 'Take the play off!' Any moment now, I thought, I'm going to be hit with a bottle. It was just like the old days when they attacked the actors in Synge and O'Casey on the Abbey Theatre stage. I wasn't at all angry; in fact I was sorry when it came off because I was enjoying it. We played the second night, but on the third night they told us there would be no further performances unless we made certain cuts. Donleavy would not make the cuts and Philip Wiseman, the producer, and I had agreed not to make them. We knew that the curtain would not go up on the fourth night. At one stage, during the meetings in our dressing-room, I formed the impression that Donleavy would have been willing to cut the play for the sake of keeping it on, but I did not see why cuts should be made when we had not been given an official reason by any particular body. This did not annoy me, but it made the situation more intriguing. We learned from Louis Elliman, the owner of the theatre, that he had been asked to make the cuts. We knew that a Father McMahon, who was secretary to the Archbishop of Dublin, had been in Elliman's office and backstage, so we assumed that the approach had come from him. If I remember rightly they wanted to cut the references to Confession, and maybe my attitude of crucifixion at the end of the first act was on their list.

I wanted to defy them. I had received messages, unofficially and indirectly, that as a Catholic I should not appear in plays of this nature. I telephoned Father McMahon and asked him why he thought the play was anti-Catholic and why I should not appear in it.

I asked him to tell me specifically what was wrong with the play and what references were offensive to the Catholic Church. I told him I would like to know what position the Church took in the matter. He said it had nothing to do with him. 'But,' I said, 'you were around the theatre. We saw you here.' He answered that Louis Elliman had taken the play off. 'As a Catholic,' I asked him, 'don't you think I should have a chat with you?' He answered: 'Go and speak with your spiritual adviser,' and hung up.

It would not have been hard to outsmart me in those days, and I was left with no definite conclusion as to who was responsible for the play's closing. The sad fact about *The Ginger Man* is that it is now old-fashioned. It could have been a monumental movie, but Donleavy waited too long. It's poetic and the cinema has been moving away from verbal poetry. It's too eloquent, and styles and techniques have changed. In those days it is what the Ginger Man said rather than what he did that was captivating. In a movie his actions would be more important than his words and his actions are commonplace. Christ, my life story is more interesting than his. So is Malachy McCourt's. We did far more Rabelaisian things than the Ginger Man ever thought of. Every fifteen days I did something outrageous. I admit I was excited by *The Ginger Man*, and absorbed myself in the character, but that goes with inexperience.

When I was sick with tuberculosis as a young man I read Stanislavsky from A to Z. But having stewed myself in his writings I am now willing to discard them. I still use his preparations, I suppose, but the idea that Stanislavsky introduced a style is a fallacy. The Americans introduced a style to acting that had nothing to do with Stanislavsky.

I had never worked very hard at school. My father would say: 'Let him go his own way.' When I didn't turn up for school I imagine that the Jesuits who taught me were actually pleased; I think they considered that I lowered the standards of the school. At one time I was a very good footballer and was once spoken of as a future international. I was capped in Rugby as a junior for my province the year I caught TB. My ambition at the time was to be a footballer and if I had not caught TB I would not be sitting here now talking to you. I didn't go to a sanatorium, but was confined to bed in my home for three years. I had been badly educated. The Jesuits were not to blame; they had offered me an education and I hadn't availed of it. But when I was sick I began to read and this reading formed my mind. When I wasn't reading I used to conjure people from light bulbs and pillows and glasses and teacups. I used to speak to them and recite Shakespeare for them. This provided me with a curious introverted stimulation.

When I was finally told I was clear of TB I had decided to become an actor. I was twenty-four and a late starter. I had seen McMaster and Mac Liammóir and Siobhán McKenna when they toured in Limerick, but they had no influence on my deciding to become an actor. My motivation came from my reading. Had I applied to join one of the companies in Dublin it might have taken me years to get a part, so I decided I would try to cram a quick course in London. I didn't know anybody in Dublin, so though London would also be strange to me it had the best academies available.

I was turned down first by Central School because I was a little old and I was ugly, and it wasn't the day of the ugly young man, but the day of the John Nevilles. Finally, when it came down to brass tacks, I suppose I wasn't very good. When Central School turned me down I applied to the London Academy of Music and Dramatic Art and they took me in. I performed the same audition piece for them: a bit of *Richard III*, a bit of *Cyrano de Bergerac* and some improvisations. I wasn't a very good student, and most of the other students were seventeen and eighteen years old and I was twenty-four. But probably because I was older I twigged after a short time that academies are geared for failures. Eighty per cent of the academy's curriculum was concerned with stage management, make-up, carpentry, wardrobe. I decided that if I were to fail as an actor I wasn't going to become a stage manager or a carpenter. But fortunately LAMDA was the only academy in London with a Stanislavsky class, and that was the class in which I excelled. I couldn't be bothered with anything else. I was more keen on directing than on acting; I had thought of becoming a director before deciding on acting. There are no classes in London for directors, but I soon found myself directing students in end-of-term shows. I directed scenes from Shaw's *St Joan* and from Miller's *Death of a Salesman*. I even condensed *The Playboy of the Western World* into a one-acter. But it was to be fifteen years before I got my first chance to direct professionally.

It was after I had been a year at LAMDA that I was drinking in a pub one night with the poet Desmond O'Grady, another Limerick-man. He had some money and I had none and he was buying pints of cider. We heard somebody in the next alcove saying that Joan Littlewood was casting for Brendan Behan's play, *The Quare Fellow*, for Theatre Workshop. I borrowed some change from O'Grady and rang the Workshop and spoke to Gerry Raffles, the manager, and asked him if I could come for an audition. He said there was only one part available. 'How old are you?' he asked. When I told him twenty-five, he said: 'The part is for a fifty-year-old.' I said: 'I promise you I look fifty. I haven't eaten for months or slept for weeks. Don't turn me down. Let me come and see you.' After some hesita-tion he said: 'If you want to come out, I'll see you.' I borrowed more money from O'Grady and took a tube train to Stratford East. Half-way through the audition, for which I used the improvisation on which I had worked quite hard at the academy, Joan Littlewood stopped me. She said: 'Look, you're far too young for this part. But there is another part, the part of Mickser, and I'm not too happy with the casting. Would you like to play it for ten pounds a week?' I almost collapsed with delight and fright. An aunt of mine had left me some shares in Guinness's and these had put me through the academy. When I had paid my fees I had two pounds a week with which to pay for my room and food. That was how I had regulated my income. But halfway through my studies I invested all the money in a play in the West End called *The Country Girl* and lost everything. I had paid my fees in advance, but I could no longer afford a room. Some nights I would sleep on a sofa in a friend's room, or a girl friend would let me stay in her flat until the affair broke up.

After *The Quare Fellow* I spent two seasons with Theatre Work-shop. Finally Joan Littlewood told me that I was going to star in the next production, *Man, Beast and Virtue* by Pirandello. I was petrified, more so because Joan Littlewood was going to Czechoslovakia to swap places with a man called Franz Yamnick. Yamnick was to direct Pirandello and I was to read for him the next day. I went home and told my wife that I would never get the part. I am the worst reader in the world. When other players are reading their lines and showing how good they are I am mumbling and not knowing what the hell it is about. That evening I got a copy of the play and read it all through the night. I was determined not to disappoint our Czech director. There were two parts: a neurotic tutor and, a much smaller part, a rough sea captain. I thought Joan Littlewood had made a mistake about my playing the tutor, so I learned the part of the sea captain. But she hadn't made a mistake; when it came to the reading two of us began to speak the sea captain's part simultaneously.

When the play opened I played the tutor and the reviews were good, especially Kenneth Tynan's. The play was to be transferred to the St Martin's in the West End or the Lyric in Hammersmith; the St Martin's meant waiting for two weeks, but the Lyric meant going in immediately. Business wasn't all that good at the Workshop, so they opted for the Lyric where the play died a death.

It was at the same time that the director Cliff Owen was preparing a play for television, *The Iron Harp* by Joseph O'Connor, and looking for an Irish actor to play the part of a blind man. It was on the last night of our play at the Lyric that Owen was walking past the theatre and saw my name on the billboards. He had never heard of me, but the notices said I was an Irish actor so he went in to watch the last fifteen minutes of the performance. On the following Monday I received a message from an agent inviting me to give a reading for a part in a television play. It was then ten minutes to four and the reading was at four o'clock. We were living in Earl's Court Road at the time, opposite the tube station, but if I was to travel by tube I would not make the appointment. I said to my wife: 'Look, I'll have to invest in a taxi fare if I'm not to be late.' We broke open the gas meter and I took the money to pay for a taxi. I arrived at the agent's on time and he kept me waiting for over an hour. By then I didn't care if I got the part or not. I could have travelled by tube for sixpence and I had spent ten shillings on a bloody taxi. When the agent saw me I gave vent to an outburst of indignation. I can remember the dialogue. 'I suppose you don't realise what ten shillings means to me,' I told him. 'Ten shillings means four meals for me and my wife and I have spent that money on a taxi to get here.' He was impressed and said that despite everything I ought to take home the script to read. When I went back to him I got the part and was paid fifty pounds for it. I had been earning six pounds a week in the Workshop.

Bob Evans, an executive of Associated British Picture Corporation saw the last twenty minutes of the play on television and there I was. As soon as transmission had finished he telephoned me and said: 'Don't sign with anybody, but come and see us on Monday.' I went to see them with my agent and they signed me for seven years. They took fifty per cent after they had paid me my weekly salary. I got thirty pounds a week for the first year, forty for the second, fifty for the third, and that's how it began. They put me into a few movies and I was soon getting good featured parts. With *This Sporting Life*, the rest of my career seemed to fall into place. I never cared very much about the money I was earning so long as I could eat. I ended up by getting around five hundred pounds a week for a movie. ABPC were paying me sixty pounds a week; they would deduct my sixty pounds from the five hundred and then split fifty fifty. Due to some misunderstanding I had signed for eight years. They would not release me from the contract, even when I told them I did not want to spend that eighth year with them. I said: 'You've made a lot of money and I've done very well, but it's ludicrous that I should continue paying you this money under contract. I'll take my salary this year and stay out of work.' Finally there was a meeting at which they asked me about my plans for that year. I told them I had been offered nothing, but I would give them twenty-five thousand pounds for my last year if they let me go. When everything was signed I put my hand in my pocket and pulled out a contract for five hundred thousand dollars which I had signed weeks beforehand for the movie of *Hawaii*. 'You codded me out of my eighth year,' I told them, 'and that's the name of the game.'

I am rich today. I don't have to act or direct to make a living. But I will act, and when I do I will have complete control. The mistake

I made as an actor was to give too much of myself. Now that I have directed myself in a movie, *Bloomfield,* I have learned to keep part of myself outside of what I am doing. On that movie I was relaxed; less concerned about myself and more concerned about the overall subject. Except for *This Sporting Life* I had never been satisfied with the results of any of my movies. To me *The Molly Maguires* was a heartbreaking experience. It was not the movie that I agreed to make. I set out to make a movie about a subject which was very much a part of Martin Ritt's background, and I knew he was dedicated to it. It was a story of an Irish informer who joined the Molly Maguires in the Pennsylvania coalmining district in 1870. Ritt took the story and related it to those people who had betrayed his own kind during the McCarthy witchhunt. Ritt was very bitter about this period and wanted to make the film as a personal statement. He was also attempting something even more subtle: he was exposing the treachery on which America exists and the men who will climb any kind of ladder to reach the top. His Mister Success would be an Irishman who gets off the boat willing to do anything to become successful, even betray the people he loves. He believes the issues at stake are right, but because he is alone he has no choice except to become an informer. When I saw Ritt's first version of the movie it was shattering and brutal, intellectually brutal; but, because of whatever pressures one must assume were placed on Ritt during the editing, the film was watered down. The film became a great compromise on the screen in which one was never involved.

In the movie industry one is subject to a gigantic machine which has no interest in good performances. The men who operate this machine are interested in getting your name into a movie in the hope that people will want to see you, but never for the reasons that you may be good or bad in it or for what you may be trying to achieve. Giant corporations have taken over the studios in America and are out to make money from motion pictures. Their bosses sit in on 'rushes' and criticise matters they know nothing about. A director can demand the right to the first cut, so they give it to him because it is obligatory. But once he has presented his movie they have the right to change it. A producer or director may use me to fight the studios, but no matter how much fuss I make they'll put out the version they think fit. Despite the shouting, they will claim it is their nine million dollars; and, indeed, with such financial investment involved they have the right to make changes.

All I know is that the movies I make myself will be my movies; they will be independently produced and nobody will dare touch them because I will have the final call. The distributors will buy my version or no version. To do this one cannot make the movies too expensively. One cannot pay enormous salaries. To some extent it must be a labour of love. If it is a success you make money; if it is not you go down with it, and that's the risk you must be prepared to take if you want to make a personal statement. But you've got to be strong. On *Bloomfield* I broke the rules in many ways. Whenever they told me something was impossible I wanted to know why. I had no preparation before the film began, because I did not know I would be directing. When the director resigned after ten days' shooting I used to sit up at night planning and rewriting the scenes for the following day. When we had rescheduled the shooting I realised I could not be back in London in time to play in the movie of *Scrooge*. My producer did not want me to lose six hundred thousand dollars and was willing for me to shoot the end of *Bloomfield* after I had made *Scrooge*, but this would have meant handing over the editing of my movie to somebody else and I said I wouldn't do that. I know famous directors who hand over their work when they have finished directing. They see the editor once a week and make suggestions while they're off doing other jobs, and then they believe they have cut the movie. But you must be there every day and look at every frame. You must supervise the laying of the soundtrack and the dubbing of the music; otherwise you have no right to call it your movie. In a way you place your head on the block because you must assume you are always right. I began *Bloomfield* with the experience of working with good directors, and this stood to me. I think the crew imagined I wasn't going to do it, or if I did it it would be an actor's brief indulgence in direction. We shot for sixteen weeks on a budget of one and a half million dollars. I had never worked on such an inexpensive movie in my career. My previous three movies had cost twenty-eight million dollars between them. But once I began to go through the accounts on *Bloomfield* I realised the fantastic wastage in the industry. The wedding dress Vanessa Redgrave wore in *Camelot*, a dress which was filmed through the flame of candles, cost twelve thousand dollars. Her gloves cost seven hundred dollars and she never wore them. From the crew to the catering staff, people steal. When you see the end product on the screen you wonder how it could have cost so many million dollars.

Nothing interests me enough to return to the stage. I would like to appear on the stage again, but I wouldn't care to spend six months in a play. You become a civil servant going into the theatre every evening at seven and coming out at eleven. I was never asked to play in Dublin by the Abbey or any other company. I would like to live on and off in Ireland. I have no roots. I have a house in Kilkee, in the West. I have a house in London that I prefer to treat as a weekend house. But I don't want to settle in London. I find it dull and obvious. I was terrified when I first went there because I didn't know anybody. Today it seems to me a series of restaurants that open and close; the menu is the same but the prices change, the address is the same but the *décor* is new, the music is the same but the sound system is different. Everybody thinks how exciting and fantastic it is, but it is only the same place with the same people. You walk in and Ringo Starr is at one table and Michael Caine at the other. It's like a huge family that cannot escape from itself. London is a place where people cannot sit down and spend an evening alone. It's wickedly sick. I was obviously a part of it at one stage of my life, but when I complain today about the lunatic way they live their lives in London they think I'm getting old. They believe that London is finishing and they want to be there to drain the last drop of juice.

I love my house in London because it is not a part of this. When I had no place to sleep in London I found this doomed Gothic Victorian house in Melbury Road one night. It was strange, but absolutely beautiful and I loved it straight away. For many nights I slept beneath a tree in the garden. When I had enough money in 1961 to buy a house I took my wife Elizabeth to Tower House and we broke in through one of the back windows. The house was locked and had not been lived in for eighteen years. It was a shambles inside. It looked as if the German Army had excreted everywhere. Statues and walls had been desecrated.

When I came back from America after making *The Molly Maguires* I read in the *Evening Standard* that Liberace had bought Tower House. I telephoned the agents immediately and described the house in detail and my part in having it preserved through the National Trust. They met me at the house at nine o'clock the next morning and by twenty minutes past nine I had signed a cheque and the house was mine. Liberace had not put down the deposit, so I beat him to it.

Tower House was built by William Burgess, the architect of Cardiff Castle. He preferred French to English Gothic and only about twenty of his buildings are in existence. He built Tower House for himself, but he died before the interiors, which were to be the epitome of his ideas in domestic decoration, could be finished. More than half his designs were not completed, but the plans were on display in the Victoria and Albert Museum. The Museum loaned me these plans to finish the house that Burgess designed more than one hundred years ago. Burgess was a man of genius in design, but his weakness was that he did not know how to display his house. He cluttered the place up and one couldn't see the walls for the furniture. The decoration he designed for ceiling, walls, drawers and floors has been completed for me by the descendants of the firm of craftsmen who carried out the original work.

When I go into Tower House and close the door behind me I might be anywhere. By nature I am nomadic. I like to travel and move into different areas among different people. I like to keep moving, and this in a way is the Irish thing.

I have no reason to be disillusioned about Ireland or about Dublin, because I have never lived in Dublin. But I like being Irish and I have found no prejudice against the Irish in London. After all, if the Irish pulled out the theatre and the cinema wouldn't be half as interesting, half as volatile, half as amusing, half as artistic.

14

☙ ☙ ☙

The Odds Against the Globe

To WATCH THE Globe Theatre company perform in the late fifties audiences made their way among the latest cookers to a tiny theatre above a gas company's showrooms. The Abbey Theatre at the time was in the doldrums. Its players performed in the shabby old Queen's Theatre, and usually its first nights stirred nothing but the cobwebs. Lord Longford's company at the Gate kept alive an interest in the classics. Between their own productions at the Olympia, Stanley Illsley and Leo McCabe kept their theatre open with visiting English or continental companies. Hilton Edwards and Micheál Mac Liammóir shared the Gaiety with musical comedy and pantomime; and audiences showed no surprise when Mac Liammóir played the Demon King at Christmastime.

The new Globe company was like a fresh breeze blowing down the Liffey; more correctly across Dublin Bay, because the company's little theatre was in the seaside suburb of Dun Laoghaire.

The driving force behind the Globe was Godfrey Quigley, who was working by day in an advertising agency. He gathered around him the most promising theatrical talents in Dublin, among them Norman Rodway, Pauline Delany, Milo O'Shea, Maureen Toal,

Genevieve Lyons, Michael O'Herlihy, Jim Fitzgerald, Anna Manahan, Donal Donnelly, T P McKenna. The company might have become a significant force in the Irish theatre, but it was defeated through lack of funds (it received no subsidy) and the need for a permanent home. Against these odds the members drifted away. Two of the younger players, Donnelly and McKenna, who found their true level outside Ireland, recall the period.

* * *

DONAL DONNELLY: The Globe was a great idea of Godfrey Quigley's. There were T P McKenna, Bob Gallico, Pamela Duncan, Genevieve Lyons, Pauline Delany, Norman Rodway, Godfrey and myself. We were told that the directors were Godfrey, Michael O'Herlihy and Denis Brennan. But to me the Globe was Godfrey. He was a real leader. We had many serious crises when morale was at its lowest, and he would then move in and lift everybody up and soon you were back with your enthusiasm again.

The Globe was worked on a share basis and we each got thirty shillings a week. We were young and played parts which were completely wrong for us. We lived and worked in Dun Laoghaire and we seldom saw the city. It may sound like a little seaside repertory company, but it meant much more to us. We presented a cross-section of plays: startling American plays like *Detective Story* to plays of commitment like *Monserrat*. We played Paul Vincent Carroll, O'Casey, even Farquhar. Jim Fitzgerald came in as producer. Godfrey did not know him, but I had known him when we were teenagers and I was in his amateur company. He was a very gifted young person. He was working in British Railways when Godfrey asked me to write to him and invite him to come on a three-month trial. He brought inventiveness and style and one kept wondering where he got his knowledge from.

When they co-opted Milo O'Shea to the board and turned the Globe into a company the actors were paid a basic six pounds a week.

165

When they asked us to appoint a shop steward who would be our spokesman we chose Norman Rodway, who was in Guinness's and very efficient in procedure. They then decided that the shop steward could be co-opted to the board and in a few months Norman became a director. We now had no shop steward, so it was merely a situation of employer and employee. I suppose it could not have lasted.

When I left school I had been doing walk-ons with Lord Longford's company at the Gate, hoping to find a permanent position. When I was twenty-one a vacancy occurred in stage management and I got the job. It often seemed to me that because of Lord Longford's heritage an assistant stage manager to him was like an under-gardener on his estate in Castlepollard. I thought I was wasting my time, but with every year that passes I value the experience. There were no drama schools in Dublin as such, so Lord Longford's theatre was a place in which to work and train. I was a sweeper, a carpenter's mate, a paint-mixer, a prop hunter, a prompter, a teamaker, a callboy. I was very frustrated, but I now realise what people must learn in the theatre. In these days of instant success there are pressures on boys and girls in the commercial theatre to reach stardom by twenty-three. Because they are young they panic. If they think they haven't crackered, which is the word they use, they become almost hysterical. Longford was the king of the Gate as Blythe was the king of the Abbey; but at least he would raise your hopes and maintain your enthusiasm. He made a direct appeal to my intelligence because he cared.

My time with the Gate ended when Godfrey Quigley told me he was forming a new theatre company and invited me to join. I went to Lord Longford to give notice. I had never really got on with him, and he just said: 'You can't get out.' I went back for my cards and he asked: 'Why are you leaving me?' I told him that I did not think there was potential for me in his theatre and that I felt no sense of excitement. He grew very subdued, and it was rather a sad goodbye.

When I left the Globe it was because I had become snug. I was a bachelor of twenty-five, earning six or eight pounds a week and, in addition, playing in late-night revues and doing a radio programme. I had my little Austin Ruby and I was cosy. I was settling into the belief that everything of importance was happening in Dublin. But I knew this wasn't my life. When we took *Juno and the Paycock* to Liverpool I received a telegram from Jack MacGowran inviting me to come to London to play in *The Shadow of a Gunman*; I had been debating what I should do when this invitation came. I went to London and acted in *Shadow* with Jack's company and then followed with *Juno and the Paycock* and *Red Roses for Me* for the BBC. I suddenly realised that in London I could do what every Irish actor and actress has a right to do: play in the dramas of their nation. In any other country young students can do this, but in Ireland it's only possible if one is a member of the Abbey Theatre company. But we had done it at the Globe.

I played O'Casey, Yeats and Joyce with the BBC or the Mermaid Theatre. Then I began to have difficult times. I was able to live on six pounds a week by working as a waiter or a post office sorter, but I was unable to act until I found Sunday night work at the Royal Court. It was here that I first met Lindsay Anderson. I did Sunday night plays for him which kept me sane, and then he formed a late-night acting school at Ronnie Scott's Jazz Club. We used to arrive at eleven at night and work until three in the morning. Lindsay ran the school and Anthony Page, just down from Oxford, was his assistant, and our class of about twenty included Tom Bell, Ian Bannen, Maggie Smith and Alfred Lynch. It was a place where you could make every sort of outrageous experiment. We used to work out our auditions there. Georgia Brown was another of us, and I worked with Georgia on her audition for *Oliver!*

Then George Devine heard about us and brought us into the Royal Court. The atmosphere which Lindsay Anderson had built up was killed. Suddenly we were in a schoolroom with George standing at the top of the class. However, the school created opportunities for me and Brendan Smith asked me back to Dublin to play Christy Mahon to Siobhán McKenna's Pegeen in *The Playboy*. It was the success of the Dublin Theatre Festival. We took it to London for three weeks and stayed for fifteen. From then on it was the usual thing of being known.

I don't love London, although I think it an incredible and fantastic city. I love Dublin, which isn't incredible or fantastic. When I first went to New York for *Philadelphia, Here I Come!* I felt more integrated in two weeks than I have felt in London in twelve years. The opening night on Broadway was scarifying. The fear of the unknown seized us. When we asked anybody beforehand how they thought the play would do, they would answer: 'Oh, gee, I dunno.' You must not be associated with a forecast on Broadway in case you forecast wrongly.

Everybody goes to Sardi's after a first night opening; Patrick Bedford and I were so shaken that we made a mess of it. Everybody was waiting for us to make our entrance, and we didn't realise it. We were looking around us like two yokels when a woman rushed up to us and said: 'The reviews are raves.'

London and Columbus, Ohio, were the only cities in which *Philadelphia* didn't mean a damn thing. Columbus is conservative, hypocritical Goldwater country where *Fiddler on the Roof* lasted ten days. In London the Chinese Embassy staff came to *Philadelphia*; the Americans and the Irish came; but not the English. Oscar Lewenstein said: 'Please stand at the box-office with me and I'll be surprised if two English persons ask for seats.' That night there wasn't one. Lindsay Anderson believed that the English hated the play because it described sensitive human relationships. The critics could not see the dilemma. One man who came to my dressing-room remarked: 'Here you have this boy living in this ghastly village with his loutish friends and his awful father and dreary housekeeper, and his time is spent in deciding whether he should leave this dreadful set-up. Where's the dilemma? He should get out.'

I played in *Philadelphia* in America for eighteen months, and that was too long to be away from Ireland. It is a mistake to stay away from the place that nourishes you. But it was whilst I was in America that I decided I wanted to spread myself by proving or disproving that I could direct. In the theatre an actor is inclined to accept and become part of a situation in which he sits and waits to be called. His lifeline becomes a telephone with an agent at the other end. The decision as to whether he is employed very often rests with people he has never met. I decided I no longer wanted to be a commodity to be used at the whim of people I didn't know or didn't want to know.

London has been good to me. But I have mentally rejected the notion that everything must be done in the West End. I shall still work there, but I know now that I shall not become that permanent resident London actor doing pretty well.

T P MCKENNA: At the age of fifteen I knew I wanted to be an actor and nothing else. I had played in Gilbert and Sullivan operas at my boarding school in County Cavan. But County Cavan is an unlikely place for an actor. When I left school I wanted to find a job in a city where I could be near the theatre. I passed a bank examination and expected to be posted to Dublin or Belfast. I was sent to Granard in County Longford. From there I went to Trim in County Meath, where at least they had a dramatic society.

This illustrates how difficult it is for a boy from an Irish country town to become an actor. It took me the best part of five years after I had left school to become a professional actor, and that was achieved by sheer determination. In England there are scholarships available in the provinces. I have known actors in London who had worked in the pits or on the boats in Hull or in grocers' shops. They became actors after a short time in a training school.

I arrived in Dublin at the age of twenty and I immediately set about getting to know the professional actors, particularly Godfrey Quigley and Milo O'Shea. I baulked at my chance of joining the Gate Theatre when I suggested to Dan O'Connell that I should leave my secure job. If the Earl of Longford should die, I was asked, and the company should disband, what would I do? I stayed in the bank for another two years, still doing semi-professional work. Eventually the bank transferred me to Killeshandra in County Cavan, back to where I had begun. A bank inspector suggested that I had not completed my bank examinations because of what he called my 'extra-mural interests'. So when my transfer came I left the bank without having a job to go to in the theatre.

It was 1954, the year of the Pike Theatre revues, and I was twenty-four. I played in some of these revues, and I remember saying: 'My God, Milo, twenty-four is a very late age to be starting!' Godfrey Quigley found me a job with the Longford Company at the Gate and between the Gate and the Pike we survived the summer. Then the Globe company, which had blossomed the previous year, was presenting a season at the Gaiety. I joined Milo in *The Seven Year Itch* with Godfrey directing. Milo had a car, and after the final curtain we would dash from the Gaiety along Baggot Street to the Pike and whip in for an eleven-thirty curtain up. At the same time we were rehearsing by day for a season of plays which Anew McMaster was preparing. So I worked from half-past ten in the morning until half-past one the next morning.

It had been thrilling for me to see McMaster playing *Hamlet* and *Macbeth* on his provincial tours, and now I was in his first production of *King Lear* in Dublin. That opening night in the Gaiety in 1954 was his first before a full audience. I played the Duke of Albany, one of five parts in that two-week season. I had rehearsed the parts in three weeks whilst playing in *The Seven Year Itch* and the Pike revues at night. I played Horatio to his Hamlet (and McMaster was in his sixties then); Lucentio in *The Taming of the Shrew*, which Hilton Edwards directed; Solanio in *The Merchant of Venice* and Montano in *Othello*.

When the season was over the Globe actors moved to the little theatre in Dun Laoghaire. Godfrey, Milo, Jack MacGowran, Michael O'Herlihy and Denis Brennan were the seniors; Donal Donnelly, Norman Rodway and I were the young fellows. We initiated the season with a play called *The Biggest Thief in Town*. It was a disastrous beginning. We were on shares and averaged about fifty shillings a week. Godfrey was carrying everything on his back. Unlike Donal and Norman, I was not living at home and my parents hadn't money. I knew I could not continue.

I started to battle for a place in the Abbey Theatre and in those days that was betrayal. There was a ferocious bitterness among actors about the Abbey and it took me years to lose my sense of having betrayed them. There was an antipathy towards the Abbey because it was a subsidised theatre and the other companies were out in the cold. Many actors were antagonistic because they had been rejected by the Abbey for their lack of Irish or for some other reason given by the management. But I thought that if I was given two or three years at the Abbey I could settle down and slowly learn my craft as I believed it should be learned. The desperate running around between one theatre and another did not encourage relaxation in acting or the proper approach to the profession. I had to say to Godfrey: 'Look, I can't keep this up. Things are too bad.' I suppose it was a lack of faith on my part, because after I left things did pick up for the Globe with the production of *Monserrat*. But I was not the only member to leave. Michael O'Herlihy, Denis Brennan and Jack MacGowran left, but Godfrey stood firm like a great oak tree. To this day there is no rationale about the fraction of the Globe; but you cannot run a company like that without subsidies.

I went to see Ernest Blythe. He said: 'There's nothing for you here,' but I was persistent. When Ronnie Walsh and Joe Lynch were brought before a 'disciplinary court,' McKenna was called in to fill the gap. My first performance at the Abbey was to speak five or six lines offstage in *Is The Priest At Home?* That was at the Queen's in the spring of 1965. You were never told you were a member of the company because there were no contracts. You were kept in a state of tension for years.

I spent eight years at the Abbey and was pushed fairly early into big parts. Now that I see how theatres are run from an administrative and planning viewpoint those years at the Queen's were monstrous. Plays were thrown on and there was no attempt to train actors. Ria Mooney produced almost every play, which was lunacy. She directed an average of ten plays a year. All the management seemed to be interested in was a comedy that would run for a hundred perform-ances and pay the bills. It didn't matter what rubbish went on so long as it was an Irish play by an Irish playwright. Acting with the Abbey was valuable in the sense that one got experience in different types of play; but looking back on those eight years I realise that I could have learned more quickly and in a more disciplined manner in a good

171

theatre. One accumulated bad habits; you can see them today among Abbey actors.

I was becoming depressed as one year succeeded another. The company was holding on to the hope that next year the new theatre on the site of the old Abbey would be ready. But it took eight years to get the damn place built. Because the Abbey was constantly under attack there was no sense of dignity left in the company. You felt incompetent. There was also a sense of alienation between the Abbey actors and the actors outside.

After the collapse of the Globe other companies sprang up. Around 1960 Norman Rodway and Phyllis Ryan began putting on plays at the Gate. Godfrey and Donal had gone to England, and Milo was doing everything: pantomimes, plays, revues, cabaret. Suddenly the theatrical year began to orbit around the Theatre Festival. Brendan Smith, a very able administrator, began to build up the Festival. One of his objectives was to interest English managements in Irish plays; and his first success in this direction was the production of *The Playboy of the Western World* with Siobhán McKenna and Donal Donnelly.

The next Festival success was *Stephen D*, Hugh Leonard's adaptation of Joyce. Norman Rodway played in it and Peter Bridge bought it for London. One night Norman came to me and said: 'Will you play Cranly in *Stephen D* in London? They are saying, of course, that you won't come because you are stuck in the Abbey for good.' I went to Blythe and asked to be released. In a strange way he was fond of me and I felt he did not want to lose me. But I think he knew that if he refused I was going to resign. So he gave me a year's leave of absence. The play was a great success in London and I did not go back to the Abbey. At the end of a year I wrote a letter of resignation.

I joined Donal Donnelly in a television play by Tom Murphy for the BBC, *The Fly Sham*. I felt rejuvenated, and I have been commuting ever since. I have tried to limit my television appearances to three or four prestige plays a year. I have appeared in films, although the parts have not been good enough. I had a good part in *Young Cassidy* until John Ford and I had a disagreement about a line in the script in which I was to refer to Daniel O'Connell's bastards. He said the line was a slur on O'Connell. I said it was true. He tore the pages out of the script in front of me and left me with about five lines.

My part for Tony Richardson in *The Charge of the Light Brigade* suffered when the film was cut by an hour and a half. Some actors who had good parts disappeared. I became very depressed. When Stuart Burge telephoned me to say he was taking over the Nottingham Playhouse from John Neville and intended to launch a new régime I agreed on an impulse to appear in two plays. I played the Bastard in *King John* and Surface in *The School for Scandal*, with Jonathan Miller directing. Miller asked me to stay on to play Trigorin in *The Seagull*. By Christmas I was tired and was thinking of going home. Then Stuart asked me to play Macduff. I did not want to play Macduff, but we had talked about a production of *The Playboy* with two talented young people in the company, and Stuart said: 'If you play Macduff you can direct *Playboy*.' I felt a whiff of excitement. I stayed on.

It was my first experience as a director and I found aspects of myself I had not known about. I found it reassuring to hold the reins. The players felt that I knew more about the play than they did. It was an Irish classic and I was an Irishman, whereas they were English. It was a psychological advantage, but I did not exploit it. I knew just how I wanted to direct the play.

The theatre has always thrived on revolution. The Irish theatre has come alive in times of ferment. Rebellion produced O'Casey. But since 1922 Ireland has settled into a middle-class morass. Even the Abbey has brought all its old reflexes into its new building. We are the most conservative country in Europe. We don't want change. The Church has infiltrated its teaching of respect for authority, age and constancy. The Irish were oppressed for years with only religion to cling to. Now, suddenly, the new God is Mammon. When I meet men I went to school with, the only question they ask is: 'Have you made any money?' You observe this in Ireland's Government – the lack of respect for the arts and the tearing down of beautiful buildings. This opportunity to make money is destroying the fibre of our people.

When I went to the Cork Film Festival I was appalled to see a play-thing in the hands of a clique of bourgeois people. Don't you realise, somebody said to me, that it's a Victorian city of merchant princes? Only in Dublin do I sense a feeling of unrest and social conscious-ness. This may seem irrelevant to the Abbey Theatre. But it's not. The Abbey's board consists of men mostly over fifty who have not kept in touch with European theatre. Europe had a war, and you cannot separate a country's literature, drama or art from its political life; they are intertwined. In England the class system began to break down and suddenly London was flooded with young fellows from Hull, Bradford, Wakefield, Liverpool – the O'Tooles, the Finneys, the Richardsons, the Halls. The gates were thrown open by the Labour Government and Northerners descended like hordes on Oxford and Cambridge. Young men full of vitality tore the English theatre apart. Yet they had the good sense not to guillotine Gielgud or Olivier. They staged their revolution without cutting off the heads of the men at the top. Peter Hall was given total charge of the Royal Shakespeare Company at twenty-six. The idea of handing over the Abbey to a man of thirty-five would seem horrific.

The Abbey is a beautiful building with a bad stage, as if funds had been cut to enable more money to be spent out front. The backstage facilities are primitive; the stage itself has no revolve. There is no department of design, yet every theatre in England worth a damn has a head of theatre design. Such things require money. Peter Hall ran Stratford into debt to preserve standards. When they said: 'You're £50,000 in debt,' he was able to answer: 'Ah, but look at our standard!' and they gave him another £50,000. But nobody is doing that in Ireland. The national theatre becomes a prostitute unless you have people of strong artistic integrity. The men at the top must not bend to the Government because they need money. Our present Government members are bullies, and I do not think the Abbey would be prepared to stage a play attacking the Government. We are not mature enough. We still produce good writers, but they flee in dismay. Ireland is running itself into a frightful middle-class philistinism. It scares the life out of me.

I have continued to live in Ireland. I do not like exhibitionism passing for patriotism, but I have no need to wear my patriotism on my sleeve; that would be indulgence and an embarrassment. My family have lived in the same village since the turn of the eighteenth century. My grandfather was a friend of Parnell's, my uncle was in the first Dáil and my father fought with guns in the War of Independence. I want my children to have roots and I can't find it in me to sell out here. I don't want my children to be exiles. Displaced persons are rather sad.

15

❧ ❧ ❧

Rodway : Stephen D and After

ON SAINT PATRICK's night, 1970, Norman Rodway arrived in Dublin
with four colleagues from the Royal Shakespeare Company's
Theatregoround to perform their repertoire of readings, *Pleasure and
Repentance.* It was a homecoming for Rodway who had left his native
city some years previously to pursue a career in London; yet this was
to be his first appearance on the stage of the Abbey Theatre. The
playgoers who applauded him that evening no doubt remembered
his days in Dublin with the Globe company and, more particularly,
the impression he had made on them as Stephen Dedalus in the first
performance of *Stephen D.*

A few weeks after that night at the Abbey Rodway was playing
Richard III with the Royal Shakespeare Company at Stratford-
upon-Avon. The London reviews were mixed; the critics seemed more
concerned with Terry Hands's direction than with Rodway's
approach to one of Shakespeare's most compelling characters.

Rodway, who has been described as an intellectual of the theatre,
is a versatile actor who might pass for an English actor in Ireland. He
is small in stature, yet has a remarkable stage presence. He is so
absorbed in the theatre that one feels he would be happy any place

in the world in which there is a stage from which he could communicate with an audience. In London we talked to him after he had spent a gruelling day in rehearsals for *Richard III*.

* * *

After I had appeared in the Dublin Theatre Festival production of *The Passion of Peter Ginty*, Hugh Leonard's adaptation of *Peer Gynt*, in the same Festival in which Mac Liammóir introduced *The Importance of Being Oscar*, Jack (Hugh Leonard) came to me and said: 'I've got a marvellous idea for you – a one-man show of Joyce's *Portrait of the Artist as a Young Man*.' He went back to London and we kept in touch with each other about the project. When he sent me the rough draft I told him: 'This is ludicrous. You need Peter Sellers for this.' 'Well, I could make a play of it,' he suggested, and this was what he did. To me it was just another show. When we put it on for the following year's Festival we had three weeks' rehearsal and my only concern was to learn the part of Stephen Dedalus.

Our producer, Jim Fitzgerald, had fallen in love with the play, but I recall that we had no dress rehearsal. There were one hundred and fifty lighting cues, which we finished rehearsing ten minutes before the curtain rose at eight. Jim wished me good luck and I answered: 'It's just a question of walking round the stage and hoping that Arthur turns the spots on at the right time.' Arthur never missed a cue. The notices in the Dublin papers next morning were not marvellous, but the English critics were enthusiastic, and this astounded us. We brought the play to London and it was a success.

People warned me after the run of *Stephen D* in London to be careful about what I chose to do next and predicted what might happen in three years' time. Although I reached the stage of thinking that I just wanted to work, I didn't act again until I returned to Dublin three months later for the next Festival and *The Poker Session*. After Dublin this play ran for only five weeks in London. When it closed I stayed on to do television and films, which occupied me for a couple of years, except for a spell at the Nottingham Playhouse.

177

I joined the Royal Shakespeare Company in 1966. It was something I didn't will to happen. At the time I was thinking of going back to Dublin. I was earning a good living, living happily and free from responsibilities, but as an actor I decided I was banging my head against a wall. Out of the blue came the Royal Shakespeare offer. That was the year the Company revived the *Henry Fours*. Roy Dotrice, who had been with them for a long time, had left. He had been playing Hotspur and opted out at the last moment. Peter Hall knew I had played Hotspur in Orson Welles's film *Chimes at Midnight* and asked me to audition for the part. I played Hotspur in the *Henry Fours* and Feste in *Twelfth Night*.

Apparently it was Kenneth Tynan, who had given me an excellent notice for *Stephen D*, who suggested me to Welles. I auditioned by reading the first speech of Hotspur's in *Henry IV*, which I read appallingly. He said: 'Great! You're dead right for the part.' When I went out to make the film in Spain three months later I spent a week looking for him.

I went first to Madrid and found a message instructing me to go to Valencia and when I got there a message arrived telling me to return to Madrid. When I went back to Madrid there was a message telling me to go to Barcelona. In Barcelona there was a message for me to continue to the Pyrenees. Four days later I found him and he exclaimed: 'Where the hell have you been?' It was all very bizarre. The continental crew were often not turning up or having rows with Welles or leaving. It was an hallucinatory experience and the final film was badly dubbed and not a great success. Although it's a fragmentary piece, there are some marvellous moments and pictorially it's very beautiful. For me it was an experience to work with Welles. He is a genius.

I had desperately wanted to play Shakespeare. It was an area in which we had no opportunity to work in Dublin because the costs were prohibitive. We had talked about a production of *Hamlet* at the Globe for a long time, but we never actually managed it. Apart from *Chimes at Midnight* I had never played Shakespeare before joining the Royal Shakespeare Company. Not only had all the other players performed in Shakespeare, but they had already presented *Henry IV* and I was in the embarrassing position of taking over from one of their leading actors. I had been influenced by Peter Hall in the sense that I had been to see *The Wars of the Roses* when *Stephen D* was playing in London and been impressed by his approach to Shakespeare and the manner in which he had formed the company. When I was asked at length to play Richard III I decided to treat the play as just another new script that had dropped through my letterbox. In purely theatrical terms Richard was a more demanding part than that of Stephen Dedalus. Stephen was something personal to me, I loved Joyce and I knew the book well. In fact, Stephen to me was an easy part for which I just had to learn the lines. My capabilities were suited to the role and I knew I could do it. It gave me no nightmares and I never considered it an enormous challenge. However, the more I studied the part of Richard the more I decided that, with the possible exception of Mozart, Shakespeare was the world's greatest genius. His plays are an inexhaustible mine of knowledge of what life is about, and in some ways they are always applicable to what is happening in the world.

Unfortunately, one of the things wrong in the Royal Shakespeare Company is that it has become a director's theatre. This has happened in the West End, and it has certainly happened at Stratford. The pendulum has swung too far from the actor, although it may fairly soon swing back again. Primarily, it should be a writer's theatre, but the balance of power between actor and director has swung heavily in the director's favour. They talk about Peter Hall's *Hamlet* as much as they talk about David Warner's Hamlet. If the critics are largely to blame, the Stratford system is also to some extent to blame. What is inclined to happen is that in the last two weeks of getting a show on stage in that gigantic theatre with all its machinery the actors are lost; with the result that the critics come to look at what the director is trying to say through the play rather than looking at what the actors are doing. It has happened that when the play has been run in and transferred to London then, and only then, do the actors receive the notices they deserve.

I don't believe there are separate attitudes towards the Shakespeare and the commercial actor in London. Those who have spent a long period in the Royal Shakespeare Company can become insulated from everything else in the theatre; conversely I don't think it is true to say that people divide actors into categories any longer. Any distinctions have been smoothed out.

Shakespeare is perhaps more difficult than any other dramatist. In fact, anybody else is easy after Shakespeare. Being a member of the RSC does not mean that one is cut off necessarily from the stream of world drama. Shakespeare's is the most stretching and exacting theatre in which you can play. The RSC is a small company, which means that everybody is playing both large and small parts and understudying. How a production will turn out one doesn't know, but we know that from the point of view of work it will be sheer bloody murder. If you are rehearsing and playing at the Aldwych you work fourteen hours a day; you go into the theatre at ten in the morning and don't come out until midnight. The salary ceiling of four thousand pounds is not good for London; you can earn more than that by working as a freelance; indeed you should be able to earn from six to seven thousand a year. A lot of actors won't go to Stratford because they think they can't afford it, or because they cannot afford to lose opportunities in films or television for such a length of time.

I don't believe that on any given night in any theatre there can be more than twenty-five per cent of the audience who want to be there or who are enjoying it or who will carry anything away from the performance. But I think you must accept that there are perhaps twenty people out there for whom the evening is an experience; apart from this you cannot go on believing that everybody in the theatre is hanging on your words. This is manifestly untrue. This applies more so in Stratford where you find American tourists who have come just to take the programme back home so that their friends in Arkansas will know they have been there.

If the Royal Shakespeare Company offer had not come when it did I would probably have gone back to Ireland. I was in no way disillusioned when I left Ireland. Of course I experienced the customary frustration at not being able to earn a living because people didn't care about the theatre. But you find that everywhere.

When the Globe Company in Dublin finally disbanded we needed something like two and a half thousand pounds to keep us going, and we couldn't get it. We were never done seeking subsidy. We received three hundred pounds from Clayton Love and occasional grants from the Arts Council over the years. What we needed to keep the company going would just about pay for the costumes for one production at Stratford.

My parents were English and they came to Dublin around 1927, and I was born in Dalkey in 1929. I was always regarded as English in Ireland just as I'm regarded as Irish in England. The first time I went to the theatre was at the age of thirteen to see McMaster as Macbeth. I was working in the Guinness brewery when I made my first appearance with professional actors at Barry Cassin's 37 Club in an English comedy called *George and Margaret*. When Godfrey Quigley was offered the opportunity of a little theatre in Dun Laoghaire which held only one hundred and ninety people he took it, and I became the business manager because I understood figures. We had staged two productions without doing business when Godfrey decided to try just once more. We presented an old farce called *See How They Run* and it ran for six weeks. I left the brewery and became a professional actor with the Globe, playing in Dun Laoghaire and making excursions into the Gate and the Gaiety and the Olympia. I don't think any of us had a clear vision of what we had set out to do. Godfrey had returned from America deciding to form his own company which would be a breakaway from Hilton Edwards and Micheál Mac Liammóir, which I think Denis Brennan also wanted. The nucleus of the group became Godfrey, Genevieve Lyons, Pauline Delany, Donal Donnelly, T P McKenna and I. Donal knew Jim Fitzgerald, who was working on a building site in London, and brought him back to direct the plays.

As time went on we began to realise how much we were a breakaway group from the Abbey and the Gate. We represented a new movement in Dublin which, I suppose, was paralleled by the Royal Court in London. I could not have joined the Abbey because I could not speak Irish; but I was not interested in the Abbey which seemed to me to be working in an outmoded tradition. I worked for

181

Lord Longford's Company from time to time, but I would not have become a member. Longford deserves great credit for staging the classics in Dublin, yet basically the company seemed a tired civil service with players who were more interested in their homes and families, It was very much the sort of company in which acting is what you do during the week to bring the money in.

At the time when we asked for money for the Globe it wasn't forthcoming. After about seven years we decided that enough was enough and we should go our own ways. We were quite exhausted. We had been earning salaries of six or seven pounds a week, although I think I earned ten pounds because I was also business manager. Yet I count some of the productions in which I played at the Globe as good as anything I have done since. Before I joined the Royal Shakespeare Company I knew I could stay on in London and earn a very good living, mostly from television plays. But this was not what I wanted from acting. I believed in the permanent company of people, such as we had in the Globe, working towards an object. I'm not interested in fame or money or in being a face on the cover of the *TV Times*. If I become bored with acting I might turn to direction. I had always wanted to play Richard III and in ten years' time I would like to play Lear. I consider Olivier the greatest living actor because of what he dares to do. His nerve distinguishes him. But McMaster at his best could hold his ground with anybody and his Othello was something I shall never forget.

I think the Abbey as a national theatre should have at least one Shakespeare in its repertoire and Goldsmith, Wilde and Shaw, too. I have never been asked to play at the Abbey, and don't particularly see why I should be asked. Wherever I am I suppose I'm a displaced person. I don't really belong anywhere. The last time I went to Dublin I found it very changed, physically uglier with a new breed of people. The meritocracy, which the Government has created, is very American, very plastic and very philistine. And Dublin was never philistine.

16

❧ ❧ ❧

Ulysses : Playing for a Percentage

THE BARE-CHESTED lover of Molly Bloom on the cover of the paper-back edition of *Ulysses* is an Irish actor, Joe Lynch. Lynch played Blazes Boylan to Milo O'Shea's Leopold Bloom in the film of the novel. Joyce has been as kind to these actors as he has to Hugh Leonard.

The leading players in Joseph Strick's film accepted minimal salaries for a guaranteed percentage of the profits. Lynch said: 'Joe Strick's *Ulysses* was the nearest we ever came to an Irish film. The actors complained because they were not getting big money; now they get a regular share of the profits and they are happy.'

Ulysses was never screened publicly in the Dublin in which it was filmed, yet it brought recognition outside Ireland to O'Shea and Lynch. Two years after *Ulysses* was completed Milo O'Shea was so much in demand that he found himself making films for Vadim and Zeffirelli at the same time. On Broadway he played opposite Eli Wallach as a homosexual barber in *Staircase* and in *Dear World* as a singing sewerman opposite Angela Lansbury. Whilst in *Dear World* a film company bought out the theatre for a weekend so that O'Shea could fly to Rome to film extra scenes for Zeffirelli's *Romeo and Juliet*.

Between films O'Shea plays a mother-dominated Irish bachelor with Anna Manahan as the matriarch in a British television series, *Me Mammy*, written by his friend and fellow-Dubliner Hugh Leonard; just as Joe Lynch between appearances on the London stage portrays an Irish Catholic tailor in another British television series, *Never Mind the Quality, Feel The Width*. Lynch has said: 'The theatre in Ireland is dying so fast it is becoming a memory and Irish playgoers are like watchers in a funeral parlour.'

Although Lynch has not appeared on the Dublin stage for some years, he continues to make his home in Ireland, as does Milo O'Shea, who lives in an old house called Sorrentoville, in which James Joyce once taught school, overlooking Killiney Bay.

MILO O'SHEA: About five years before we filmed *Ulysses* I had played Bloom in an adaptation for the BBC called *Bloomsday*. Although I didn't know it at the time, Joseph Strick had seen my performance. When he came to Dublin and introduced himself he asked if I would like to appear in *Gallows Humour*, the play he was directing for the Theatre Festival. I appeared in it, with a number of other Irish players, and it was quite successful. Afterwards Strick said to me: 'The reason I asked you to do this play was because I have written an adaptation of *Ulysses* and want to make it into a film. I have seen you playing Bloom and I would like you to play the part in my film.' Although I was sceptical about an American adapting Joyce, I read the script and found it quite brilliant. Originally it was lengthier; Strick wanted to make a film that would run for three and a half hours. He was so enthralled with the idea of filming Joyce that he had come to Dublin two years previously to see Irish actors performing in theatres and clubs. Not only did he soak himself in the Dublin scene, but when it came to casting the film he knew exactly where he stood.

Basically, the Irish and the Jews have a lot in common. We both had the shit beaten out of us for so long that there is a basic sympathy between us. I formed the character of Bloom out of my head, but I threw in a bit of Robert Briscoe. I was doing a show in Vancouver at the time he was Lord Mayor of Dublin and I asked him to give me a recorded message to take to the Vancouver Irish. He made a recording which I brought with me; I held on to it, and when I was asked to do *Bloomsday* I played it over and over to study how he spoke. Before we made *Ulysses* I met him again and listened to him and looked at him carefully. I also had Jewish actor friends in Sammy Lynn and Bob Lepler and I watched them and studied how they spoke. I got many ideas from them, but the part was not an impersonation.

I didn't think I was taking on a controversial part. When I played in *Bloomsday* nobody had thought it controversial. When the film opened in America the critics were enthusiastic, and it was approved by the League of Decency and went on the Catholic University circuit. Nobody suggested it was *risqué* until Lady What's-Her-Name in England stood up and said so, and the Press took up the story. I was amazed. So far as I and the other actors were concerned, we had agreed to play in a film of artistic worth: and this is what it turned out to be, mainly because Strick was adamant that we should adhere to the letter of Joyce and try to give an honest presentation of the book on the screen. Before the film opened I went on a promotional tour of the United States. I thought I would have to explain about Joyce and his writings, but my audiences knew it all.

It was nice going back to America then, and again a year later to play with Eli Wallach on Broadway in *Staircase*. It rounded off a chapter which had been very tough in the beginning. I first went to America in the fifties. Maureen Toal and I were just married and we had twenty dollars between us. We eked out an existence. We toured in Irish plays with the first Ronnie Ibbs's company. Most of the players went home to Ireland after the tour, but we elected to stay on. We joined a group of touring players and did good plays, mostly in the Southern States, because the winter was coming on. After five months we went to New York to act in summer stock, and then hocked everything to go to Canada. Eventually we returned to New York to play in a show which folded. Neither of us had any money, so I went round to the Waldorf-Astoria and took a job as an elevator operator. I was paid thirty-four dollars for my week's work and gave it to Maureen. We decided to go out and eat. Then her purse was stolen and we had no money at all. I had to sell my blood for five dollars. I began to think that my father's misgivings had proved true. When I was a schoolboy at Synge Street I had played Ptolemy for Hilton Edwards and Micheál Mac Liammóir in *Caesar and Cleopatra* at the Gaiety and a cabin boy in a play called *Lifeline* for Stanley Illsley and Leo McCabe at the Olympia. I played Emil in *Emil and the Detectives* at the Peacock, and when Eamonn Andrews formed a drama group made up of former Synge Street students I joined them. He presented his own play. *The Moon is Black*, at the Peacock and gave a very good performance as Danny in *Night Must Fall*. When I was seventeen my father asked me what I intended to do. When I told him I wanted to be an actor, he said: 'I'll cure that.' He had been a semi-professional, and when the summer holidays came he sent me around Ireland with a fit-up company to teach me a lesson.

I joined as an electrician and played juvenile leads. I went on stage as O'Flingsley in *Shadow and Substance* in a town called Manorhamilton. And when I was halfway through my scene with Bridget the lights began to go down. Soon the stage was in complete darkness. I rushed off to examine the fuse-box, but the fuses were all in order. I found that the meter needed shillings and had to go back on stage and ask the audience for shillings. They threw them at me.

When I came back to Dublin I was given walk-on parts with Lord Longford's company at the Gate, until I earned the Boy's part in *Our Town*. I had won a scholarship to Ria Mooney's Gaiety School of Acting. Eamonn Andrews was there, so was Jack MacGowran. I painted scenery and took dancing and movement classes. I was a very shy person in company and I found that the answer to my shyness was to clown and be funny. I had been in a Red Cross entertainment corps during the war and when we went to the Curragh internment camp I performed my funny patter routine before an audience of Germans and Italians. They didn't know what I was talking about and my act died the death. Afterwards I watched their reactions to old Chaplin films and it struck me that here was an international language. The next time I went there I had worked out a mime about a drunk coming home from an all-night binge. They cheered this, so I did it again because I didn't have another mime. Then I saw Marcel Marceau at the Gaiety and I discovered a balletic style of mime which I became very keen on, but it didn't suit me. When I came back from America I began to include mime in the acts I did for revues and cabarets. It was difficult to make ends meet as a legitimate actor, so I concentrated on musicals, pantomimes and revues. I created an image in Dublin of a comedy artist which is completely at variance with my image abroad.

I never wanted to become identified with any character. Jimmy O'Dea had been a tremendous influence, but I did not want to be forced into the position in which Jimmy had found himself. He had begun as a straight actor playing Chekhov and Wilde until audiences discovered his comic genius. When he capitalised on this image he found that he could not escape from it. The public would not allow him to escape. Jimmy had also decided that Ireland was to be his home and he did not want to leave. He turned down Broadway and Hollywood offers and had to be forced into a film for Disney. I remember being told that Jimmy had said of me: 'There is the next Jimmy O'Dea.' But I did not want to be the next Jimmy, even a pale imitation of him. I wanted to be Milo O'Shea and I did not want to be forced into the same situation. I am a Dubliner and I enjoy living in Dublin, but I want to be able to play in London, New York, Hollywood and Rome.

When I was playing small parts at the Gate I used to stand at the side of the stage and watch Micheál Mac Liammóir and Maurice O'Brien. O'Brien was brilliant in Restoration comedy: his timing was impeccable. I wanted to join the Abbey, but eventually I joined a group called the Players' Theatre which had broken away from the Abbey and included Liam Redmond, Gerard Healy, Eithne Dunne and Harry Webster; and in that way I got part of the Abbey. In 1953 however, when I came back from America, I finally appeared on the Abbey stage in a Gaelic pantomime.

At this time I was playing small parts in films and I remember my first film was a disaster. Cecil Forde, who was production manager on a film called *I See a Dark Stranger*, with Trevor Howard and Deborah Kerr, sent me a telegram instructing me to be at Kingsbridge Station early the following morning with my suitcase. My mother said: 'That's absolutely marvellous. You're off on location. But it's cold and you had better take your woollies.' I packed everything into that suitcase. When I got to the station I found I was to play an extra heaving his suitcase up and down the platform all day. In my second film Ronnie Walsh and I played two soldiers who had to shoot Rock Hudson as Captain Lightfoot. Our own Captain, Geoffrey Toone, was shot in the film and we had to haul him from the edge of the River Boyne. The director told us that he was an important actor and we must be careful with him. Ronnie decided that he would do the shooting and I would drag Toone from the bank. But the cows had been there before us and of course I dragged him through cow dung. That was the end of me; Ronnie was kept on.

When I first returned from America I was asked by the Globe Company to play in *The Seven Year Itch* at the Gaiety. Later I was asked to become a director and for two or three years Godfrey Quigley, Norman Rodway and I ran the company. We found that the more serious plays which Norman and Godfrey wanted to do were inclined to lose money. So every second or third play would be a comedy and I would go into it. I became known as the funny man of the Globe and a sort of moneymaker. This did not please me at all. I fought tooth and nail for serious parts. I was finding work outside the Globe with Micheál and Hilton and doing television work in London. Soon I was unable to devote much time to the Globe and when they decided to put me in a comedy to get their money back I was not available. 'Look lads,' I said, 'let me bail out.' Shortly after that the Globe folded. It was unfortunate. The company had all the aspiring young people at the time: Genevieve Lyons, Pauline Delany, T P McKenna, Donal Donnelly, Jim Fitzgerald, Godfrey, Norman, myself. There was a wave of excitement in that theatre. We earned about six pounds a week and it was inevitable that we should outgrow this and begin to look to London and elsewhere.

JOE LYNCH: Film people who once told me that we in Ireland were crazy to sign for the film of *Ulysses* on the strength of a percentage of the profits now come up to me in London and say: 'We hear you're collecting.' It never occurred to me that Joe Strick was anything but an honest man. The only pity is that he could not make his film as he wanted to – more expansively and in period; but with the cloth at his disposal he made a very nice suit of clothes. Censorship has been applied in the Irish theatre by the players and directors, because actors are stuffy people who would not be a party to anything they thought was not quite right. Nobody has ever said to me that *Ulysses* was a dirty film because I can throw a good right cross.

Ulysses was cast in Ireland. Yet no other foreign film company has shown such confidence. When an outside film company arrives in Ireland they behave as though we were living in the days of the Famine. A big casting director, himself an Irishman, once remarked: 'They're only Irish actors.' Yet the theatre of Shakespeare was filled with Irish actors. If a foreign company wants to use our actors they should pay them their proper worth. If we have not got our own film industry, it is because of the old story of the cromlech. The little boy told his father: 'I know how they put one stone on top of the other two stones. They got three hundred Irishmen with ropes and they all pulled together.' We shall never have an Irish film industry until three hundred Irishmen can pull together again. The theatre as we know it in Ireland is at a standstill and with insufficient money. Until the Irish see the corpse they won't believe that the theatre is sick. It is true to say that theatre cannot die, but in Ireland it may go underground and be waked before long. Only the Abbey will be left and it can become an international theatre only by forgetting the plays with kitchen scenes and the loaf of soda bread leaning against the window.

When I joined the Abbey at their request to play Christy Mahon in *The Playboy of the Western World* I found a lack of discipline. I had been taught Shakespeare at a very early age in Cork by Father O'Flynn. When I returned to Cork from boarding-school it was the tail-end of the war years. I joined James Stack and we cultivated an audience when there were no touring companies from England.

Eventually we were able to fill the Opera House with *A Midsummer Night's Dream*. Stack was a disciplinarian, and I was shocked to find such a looseness in the Dublin theatre. An agent once told me that the Irish, the Welsh, and the Scots all lacked discipline. Yet the good actors are disciplined and this is known abroad. The days of the drunken Irish actors are gone.

I have been travelling backwards and forwards to act in England for the best part of twenty years. This has its rewards, but the tragede is that you cannot do such work at home. In the Dublin theatre ony feels like Blind Raftery *'ag seinimh ceóil do pócai folamh'* (making music for empty pockets). That solid group of Irish actors, who would be difficult to equal in any country, are struggling to earn a living. One doesn't know how they manage. No actor can remain independent by working and living solely in Ireland. It never happened in the past unless one was an actor-manager; and the monkeys never run the zoo. Most actors are a poor judge of a play and most actors need direction. But this has always been the Irish dilemma. If all the Irish actors who are working outside Ireland came home there would be an ocean of talent.

17

  ❦   ❦   ❦

Leonard: Difficult to say 'No'

IN THE LATE fifties, when the Globe Theatre was having its best years, a young Dublin Civil Servant, who cycled every morning to his work in the Land Commission, was writing plays in his spare time. John Keyes Byrne was soon to become Hugh Leonard, one of the most prolific writers living in Britain. When Leonard's Joyce adaptation, *Stephen D*, reached the West End, two former Globe members, Norman Rodway and T P McKenna, were to make an impression on London audiences with their performances as Dedalus and Cranly.

By this time Leonard had cut his apron strings with Ireland and was a script editor with Granada television, commuting during rehearsals between Manchester and London to put his case to the Lord Chamberlain who had demanded cuts in the play. Leonard has become the most commercially successful of Irish playwrights, yet he has remained consistently loyal to Irish actors by providing them with rewarding roles in his stage and television plays. Although committed to his work in London, he has presented the Dublin Theatre Festival with a new work every year.

When he talked to us it was at his home at Barnes, near London.

a large house with an Aston Martin in the garage. But a few months later, in the spring of 1970, Leonard decided to return with his Belgian wife and their daughter to live in a house at Killiney, over-looking Dublin Bay, not far from the house where Milo O'Shea lives and in which Joyce taught school, or from the house which Dan O'Herlihy has bought himself.

* * *

All I ever wanted to become was a writer. I remember writing my first short story at the age of eight. When I joined the Land Commission at eighteen I wrote a few plays for amateurs: *Nightingale in the Branches*, which became *The Big Birthday* when the Abbey staged it; a sequel, *Another Summer*; a one-act play about Parnell, *The Man on Platform Two*, and *The Italian Road*, which was the first play I submitted to a theatre. I entered it for an Abbey Theatre competition, but the standard was so low that they made no awards that year. When they turned down *The Italian Road* I sent them *Nightingale in the Branches* and changed the title to *The Big Birthday* and gave myself the pseudonym Hugh Leonard, which was the name of the hero in the play they had rejected. They accepted the play and within a few weeks I found myself lumbered with a name I did not really want.

I had been knocking the Abbey in a critical column in a Civil Service magazine. When I submitted *Nightingale* I told myself I would not give them the excuse of refusing it because I had criticised them; I went back to *The Italian Road* and took the name of a young psychopathic character called Hughie Leonard. When Ernest Blythe discovered that it was a pen name and that the play had in fact been presented by amateurs five years previously he was extremely angry.

I had always wanted to become a professional writer. I enjoyed my time in the Land Commission, but hated the actual work. Within a few years I was able to become a fulltime writer by writing serials for sponsored radio. I was not conscious that this was a big

Colin Blakely as Astrov in the Royal Court Theatre production of *Uncle Vanya*.

Donal Donnelly and Zena Walker in the Broadway production of *A Day in the Death of Joe Egg*.

[*To face page 192*

Sean Kenny, Irish architect turned
world stage designer.

Norman Rodway in the costume of
Richard III at Bosworth field.

T. P. McKenna in the film *Villain*.

step, yet people telephoned me to say I was made. When I married I was earning five pounds a week in the Land Commission and with the marriage allowance this became seven pounds. When I resigned after fourteen years' service I was earning ten pounds, eight shillings, and I had a wife and child. The serial *The Kennedys of Castleross* paid me sixteen pounds a week and I had three other sponsored radio programmes at six guineas apiece. So I was earning three times my salary in the Land Commission. Becoming a fulltime writer in Ireland never worried me, except for the early days when I used to wake up in the morning with the idea that this was the day I was going back to the Land Commission. I could not rid myself of an inborn dislike of working for somebody else.

I was thirty-two when I left the Civil Service, a little late perhaps to throw up a job; but for a year I churned out five sponsored programmes a week whilst trying to write plays for the Theatre Festival. On a point of stamina I realised that I could not continue like this. Then Granada asked me if I would work for them. I agreed, but at the time I had no intention of leaving Ireland. For a year I commuted between Dublin and Manchester, flying to Manchester every Monday morning and flying home to Dublin on a Thursday evening. It was a Jekyll and Hyde existence. Finally my wife persuaded me that we should move to Manchester. I signed for a second year with Granada and when the two years were up I decided that that was as much as I wanted. Granada had only four writers at the time, and there was some mystique about me because I was an original playwright. I was not allowed to write an original word, and I was dying to write. I edited *Knight Errant* and *Family Solicitor*. My last job was an adaptation of some plays by Tennessee Williams.

I came down to London and changed my agent. My agent doesn't read my television scripts or inspire me, but he takes care of me in the business sense. He signs contracts for me because he knows that if he sends me a contract I shall put it aside and forget to return it. England did not mean a great change in our lives. My wife, who is Belgian, had spent the war years in Moscow and Los Angeles before moving to Ireland, which was her first permanent home. Life in London has a great deal to offer, but the social values do not go deep. As E M Forster said, the English have incomplete hearts. I often asked my wife if she left England where she would like to live, and she always replied Ireland, long before she would live in Belgium. For me, I think of what Shaw said, 'You don't know what your own house is like until you get outside it.'

I was working in Manchester when the idea for *Stephen D* came to me. I was lunching in Dermot McDowell's flat in London when he played me Cyril Cusack's recording of extracts from *A Portrait of the Artist as a Young Man*—the Christmas dinner scene and a couple of other passages. I thought of what a marvellous one-man play it would make. Cyril was the wrong age for the part of the young Joyce, but I thought of writing a one-man play for Norman Rodway. He liked the idea and I wrote ten pages. When I showed them to him he went white and said he didn't feel he could do it. I then suggested writing a fullscale play and from that the idea grew.

I spent only three to four weeks in writing it; and when you spend such a short time on a play you feel very cold about it. One may feel professionally proud of a play without having any great liking for it. I could not understand why Phyllis Ryan was so enthusiastic about it. Jim Fitzgerald made a splendid producer and the play became a great success. But I could never understand why. I admire the content of *Stephen D*, but I have never really liked it because it wasn't my own. To me it was always Joyce and it was more of an arranging job than anything else; not only an arranging job but a matter of instinct, a knowledge of what would work on the stage even though one did not know how to stage it. I knew whether certain things were possible and whether they worked dramatically; and that, I think, was my only contribution to *Stephen D*.

I have written a great deal because I have always found it difficult to say no. It takes me from six to eight weeks to write an original television play. But I can write an adaptation at the rate of an episode every two days, with a day at the end to recuperate because I work intensely; this was how I adapted *Nicholas Nickleby* and *Dombey and Son*. If I choose the adaptation, as I did with Dickens, I find it easy. But when I adapted *The Possessed* in six one-hour episodes for television I found it difficult. The book was almost unreadable, and I did not trust Dostoevsky. I kept thinking his scenes were not making sense and I did not have the patience to stick with them. It was my own fault. When I managed to read the book I found that the scenes made up a mosaic and I was able to finish the adaptation within a month.

I made the mistake of becoming a compulsive worker. Writing film scripts has helped me pull myself out of that trap. Film writing gives one more time and there are lengthy breaks between the first and second and third drafts. My first film script was never filmed; most film scripts aren't. It was an adaptation of Iris Murdoch's *The Unicorn* for Tony Richardson. Then I tinkered with a script for a man who went broke. I then wrote *Great Catherine* for Peter O'Toole. When I wrote the script of *The Scarperer* for O'Toole I thought it the best I had done. I was rather proud of it. But O'Toole wanted to direct it himself and handed it over to another writer. I wrote *Interlude* in two weeks. My work consisted of destroying the original script and substituting another whilst keeping the scenes of the original in their order, although the content was completely different.

Some producers mess you around and bring you to script conferences because they are lonely and need someone to talk to; others like David Deutsch or Philip Mackie will simply talk over the subject with you and allow you to go away to write your script. When you have finished you give it to them and a week later you talk about the second draft and they ask you to stay with it. With some people screen writing can be delightful; with others it can be torture, and you end up almost in tears.

The only way to maintain control over a film is to direct it. Quite properly the word is subservient to the image. If you have a picture in your mind, a dream of how something should be done, you yourself must carry it through to produce the image. I would like to direct a film some time, but it is not a burning ambition. I prefer television to film writing because one has more control. With the BBC in particular you simply have a chat about the subject beforehand and then you go away and shape it yourself. It's your idea and your conception and you stay with it to the end.

First and last I flatter myself as being a writer for the stage. I don't think there's anything so good as writing for the theatre; but it's difficult to live on theatrical earnings because your play can be destroyed in a night, or, of course, you can be famous in a night. If that happens you can make a fortune and sit back for twenty years re-writing the same play and forgetting everything else. But to achieve this is like drawing a winning ticket in a sweepstake.

More than anything else television has made me financially independent; so, more recently, has film writing. This is inclined to make one greedy. When jobs are offered you say yes, I'd love to do that, thank you for asking me. You go ahead and do it and at the end of the year you find yourself in a tax trap. To pay your taxes you will have to work harder the following year, and on that year's earnings there will be more tax. You reach the stage where you must buckle down to not making much money and not spending much either. The alternative is to flee to Ireland and put your tongue out at the English taxman.

My working methods vary between films, television and stage plays. With a stage play I have a perverse way of working. I begin at the top of a page with the first line and keep working on this line until it is right. Then I write the second line and re-write the first and second until they are right. By the time I get to the bottom of the page a day has probably passed. The trouble with this method is that one's work is so tight that it becomes almost impossible to cut. It may need cutting, but you cannot get a wedge in because each line fits into the next. I usually work from two in the afternoon until six. I may go out for the evening or watch television or read, but I start again at half eleven and work through until three. I rise so late in the morning that I am regarded by my neighbours as the original slob of Barnes.

The concentration needed for a stage play is so enormous that unless you have a good day the edge goes off after a few hours. When I'm writing a stage play I watch what I drink because it will affect tomorrow's work. If I'm a little tired it means I have lost a day. I try not to become too obsessed with this; otherwise I should lock myself away like a hermit. With television it's different.

Television is a more fluid medium, and I can write an adaptation very quickly. I keep the same working hours, but there is no longer the necessity for this up-and-down-the-page method. I re-draft a page twice, perhaps three times, and press on. I don't write second drafts of the final script because I could not bear the thought of returning to a job that has gone cold; all I do is go over the manuscript and make cuts. I have a fetish about tidy typing. If I make a mistake I scrap the whole page.

I have two typewriters, but one of them was left behind by a typewriter company. I use a taperecorder only to tape music for enjoyment. I use a video recorder to preserve my television plays after the studio has wiped them. I possess the only copies of such plays of mine as *The Great Big Blonde* and *I Loved You Last Summer*. I keep these as mementoes and sometimes run them if a producer wants to see a particular Irish actor I have recommended. I use an electric typewriter because it is fast and clean, and there are books on which I draw from time to time. But I use no other aids and never speak into a taperecorder. I cannot write in longhand: my handwriting has become infantile and I have to type even Christmas cards.

I find time for a little drama criticism, usually one or two plays a month, which keeps me near the theatre. I spend one night in the week on the town because working here in one's own house and meeting nobody is a claustrophobic existence; one needs to get out and shake away the cobwebs. I go out with Norman Rodway or Philip Mackie perhaps or with an Irish friend if there's someone in town. Being in Barnes I can stroll around the Green, or if I'm really fed up I go for a drive, usually to my bookshop in town.

But the age of the bookman is vanished. You cannot talk of the English literature scene any more. The day has gone when Hugh Walpole could walk along the street signing autographs. Now when you say you are a writer it's exactly as if you said you are a doctor or a dentist. There is no glamour attached to being a writer. I'm a member of the Dramatists' Club, the members of which meet for dinner about three times a year—Bolt, Pinter, Mankowitz, Waterhouse and Hall, Morley, writers like that. We just sit in the Garrick

197

Club and get sloshed. Otherwise writers don't congregate. You meet many more actors and directors than writers.

Looking from London the temptation is to think of the Irish literary scene as being very small. I haven't written for the Abbey since my second play in 1957 and I'm just on nodding acquaintance with the actors. Apart from writing *Insurrection* a few years ago, I have had nothing to do with Irish television. But I have kept up a great friendship with Phyllis Ryan who has presented a play of mine at the Dublin Theatre Festival once a year for about nine years. But it is impossible to know how large one's name looms on the Irish scene or whether one is regarded even as an Irish writer any more.

Had I stayed in Ireland I might have written more for the stage, but since coming to England and working on every possible subject in different media I have learned craftsmanship. I certainly would not be writing the type of play I am writing now, for better or for worse. For example, the class structure in Britain fascinates me, and *The Au Pair Man* is about an outsider despising this structure whilst using it for his own material good. Class is about the only facet of English life which excites me or about which I care intensely. I certainly would not have written *The Au Pair Man* if I had stayed in Ireland. I think the most interesting thing about Ireland today is the new aristocracy, which I call the Foxrock aristocracy. It has sprung up full of new business executives, all of whom seem to be called Brendan. It's a classless aristocracy.

The Irish writer is alone in the world in the sense that in every other country the existence of God is doubted and a serious play becomes a search for a god, not God, a search for a purpose and a meaning. The Irish writer is different in that he accepts God and so do his characters. That is his starting and his finishing point, and it is inclined to put him out of step with the rest of the world's writers. Basically I think this is the reason why Irish plays are not always acceptable in Britain and America. At the beginning of every Irish play there is the presumption, which audiences cannot readily accept, that God exists. In nearly every European country among the *literati* who attend the theatre, and I am speaking of theatre in a serious sense, there is a belief that God is dead and that we must carve our own meaning out of life. This is a premise to which Irish writers cannot subscribe, and it creates an interesting problem. I suppose it would be easier to write if the problem was not there. I think any man who believes in God is a saint. The rest of us hope there is a God. As a character in a Spanish play said, we should always behave as if there is a God in Heaven, although we can never be sure until the last moment whether there is.

I don't consider myself an expatriate writer. I love Dublin and, though my parents are dead now, I get back quite often. It is only two hundred and eighty miles away, nearer than Edinburgh and the same distance as Cornwall from London. The strip of ocean doesn't bother me. I consider myself very much an Irish writer; I am always tinkering with the idea of returning to Ireland, but I will have to give myself a few more years. One really cannot live in Ireland and continue to work in films and television, which is where most of one's income comes from. You must be on the scene or you are not used. The English producer will commission an author who lives in Edinburgh, four hundred miles away, before he commissions a writer who lives in Dublin, because he thinks he cannot reach him. I like London, but I do not like its values and I shall turn sour if I stay here much longer. I would like to get back to roots and use the material I have collected in a more permanent form rather than continue to turn out plays which are concerned with current fashion and keeping up with current morality or lack of it.

I have half a novel here called *Sex on Thursday*. Missioners in Ireland preach sex on Thursday, which is the servant girls' night off. It is a kind of *Clochemerle* based on the efforts of a parish in Dalkey to put gates on the Burma Road to prevent courting couples in cars from parking there. But I don't think I'm very good at writing stories. I tie myself in knots with prose. I re-write too much and you can drive yourself silly with narrative prose if you re-write. A spoken line is neat, and there it is. You can make it quite perfect if you work hard enough at it. But great slabs of narrative, with variations, paragraphing, the juxtaposition of words, become too involved for me.

I cannot write spontaneously. I have to work at it. I abandoned that novel about ten years ago, but it is still lying around somewhere.

I don't know if it has any value now, because the Clochemerely kind of writing has gone out of vogue. The Honor Tracy and Brinsley MacNamara writing, with the parish priest and the publican running the full gamut of hypocrisy, is old hat now. I don't know if I could summon up enough enthusiasm to finish the novel. For me there is nothing that I want to say that I cannot say much better in a play, although it is pleasant to see one's work between hard covers. But there is nothing to equal the excitement of a first night, particularly a first night in Dublin.

Even from this distance I feel free to comment on Irish society. I am not out of touch because I experienced thirty-two years of Irish society, both my mother's kind of society and the society of my friends. Only the trimmings change. There is a car in the garage. The poorest old lady can wangle a television set. People who grew up believing that if they were poor it didn't matter because they were going to Heaven now discover that they need be poor no more. The trimmings are easily assimilated, but I know the people themselves so well that they will never leave me. There is a slight bewilderment as they are pulled one way and another; that is why it is fascinating to write about them. There is an intensity in the Church; but life outside the Church in Ireland is not at all religious, and these two factors are at war with each other. It is like watching a new civilisation taking shape. Ireland is becoming more American than English. Every town has a new school and when you drive through you get the impression of towns in the Middle West of America.

If I thought I was losing touch with Ireland I would go back at once. But with a writer's way of life, one lives slightly apart from the people around one. A writer cannot assume, however, that all right-thinking people feel as he does. Once you find yourself making fun of people, you realise that you are out of touch. As someone said, it is very easy to shock but when you put yourself in the place of those you are shocking you realise what a terrible thing you are doing; you are attacking the values by which they live. I do not think, although I may use shock words in plays to achieve a certain effect, that I am a controversial playwright in the sense of shocking the *bourgeoisie*. I can decry them and criticise them, but I cannot begrudge them their beliefs and values.

There are not enough good writers in Ireland. Irish writers are still copying Murray and Robinson, still involved in an incestuous kind of theatre. They do not realise what the playwrights of other countries are trying to say. Whilst playwrights abroad are making urgent personal statements, Ireland's playwrights are still dribbling on about the aunt's farm and the marriage broker.

I want to write a play about Judas. I have always been interested in the theme of betrayal. It runs through my work—the enormity of betrayal and the necessity to betray other people; not a convenient necessity, but part of the human make-up. Judas was the arch-betrayer. I also want to write a play called *The Bully and the Chap*, about an Irish writer and a television personality—a serious, literate, rational Irishman who happens to have sold out. I want to see his skin scratched and the peasant seeping through.

18

❧ ❧ ❧

Kenny : The Ireland of the Blind

SEAN KENNY KEEPS a house in Chelsea and an office above a laneway
in Soho. On his drawing-boards are the blueprints for a riverside
theatre centre; on his shelves the scripts of *Oliver!*, *Blitz!*, *Maggie
May*, *Gulliver's Travels*, *Quasimodo*. Kenny left Ireland without ever
working in theatre or films; he tried to practise as a young architect
in Dublin, but failed. His theatrical achievements have been in
England, but he looks back on his native country with a more
burning passion then any other figure in this book.

No other Irish designer has made such an impact in the theatre
abroad; yet Kenny was not invited to design the new Abbey Theatre
and has not been invited to design any of its productions. The Irish
theatre cannot afford Kenny, just as it cannot afford Hugh Leonard;
but from the beginning of his career, when he sailed a small boat to
America with three companions, he has been an adventurer abroad.

His talent might have been employed to preserve what is left of
Georgian Dublin, for which he shows concern; but if he were to
return to Ireland, he says, it would be as a politician. Yet this short,
stocky designer speaks so softly that he would seem out of place
in Dáil Éireann.

* * *

When I came back to Ireland at twenty-three to change the face of
my country, nobody would listen. I had left the School of Architecture in Dublin to sail with three other boys to America. That
voyage was something I did in the past. It was exhilarating then,
but I don't regard it of any consequence now and there is not much
to be said about it. I spent two years in America with Frank Lloyd
Wright and three years in the Pacific. When I came back to Dublin
I put up a plate which said: Sean Kenny, Architect. An architect
is like a carpenter or a painter or a blacksmith: he sets up his
sign and if nobody comes he thinks he should be doing something
else.

I wanted to get rid of the bullshit and the bigoted attitudes of
people. To me the Irish were a poverty-stricken people, psychologic-
ally and mentally poverty-stricken rather than economically. I knew
there had been a revolution. I knew this very well because my family
had been involved in it. I also realised that the revolution had begun
and ended with the changing of the flag. Nothing else had changed
very much, and I wanted to change the attitude of people to their
environment. I hated the cheapjack bungalows they were building
all over the place. I hated the cringing attitude towards the American
dollar. The Irish had become a nation of shopkeepers waiting for
the Cadillac to come off the boat before they began bowing and
tipping their caps. I knew we had no aristocracy, but I did not like
the servile attitude. The only way I could change things was through
the work I had been trained to do in architecture and design. I
hoped somehow to convince the people in Government departments
that although we were a peasant people, and are a peasant people,
we could make something of ourselves as good as any borrowed
culture.

Although I came from Tipperary, I found Dublin a good enough
place, except that everybody seemed to talk all the time. It was like
a green whirlpool which would swallow you if you weren't careful.
I stayed two years in Dublin and nothing happened, except one job
which I finished at the end of that period: a house in Derry overlooking the Foyle. I had to go somewhere to work, and I would have
wasted my time if I had stayed in Dublin. I went to Canada because

it seemed a good place, but it was no better than Ireland. It, too, had its narrowminded attitudes.

I decided to move to England or Venezuela. I had always avoided England and I thought of going to Caracas to work in architecture, but I tossed a coin and England won. I arrived to work on the Harlow New Town project, which seemed to me a disaster before it started. It took me about four months to find out what was happening and then I left. I went into television and later theatre. I was designing for television and doing things I didn't like very much.

My entry into the theatre was an accident. One night I met Brendan Behan in a pub in London. He had written a play called *The Hostage* and Joan Littlewood was going to direct it in Stratford East. Brendan told me that the play was about a house which we had all known as students in Dublin. It was a famous house and I wondered how Behan was going to put it on the stage. I began drawing the house on beer mats and that was the end of that night. The next day Joan Littlewood called me up. Behan had taken the beer mats to her and she said this was exactly how the set should look. I had never thought much about the theatre, and I still don't think it is very important. But after that setting for *The Hostage* my work for the theatre began to snowball. They said I was good, but to me it was just like selling doodles. I wasn't doing anything I cared about very much. I wrote letters home to Ireland because I still wanted to work there. Perhaps one of the reasons why I had chosen to work in London was because it was so near to Ireland where my home still is. My mother lives there and my young brothers and sisters. I wrote letters to that stupid place, the Abbey Theatre, and got no replies. Now that they said I had value in the theatre in London I thought this might mean something at home, but obviously it didn't.

Whilst I was working in television I helped Bernard Miles with the Mermaid Theatre. I helped him arrange the stage and the auditorium and build the sets. I designed the sets for the first four productions at the Mermaid, and it was there I first met Lionel Bart when we worked together on the musical *Lock Up Your Daughters*, for which he wrote the lyrics. I designed the sets for his next show,

Oliver! and then *Blitz!* and later *Maggie May.* But the theatre's middleclass, middlebrow audience don't really care what happens on the stage. It is purely lullaby activity. The theatre is not totally an idea of words. Literature is words, but not theatre. When I was able to adapt, direct and design a show called *Gulliver's Travels,* I tried to get away from this wordplay and convey the story with a lot of sound effects and visual activity. I don't work in films or television or architecture any longer, but I believe that the theatre could be much more than it is, and that is why I work in it. My fulfilment is in the future. Some day I know there will be a place where the theatre will be part of a community. This is more likely to happen in France or Germany before it happens in England. Even the oldest and most puritan theatre groups now realise that the proscenium theatre is a dead duck. I have designed for the proscenium theatre, although I am very much against it, because I have to make a living. I try to outwit the proscenium by suggesting to the people who watch this kind of theatre that it would be marvellous if one could move around and look at the other side of the set. That is what I call compromise. I don't adapt easily to compromise, but most of the time I have to, especially when it is a question of money.

When I designed for Expo '67 more money would have helped, but I had to work within a budget. The limitations can be enormous. If I work on twelve projects in a year I am fortunate if two of them become reality. I designed an underwater city for Kevin McClory for the Bahamas. But it may never be built because there is now a native Government in the Bahamas which threw out the racketeers and the ancestors of the pirates. The natives now rule themselves and there is no money for projects such as McClory's and mine because there are more essential things to build such as schools, hospitals and houses.

I know what is happening in Ireland because I read the Irish papers every day. I know there is nothing very much I can do there. Things have changed, but in the wrong way. Everything the Irish do is borrowed from English or American society. There is not very much that is new in thought, word or deed. I would not say that Ireland is philistine because that presupposes the existence of intellectuals. The few people who matter are men like Dan Breen who fought his revolution and has things to say to which nobody will listen, the poets who survive by the skin of their teeth, and maybe a couple of painters and sculptors who hang on but barely make a living. The State is more involved with its economic system: a kind of poor man's bank which sells English houses to the Germans. There has been a tradition of good work in Ireland for nine hundred years. Irish artists once spoke for the whole world; now Ireland has become a nation of little men selling leprechauns made of bog oak. It is no good using the English as an excuse by saying that Ireland was occupied for hundreds of years and that we have never had a proper schooling. Philosophy and ideas have to do with a sense of oneself and a sense of one's country.

Ireland has a great tradition of revolution, yet the revolution changed nothing. When the English moved out the Church stepped in. The thrones of the English were taken over by the bishops of Ireland. I would not want to work as an artist in Ireland. I would want to be a leader reshaping the laws, the policies, the ideas and the ambitions of my country. Nobody can be an artist in Ireland before the country is fit to live in. The only thing that would take me back to Ireland is the possibility that I might become a member of the Government. The gesture of tax concessions for artists is likely to attract every middlebrow artist in Europe. The painters and writers and musicians who live in London or Paris or New York live in these places because they want to. The English taxation system is crucifying, but we live here because the climate of art is good to work in. If you are an artist you go where the climate of work is, where it is possible to talk to fellow-artists who are also trying to improve themselves. These centres of art are London, New York, Berlin. The only artists you will attract to Ireland will be the failures. No artist works in a vacuum. No artist lives for his work totally. The work you do is out of the life you live. You cannot separate life from work. You cannot live one thing and do another. You cannot survive in the climate of Ireland that has a false idea of religion and a false idea of God. The Church puts a curb on the feelings of the people as though she were afraid there may be another revolution and that this revolution will be against the Church itself. By working in London we can do more for Ireland than we could at home. We fight against our own limitations and against the idea that Irishmen are always drunk, never on time, and unable to produce anything.

I know why Conor Cruise O'Brien on his return to Ireland joined the Labour Party. It's the best of the three parties: not a very good best, but still the best. The climate that must change first in Ireland is the political climate, and O'Brien has made a beginning. Ireland can produce artists who will break down walls in any country in the world, but Ireland itself has no imagination; it has fallen back into an old prosaic idea of yesterday. Yet all the Government needs do is to offer revolution and the people in the name of revolution will build a new country. There is no adventure in the land that produces adventurous artists. There is nothing adventurous or artistic about a country in which there is no freedom. You may paint a red Victorian letterbox green and say it is Irish, but it is not: it is still a foreign letterbox. The social structures and attitudes are formed in the Irish at school. An Irish child has no opportunities; I don't mean opportunities for learning Latin or mathematics, but opportunities to acquire a knowledge of life and a sense of himself.

I don't think the Irish language is all that important. Language is purely a means of communication; what you want to say matters more than how you say it. I wasted time learning subjects through an archaic and beautiful but impractical language. The idea of studying sciences through the medium of an archaic language is incredible. No symbols exist in Irish for the common language of science, so they invent funny words for them.

I think the reason the Irish become writers rather than painters or sculptors or musicians is because during the centuries when the Irish warred against the English the word and the ear were more important than the eye. The Irish spoke in whispers about Ireland and called their country Cathleen Ni Houlihan or the Shan Van Vocht. The visual arts were dangerous, but nobody could discover what was in your head because this was a secret and a whisper. Our eyes were taken from us in those long years and we are now a blind country. We have produced major writers, but not great painters or sculptors or architects. We find it possible to tear down beautiful squares and replace them with concrete office blocks because we are wearing green shades over our eyes and cannot see.

The first problem to face in Ireland is how to make people look about them and see for the first time. It is for education to improve the eye. Ireland needs artists, not to free them from English or dollar taxes, but to get them to teach. If I were to go back my only concern would be the children of Ireland; it is too late for the adults. I don't consider myself an international person. I consider myself an Irishman who happens to be where the work is. I have no sentimental feelings about Ireland; my love is for my mother and brothers and sisters. I don't cry because I am not living in Ireland; I only cry when I cannot do good work.

I like working in Soho because it is an unEnglish part of London, full of Indians and Greeks and Pakistanis; a mixture of people like me who have come here to work as waiters or taxidrivers or shop assistants. People who come from Yorkshire or Lancashire also feel themselves foreigners in this city. I have not established residence here. I have not settled down in London forever. One always has at the back of one's mind the idea of returning to Ireland. But every year the idea drifts further away.

Siobhán McKenna as Cass in Brian Friel's play, *The Loves of Cass McGuire* at the Abbey Theatre, Dublin.

Alan Simpson, the producer who discovered Brendan Behan the playwright.

Tom Murphy, emigrant playwright by choice.

Brian Friel, Derry playwright on Broadway.

Conor Cruise O'Brien with his wife Maire (poet Maire MacEntee) on their wedding day in Dublin.

19

❧ ❧ ❧

Behan: The Last Laugh

IN 1970, SIX years after Brendan Behan's death, *The Hostage* was running at the Abbey Theatre in Dublin and the dramatisation of *Borstal Boy* at the Lyceum Theatre on Broadway. The original, once-banned novel of *Borstal Boy* was freely on sale in Dublin's book-shops. Behan's widow, Beatrice, told a journalist: 'Everybody seems to be on a Brendan Behan streak at the moment. Everywhere you go you see his books displayed. All this would have made Brendan laugh. I remember saying to him that you could buy all sorts of dirty books in the supermarkets of Dublin, yet you couldn't buy *Borstal Boy*. At last that has changed.'

Beatrice Behan still lives in the terraced house in Dublin's Balls-bridge where she and Brendan made their home. She has abandoned the autobiography which she started shortly after her husband's death. 'I decided that one is either a writer or one is not,' she said, 'I'm not.' Instead she continues her career as a painter, often taking her children, Blanaid (born shortly before Behan's death) and Paudge, who was adopted later, on sketching holidays to Connemara.

Brendan Behan died at the age of forty-one with a play, *Richard's Cork Leg*, unfinished. It was in his native Dublin ten years previously that Behan, a rebel and an aspiring writer, made his first impression as a dramatist in a tiny theatre in a converted mews behind one of the city's Georgian streets. Despite the limitations of the stage and the shortage of resources, Alan Simpson, a former Irish Army Captain who had entered the profession of the theatre, presented *The Quare Fellow* and created a legend.

Seán Ó Faoláin, who encouraged the young Behan as a writer during his editorship of *The Bell*, an Irish literary magazine, told us: 'Behan wrote deplorably less than his potential. When he was in prison in Mountjoy I would occasionally bring him gifts. He was an idealistic boy. He reminded me in his later years of Dylan Thomas, and in a way there was a close parallel in their lives. To read him in manuscript was to discover that he was a born writer.'

When the stage adaptation of *The Hostage* was produced on Broadway, earning the 'Tony' award for the season's best play, Clive Barnes wrote in the *New York Times*:

> We are never going to get another play from Brendan, or another drink, so let us be grateful for Frank McMahon's adaptation and the chance it gives not only for Niall Toibín's rich and lusty picture of the mature Behan, but also for a young actor, Frank Grimes, to give a fascinating picture of the artist as a young man, growing up in harsh exile.

Alan Simpson left Ireland in the early sixties to work in London just at a time when Behan was spending long periods in New York. He returned to Dublin as Artistic Adviser to the Abbey Theatre in 1968, producing, among other plays, *The Quare Fellow*.

*   *   *

I founded the Pike Theatre in 1953. We had been in existence for almost a year when we presented Brendan Behan's first play, *The Quare Fellow*, in the autumn of 1954. I had known Brendan since 1945. He had been released from an internment camp and I had come out of the Army. I had been a military engineer at the Curragh when

Brendan was on the other side of the barbed wire. I did not know him then, nor was I guarding him; it was simply that we had our training-ground alongside the internment camp. But in 1945 I was out of the Army and working with Edwards and Mac Liammóir at the Gaiety. Some friends of mine had a studio over the Monument Creamery which had been leased to them by John Ryan, who was to be the editor of *Envoy* magazine, and it was here that I first met Brendan Behan. We became friends and by the time I founded the Pike he was writing for the *Irish Press*. He didn't actually tell me he was writing a play, but Sally Travers, Micheál Mac Liammóir's niece, told me that Brendan had sent a play to Hilton Edwards.

It was not Hilton's sort of play and obviously they were not going to do it, so I asked Brendan to let me have a look at it. As soon as I read *The Quare Fellow* I wanted to stage it. I liked the play and was excited by it. I suppose this was some time in the summer of 1954, but it was autumn before I was able to get it on. It was a frightfully difficult play for our tiny theatre. There was a cast of twenty-one and the play created all kinds of technical problems for us, apart from the problems of finding actors. But we produced it and ran it for as long as we could afford. After a month it became too costly to keep going. Brendan came to the rehearsals. He was easy and uncritical, not in the silly sense; he was not one of those playwrights who see everything differently to the director or try to mess him around. We re-arranged rather than re-wrote some of the play. I still have a copy of the original script, which is very rambling. A character would change subjects as though in a genuine conversation. We made Brendan sort it out so that one subject was dealt with at a time. We probably made cuts; in fact, I am sure we did, and we tied up loose ends such as curtain lines.

We never discussed his theme of capital punishment. That was a delightful aspect of his play: it was not propagandist in the ordinary sense of the word. Brendan wrote *The Quare Fellow* out of his experiences of English and Irish prisons as an almost documentary record. I would not say that he set out to write a deliberately anti-capital-punishment play.

Dermot Kelly played Neighbour, Derry Power the young Gaelic-speaking prisoner and David Kelly the part which Brendan called Fatser, but which we renamed Mickser because David wasn't by any means fat. I would not say that Brendan was conscious of having written anything theatrically important. He was delighted and enthusiastic simply because I was putting on his play. He loved coming to rehearsals; in fact, he turned to somebody during rehearsals, nudged him and said: 'I wrote that!' He had been to the dress rehearsal, but it would have been dangerous to bring him to the first night; in such a small theatre he would have made too much noise. We kept him in the office across the laneway and the manager, Tim Willoughby, gave him a drink every fifteen minutes. If we hadn't given him a drink he would have gone off to a pub to buy one. On the other hand, if we had given him as much drink as he wanted he would have been incapable of walking into the theatre to take a curtain call. During the last ten minutes of the play we steered him into the auditorium. He refused to make a speech; instead he sang *Red Roses For Me*.

The play was hailed by various Dublin critics as the best since O'Casey. Its potential was obvious to me. It was rather a shocking play for a Dublin which wasn't very sophisticated at the time, and I had been slightly afraid when I put it on that it might be libellous; indeed, somebody might have seen fit to take an action if it had received its first production in a large theatre. But obviously there was no point in taking an action against either Brendan or the Pike because neither had any money. People from Mountjoy Prison had even come down to see the play and once it was hailed as an important work they could not very well have taken an action. The nuclear disarmament movement meant that a lot of middle-class people who had never been inside a prison or approached a policeman except to ask the time now knew what went on behind prison walls. But at the time of *The Quare Fellow* prison life was still a mystery to the man in the street. Brendan's play was shocking in the sense that it revealed things which had not been revealed before. I wanted to establish the play in Dublin by putting it on after its Pike production in a large theatre. I lined up a cast which included Denis O'Dea and Noel

Purcell. I approached the Gaiety Theatre first, but they had no available dates at the time. I then approached the Olympia, but the management was suspicious of Brendan because his brother had once worked there and sold the *Daily Worker* in the gallery when he should have been operating the spotlight. It was a pity, because Joan Littlewood was able to steal our thunder by presenting the play in Stratford East. At the time we were very cross about this, but I suppose it is hard to blame the Dublin managements.

The Pike seated only fifty-six persons and with a full house, which included persons standing, we took about a hundred pounds a week. We played to packed houses, so if Brendan was working on a ten per cent basis, which I think was our agreement, and the play ran for four or five weeks, he got forty or fifty pounds. I later staged three short plays of Brendan's: *The Big House*, which he wrote on commission for the BBC's Third Programme and which I adapted for the stage with his blessing; and two other short plays, *Moving Out* and *The Garden Party*. *The Hostage* was commissioned as *An Giall* for Gael-Linn. They gave him seventy-five pounds to write a play in Gaelic and promised him a further seventy-five pounds when it was written. He spent the first advance and wrote nothing until about three weeks before the deadline. Frank Dermody directed *An Giall* at the Damer Hall and it was the first, if not the only, controversial play written in the Gaelic language for many a long year.

Meanwhile Joan Littlewood presented *The Quare Fellow* at the Theatre Royal in Stratford East and it transferred to the Comedy Theatre in the West End. It established Brendan as an important playwright. During the run of the play at the Comedy, Brendan made his famous television appearance with Malcolm Muggeridge. He was stoned. This turned him, so far as the English were concerned, into a celebrity overnight. Joan Littlewood commissioned him to translate *An Giall* into English and gave him her flat in Blackheath in which to work whilst she went off on a holiday. Needless to say, when she returned she found that Brendan had hardly put pen to paper. She forced him to translate the play and when it went into rehearsal at the Theatre Royal she and her partner, Gerry Raffles, kept him in the pub opposite the theatre in Angel Lane, so that whenever they wanted a change made or needed a new song, they could go across to the pub and say: 'How about it, Brendan?' That is how *The Hostage* got its embellishments. Half the characters in the English version were not in the Irish version.

Joan Littlewood produced *The Hostage* for a London audience and coloured it in a London way. When I came to direct the play in Gaelic for the Taibhdhearc in Galway I worked from the English version and had the embellishments translated into Gaelic. But I related the play to Galway, which is exactly what Joan did for London. Obviously an Irish audience could not be expected to accept *The Hostage* as directed by Joan Littlewood because it did not seem true to the Irish character. When you come to work on the play, however, you realise that this difference is superficial.

If I liked *The Quare Fellow* because it was documentary, I liked *The Hostage* because it was the reverse of documentary. Both plays reflect the period of their first performance, and in this *The Quare Fellow* has suffered more than *The Hostage*. I directed *The Quare Fellow* at the Abbey Theatre in 1969 at the invitation of the directors and because of my associations with the play. I think this may have been a mistake. I found that Irish audiences had lost their relationship with the work. So many of the situations had become commonplace and much of the material had been used again in *The Hostage* and in the adaptation of *Borstal Boy*.

Somebody told me that Brendan wrote a short play when he was in jail which was never published; I don't think it can have been of great importance. The short story which John Ryan published in *Envoy* was, I suppose, his first significant piece of writing. He might well have lived longer had the lionising he received by the Press in England not gone to his head and made him drink heavily. One must remember that Brendan was in no sense arty. He was an artist in spite in himself. His way of life was that of an artisan, a house-painter like his father, who regarded work simply as a way of earning money. Whether you worked with a typewriter or a paintbrush was immaterial to him. Brendan changed from the brush to the typewriter when he found that the typewriter could earn him more money. Then he discovered he could make money just by talking to people in pubs, so he didn't bother to type any more. His later works were taperecorded. Brendan made more money than he probably intended to, and this helped to destroy him. He was not a compulsive writer; he was a compulsive thinker and talker. He had wonderful ideas, and if he dispensed these ideas to some drunken fellow in a pub who went away and forgot them, Brendan was as satisfied as if he had dispensed them at a pound a line. I lost touch with him after I moved to London and he was spending long periods in America. Shortly before I left Dublin I staged a revival of *The Big House* at the Gate Theatre and Brendan gave me the royalties from the play for my *Rose Tattoo* Fund. That was 1959, the year in which I directed his brother Dominic's play *Posterity Be Damned*, first in Dublin and then in London. Brendan came to the rehearsals at Stratford East and after that period I never saw him again.

Brendan had the philosophy of a working housepainter. Out of the money you earned every week you spent so much on the basic necessities of rent and food and clothing and the remainder you spent on drink. This is a straightforward philosophy when the money involved is reasonable, but when you earn large sums of money you must adjust to a new situation. When you have a few pounds you can get stoned twice a week, but you can't get any more drunk than that. When you have as much money to spend on drink as you like, something must give. This, rather than anything else, was Brendan's big problem. He did not know when to stop drinking, and his physique just didn't stand up to it.

The plots of Brendan's plays are nothing very much. *The Quare Fellow* is a documentary and the plot of *The Hostage* is unbelievably simple. What makes these works so lively is the characters and their talk. We can meet a person in a pub and laugh our heads off at his remarks, yet how many of us can write them down afterwards? Brendan had this ability. He was a raconteur and as entertaining on the page as when he reached the right stage in drink. Even at the time of *The Quare Fellow* he was using his earnings from the *Irish Press* to keep him in drink. He was basically a shy person and quiet when sober. When he took a few drinks to break the ice he was the most wonderful company in the world. When he took one over the eight he became violent and unpleasant. He was frightfully generous, yet hardheaded about money and he would not write for nothing. He drove a hard bargain, yet would press a hundred pounds into the hand of somebody he thought needed it. He was not unlike Bernard Shaw in this respect, but when drunk he had been known to sell the rights of a work to four or five competing parties.

I always found Brendan good company, although other people considered him noisy and tiresome and something of a menace to polite society. When I first met him he wasn't a writer, so far as I knew, except for his newspaper work. When we talked it was about politics or horseracing or other people's writings. John Ryan was simply a friend to whom he gave that first short story and said: 'Would you like that for *Envoy*?' Presumably I must have seen him when he was interned at the Curragh. He would have been one of a number of men walking around in the mornings between the huts and the barbed wire.

The English, on the whole a staid people, had this love affair with Brendan who overpowered them with his flow of poetic prose. His bad language on television at a time when television was still rather pompous had almost as much to do with his popularity as his actual writing. By degrees Brendan came to realise that he was expected to behave outrageously. His personality, combined with the quality of his work, made an enormous impact. I think that a share of the success of the stage adaptation of *Borstal Boy* can be attributed to the fact that Niall Toibín was able to impersonate Brendan so cleverly. The similarity was so alarming that it upset some members of the Behan family.

Dominic is not so good a playwright as Brendan. His sense of humour is not so ebullient as Brendan's and he has the natural exaggeration of a lyrical writer. *Posterity Be Damned* was too Irish for the English to understand it thoroughly. It was concerned with the relationship between Fianna Fail and the IRA and had an appeal in Ireland as a controversial play, but it lacked that innate warmth and humanity which is to be found in all Brendan's work.

The year after I had staged *The Quare Fellow* at the Pike I wrote to

Samuel Beckett for the rights of *Waiting for Godot*. The Pike production in 1955 was the first production of *Godot* in the English language, although there was one beginning about the same time in England. Dermot Kelly played Vladimir, Donal Donnelly Lucky, Austin Byrne Estragon and Nigel Fitzgerald Pozzo. I met Beckett before and after that production and found him a kindly and delightful person, reserved but in no sense standoffish. He was cagey about publicity and has spent considerable effort in dodging newspapermen. He attracts culture vultures as a jampot attracts wasps.

He was fond of Brendan, and Brendan once borrowed money from him in Paris when he was broke. Both writers have a compassion for humanity. On the whole I would say that audiences in Dublin were less puzzled by *Waiting for Godot* than audiences in other countries. Without distorting the play I exploited its Irish aspect, which brought it near to an Irish audience. Beckett did not altogether approve of what I had done and subsequently told me so. He saw *Godot* as a universal play, but I must say that I think a theatre should relate a play to its audience. I believe I was right at the time, although if I directed *Godot* again I would not necessarily direct it in the same way.

Dubliners appreciated the Pike Theatre, but after *The Rose Tattoo* case we lost custom. Although they might not have seen *The Rose Tattoo* and knew the case had been thrown out of court, people decided that there was no smoke without fire. Since those days the law has been brought into disrepute, but at the time of *The Rose Tattoo* case ordinary people believed that nobody went to jail unless he had done something rather wicked. I believe my indictment was the first of its kind in the world. It did us harm at the Pike. Until then we had been well thought of, but now people withdrew their support because they were frightened. We had been thinking of building or converting a larger theatre, and this would have needed capital and assistance. We had received a grant from the Dublin Theatre Festival Committee to stage *The Rose Tattoo*, but we never fully recovered from the setback of the court case which dragged on for a year. During that year our lawyers would have been distressed if we had staged anything that might have been considered controversial in the mildest sense of the word; so the plays we staged were particularly innocuous.

An organisation must grow; it cannot stand still; but there was no hope of our raising additional capital. It would have been an admission of defeat if we had closed the Pike after the court case. Except for a number of friends, however, people did not want to be too closely associated with us. Our loss was not just financial; there was an incalculable loss of goodwill which slowed down our operation until it came to a halt. Perhaps it was for the best. For me, at any rate, the day of the small theatre as we knew it is gone. The Pike was exactly right for that particular decade. I am not saying that we shouldn't have small theatres today, but they should work on totally different lines.

Curiously, it was in a small Dublin theatre, the Peacock, that I directed the first production of Brendan's last play, *Richard's Cork Leg*, in the spring of 1972. Although the play was written by Brendan in 1960, most of us believed that it was unfinished and contained only one act. Early in 1972 I asked Beatrice to search her home for any manuscripts of Brendan's. It was then that she found the draft of a second act of the play. I myself completed the play.

Although most of Brendan's later work was dictated into a tape recorder, this play was written in longhand. It is set in an Irish cemetery and highlighted by the same ribaldry and wit that made *The Hostage* so entertaining. Here is an extract which Beatrice considers typical of Brendan's sense of song and insight into the Irish character:

THE HERO: (SINGS) (RISE)
> The child that I carry will have to be
> laid on the steps of a nunnery.
> The man I call my own,
> Has turned funny and screams like
> a queen for cologne.
>
> His nails are all polished and in his hair,
> He wears a gardenia when I'm not there,

218

Instead of flittin' he sits knittin'
for a sailor he met in Thames Ditton.
I must find another, for he loves me
brother, not me. (EXIT OFF L.)

CRONIN (ADDRESSING THE AUDIENCE) My wife tries to cheer me up by
saying that girls like me – that she loves me. But then she is my wife.
I mean, I don't mean that she just loves me because a wife is supposed
to love her husband. But she is a very, very, exceptional person, and
she is very kind to everyone, and particularly to me.

But I'll tell you something for nothing. There's a lot of nonsense
given out by the English and Americans about our attitude to women.
They say it just to flatter themselves. Some old Jesuit in America
attacks the Irish for not screwing early and often enough. A hundred
years ago screwing and having kids was out of fashion and Paddy was
being lambasted because he got married too soon, and had too many
kids. It's like saying all Jews are capitalists because Rothschild is a
capitalist, and all Jews are Reds because Karl Marx was a Jew – if
they don't get you one way they get you another. If they don't get
you by the beard they get you by the balls.

The English and Americans dislike only some Irish – the same Irish
that the Irish themselves detest – the ones that think. But then they
hate their own people who think. I just like to think, and in this city
I'm hated and despised. They give me beer, because I can say things
that I remember from my thoughts – not everything, because by
Jesus, they'd crucify you, and you have to remember that when you're
drunk, but some things, enough to flatter them.

The great majority of Irish people believe that if you become a
priest or a nun, you've a better chance of going to heaven. If it's a
virtue to meditate in a monastery and get food and shelter for doing
it – why then isn't it a virtue outside? I'm a lay contemplative –
that's what I am.

20

❧ ❧ ❧

Two Playwrights with a Single Theme

BRIAN FRIEL AND Thomas Murphy have been concerned with the
theme of emigration to a greater extent than any other contemporary
Irish playwrights. Friel's gentle and compassionate treatment of the
subject contrasts with Murphy's more violent approach. In the
sixties both men achieved international recognition with plays dealing
with Irish emigration: Friel with *Philadelphia, Here I Come!* and
Murphy with *A Whistle In The Dark*. Murphy's subsequent play,
Famine, also dealt with emigration, as did Friel's *The Loves of Cass
McGuire* and *The Mundy Scheme*.

Murphy himself became an emigrant because he said he could not
be an objective playwright if he continued to live in his native County
Galway. In London he writes television plays to supplement his
earnings in the theatre. Friel moved from Londonderry across the
border to the village of Muff in Donegal in the Irish Republic; but he
depends for his livelihood on the success of his work abroad.

Tyrone Guthrie called Friel a 'born playwright' and in the early
sixties invited him to Minneapolis to watch him directing Shakespeare, Molière and Chekhov. When Friel wrote *Philadelphia, Here I*

Come! Guthrie announced: 'I think we have an important dramatist on our hands.'

* * *

BRIAN FRIEL: I was born outside Omagh, County Tyrone, in 1929 and went to live in Derry at the age of ten. I lived in Derry until three years ago when I moved to Muff, County Donegal. There were two aspects to Derry: one was of a gentle and, in those days, sleepy town; the other was of a frustrating and frustrated town in which the majority of people were disinherited. From the first point of view it was an easygoing town in which to grow up, but from a spiritual point of view, it wasn't a good town. Although the Civil Rights fires had been kindled in many places throughout the North, they burst into flames in Derry, because it was there the suppression was greatest. I was a member of the Nationalist Party in Derry for a number of years, but I resigned about five years ago because I felt the party had lost initiative. I felt it was no longer vibrant and I think this was the reason the conflagration started in Derry. A lot of people thought the Nationalist Party had become like the old Irish Parliamentary Party.

We had a cottage in the Rosses in County Donegal and had spent a lot of our time there. When the opportunity came we went to live in Donegal, partly to get into the countryside and partly to get into the Republic. The sense of frustration which I felt under the tight and immovable Unionist régime became distasteful. One was always conscious of discrimination in Derry. Still, I don't think the gap is too wide to be breached. People are pliable and generous. In a family the most outrageous things may be said, yet within a week, although they have not been forgotten, they can be glossed over. The same can apply to our religious and political differences.

I began writing when I was about nineteen. I know that after *Philadelphia* it was said that I was a born writer, but I don't know what a born writer is. The craft of writing is something you learn painfully and slowly. There was no background of writing in my family and I don't know how much of my talent is indigenous. I don't think there were any other writers in Derry. Some people feel

that if you are a writer or painter you must live in a colony, but I find
writing a very private and personal existence and I was aware of no
sense of loss at being the only writer in Derry. I was a fulltime writer
from 1960, writing mostly short stories in those days. I had been a
teacher until then. I began *Philadelphia* in 1962 or '63. It was a play
about an area of Irish life that I had been closely associated with in
County Donegal. Our neighbours and our friends there have all been
affected by emigration, but I don't think the play specifically concerns the question of emigration. *Philadelphia* was an analysis of a
kind of love: the love between a father and a son and between a son
and his birthplace. This is a theme I have tried to explore in three or
four plays. *Cass McGuire, Lovers,* and *Crystal and Fox* were all attempts
at analysing different kinds of love. A writer does not look at his work
on a vertical scale. He doesn't say that one play was better than
another. In four plays I attempted to analyse a concept of love. In
Crystal and Fox I reached a conclusion from my point of view; in
other words, I had mined this vein to the end, and perhaps the vein
was not rich enough. At any rate I reached a kind of completion and
left this area to write a play in a completely new direction, *The
Mundy Scheme.* Other European countries have been warm and
generous towards my plays, but not England. I think the English are
unsympathetic to anything Irish. I don't mean this to be a chauvinistic comment; I believe the English refuse to take the Irish seriously
on any issue. On the other hand, my respect for and interest in
Broadway is nil. To me Broadway is an enormous warehouse in which
dramatic merchandise is bought and sold at the highest possible
profit. Occasionally good things happen there, but by and large it
has nothing to do with the art of theatre.

People ask why I have not written a play about the Civil Rights
movement. One answer is that I have no objectivity in this situation;
I am too much involved emotionally to view it with any calm.
Again I don't think there is the stuff of drama in the situation. To
have a conflict in drama you must have a conflict of equals or at
least near equals. There is no drama in Rhodesia or South Africa,
and similarly there is no drama in the North of Ireland. In a lengthy
address I gave about the Theatre of Hope and Despair I made the

point that American and European plays were nihilistic and concerned with the destruction of man's psyche. But I don't think this is
true any longer. Many of the young English dramatists are vitally
concerned with resurgent and hopeful man. I think the Theatre of
Hope exists in this sense. Writers like Osborne, Wesker and Livings
are optimistic people who happen to use black canvases. When you
discuss the theatre in Ireland you talk of O'Casey and the discussion
ends. But the world has become much smaller and we should now
view ourselves not in an insular but in a world context. An Irish
dramatist need not handle his material differently. The canvas can be
as small as you wish, but the more accurately you write and the more
truthful you are the more validity your play will have for the world.

It was Lady Gregory who said of the Abbey Theatre's tour of
America that the Abbey had won praise for itself and raised the
dignity of Ireland. What the Abbey achieved in its early years was
enormous; today its role must change. It cannot keep doing the same
thing year after year, decade after decade. What it must now do is
what the English National Theatre and any first-rate repertory can
do – put on the plays of the country. The Abbey has a measure of
financial security in its subsidies and can take risks as no commercial
management can. This should be its new strength, and no one should
expect it to do today what it did at its inauguration. It is a strange
situation in which the Abbey's proud boast is that it plays to ninety-
five per cent houses. That is the kind of boast the Windmill Theatre
might have made. A better claim would be that they have put on ten
plays, nine of which were terrible but one of which was good. The
Abbey directors rejected my play *The Mundy Scheme* by three votes
to one. When I submitted the play I stipulated that if it were
accepted for production I would require Donal Donnelly as director
and Godfrey Quigley to play the leading role of the Taoiseach. I
asked for a decision within one week. Let me say that I submitted
the play with the gravest misgivings and little enthusiasm. One week
later Alan Simpson, who was the Abbey's Artistic Adviser, rang
Donal Donnelly to say that the play had been rejected. I was not
disillusioned. I have never seen myself writing for any particular
theatre group or any particular actor or director. When I have

written a play I look for the best possible interpretation from a director and actors, and after that my responsibility ends.

I am uneasy about the future of the writer in Ireland. Ireland is becoming a shabby imitation of a third-rate American state. This is what *The Mundy Scheme* is about. We are rapidly losing our identity as a people and because of this that special quality an Irish writer should have will be lost. A writer is the voice of his people and if the people are no longer individuals I cannot see that the writer will have much currency. We are losing the specific national identity which has not been lost by the Dutch or the Belgians or the French or Italians. We are no longer even West Britons; we are East Americans. A writer cannot exist financially in Ireland unless his work is read or performed in Europe or America. An Irish writer can of course write serials for television or radio, but I think he would be as well off working in a solicitor's office.

I abandoned short story writing before I grew tired of it and now that I am becoming disenchanted with the theatre the chances are that I will go back to writing stories. Walter Macken once said to me that he had taken to novel writing because there were too many middlemen in the theatre. All theatre is a kind of compromise. When you write a play you have the ideal actors in mind, but you never get them; you have the ideal director in mind, but you never get him. In one way the Irish writer works under difficult conditions because of our damned Gaelic introspection. In another way he works under better conditions than if he were living in Paris, London or New York. If you write a mediocre play in Dublin you will get it staged and it will be staged reasonably well and receive a responsible reaction. If you write a mediocre play in a big city the chances of having it staged are minimal. But if a young Dubliner writes a play it will be seen, and isn't this what he wants? Unfortunately we look at this little island, which is so tiny, and imagine that the people who live ten streets away are different to ourselves. We are obsessed with ourselves and cannot see ourselves in a global context. One of our great misconceptions is that Ireland can be ruled only by its government and that the best government is composed of businessmen. This is a fallacy. I see no reason why Ireland should not be ruled by its poets and dramatists. Tyrone Guthrie has said that if Yeats and Lady Gregory were alive today they would be unimportant people. This is the way it is going to be, I am afraid.

TOM MURPHY: When *Whistle in the Dark* was staged in London I found myself one of the Wild Geese, an uprooted Irishman in England. The play was staged in Stratford East and then in Shaftesbury Avenue. It was critically and artistically well received, but commercially successful for nobody but myself. It helped to subsidise further work that I wanted to do and gave me a little security in the new life of which I was frankly afraid. I had left a good job in the West of Ireland and, I suppose, broken my mother's heart for at least six months.

I think the most important feature of my growing up was the emigration from the family. Somebody always seemed to be arriving or going away. A lot of emotion centred around the little railway station in my home town of Tuam. In Church View, Tuam, you have a street of widows. It is a pity that Lorca isn't living there to write about it.

We lived on a big housing estate which had the atmosphere of a frontier town in the old West, with feuds in which entire families faced one another in phalanxes on either side of the street. Missing members would return from England for such a day. I left school at eighteen to work in the local sugar factory as an apprentice to the welding trade. Writing and reading stopped for four or five years until I won a scholarship to train as a teacher. I taught for nearly five years at Mountbellew. Being a scholarship boy, I had a contract which stipulated that I must teach for five years. In actual fact, I taught for four years and seven months. When *Whistle in the Dark* went on in London I applied for leave of absence for two years and was refused. So I left, and they charged me £97.4.7 for the privilege.

During my teaching period I had become involved with the local dramatic society and this stimulated my interest both in reading and writing. As a young teacher I had to do a lot of technical reading to find my way in a new profession, but the theatre was a new interest for me. One day a friend of mine in Tuam said: 'Why don't you write a play?' I thought it a good idea. I was twenty-two and

225

the amateur dramatic movement was claiming my entire social life. I began to submit manuscripts to amateur drama competitions; some won and some didn't. Then I wrote *Whistle in the Dark*.

Another reason for my leaving Ireland was that the BBC wanted me to go to the Congo. The Irish contingent were keeping peace at the time there for the UN and somebody at the BBC got the idea that there was a play in this and asked me if I would go. But the project fell through because I think the Irish Government would take no responsibility for me in the Congo. Instead, I remained in London and wrote some television plays and two stage plays, *The Morning After Optimism* and *The Moping Owl*, neither of which was produced. These plays were not as brilliant as I thought. It was a difficult situation. I had seen my play staged in London and Dublin and now I had to begin learning the business of playwriting. The books I read became chalk marks on the wall. 'I have read that and that and that . . .' Tennessee Williams impressed me most by his natural and powerful form of dialogue. Later I discovered my favourite playwright in Lorca, and I was interested to learn that he had based his style on Synge's.

When I came to London I lived for three years in Kangaroo Valley in Earl's Court before I decided to move to the suburbs. Being a cocky young fellow with a play in the bag, and a London bag at that, I thought that conquering the world was going to be easy. It took me a few years to become objective in my aims. If you saw a man standing on his head in Earl's Court you would walk round the corner and forget about it. But the same sight in a small town or a suburb would set your mind and imagination to work at filling in the background. I have a natural curiosity about people, but so much tends to be happening in the centre of London that a state of apathy exists. This is what I felt and so I moved.

In my writing I began to break away from the naturalism to which the Irish theatre is clinging. In writing *Whistle in the Dark* I suppose I cheated. I had told myself it would not be a play set in the traditional Irish kitchen; I didn't go much further when I set it in an English kitchen. But I don't think I would ever throw those particular themes of emigration and violence away. They are a part of my life.

The man who goes to England and belongs neither to England nor Ireland lives in a vacuum. He has been freed from the control of parents, neighbours, the community and the Church, and this can produce explosions of violence. When you have a drink with another immigrant he will complain in the course of four or five pints about what the English did to the Irish and, if he can sustain such drinking, four or five pints later he will say that his ambition is to go back to Ireland to buy up his home town and burn it to the ground.

Talking with Irish immigrants I find that most of them seem to have left their country without a blessing. They appear to impose on themselves a sense of guilt; guilt at having betrayed somebody or let somebody down. The emotional ties are strong. When an Irishman leaves his country he is constantly looking back over his shoulder. Such people become limbo people and it is difficult to succeed if you are caught astride the Irish Channel. Wrongs, real and imaginary, take a fantasy form in the mind. There is a great confusion.

When I wrote *The Orphans* for the 1968 Dublin Theatre Festival I tried to break away from the subject of Irish emigration. The characters were mainly English; but I was still concerned with uprooted people, with people who cannot keep up with technological advances and tend to be left behind. I married an English girl who has helped my understanding of the English mentality. But when you relinquish your beliefs you realise how deeprooted they are. If you believe in something positively, whether it be right or wrong, there is always pain in relinquishing it. I am very much drawn back to Ireland. I suffer from a nostalgia which is more than a sentimental yearning for a place. I believe that there is a make-up in the body which comes out of the particular earth of the place in which a man is born.

The Irish emigrant and his religion sounds like a cliché, but being a cliché doesn't make it untrue. An Irishman is baptised by a priest, educated by priests or brothers and nursed in hospital by nuns. This clinging to religion is peculiar to the Irish. Provincial attitudes are so strong in such an insular country, in which one's religion is decided in the cradle, that when an Irishman finds himself in a country where he can be objective and free, he resents it. Somebody once described the situation as a lengthening chain.

21

❧　❧　❧

Cruise O'Brien :　The Playwright Politician

WHEN THE UNITED Nations operation in the Congo began in July,
1960, Conor Cruise O'Brien was a member of the Department of
External Affairs – the Foreign Office – of the Irish Republic. Since
1956 he had been a delegate to the United Nations. When Ireland
contributed troops to the UN at the request of Dag Hammarskjold,
the Secretary-General, O'Brien was appointed a member of the
Secretariat. In May, 1961, he was sent to Elizabethville as representa-
tive of Hammarskjold in Katanga. When he resigned from the
service of the United Nations in December, 1961, he had the
material for a book, *To Katanga and Back*, and for what was to become
his play, *Murderous Angels*.

After engaging in other concerns in Ghana and New York, O'Brien
finally returned to Ireland and stood as a candidate for the Labour
Party in the General Election of 1969. He was elected to Dáil
Éireann, the Irish Parliament. In a country where intellectuals in
politics are suspect, O'Brien has been accepted by the electorate. He
believes that the intellectual need not be an outsider in the pragmatic
affairs of State and hopes he has some contribution to make towards
shaping the destiny of his country.

A public speaker and debater, O'Brien's social commitments are real: he has marched in anti-apartheid demonstrations and spoken in defence of students who opposed the tearing down of Georgian houses in Dublin. He is accepted as an expert on international affairs, but would be regarded in Ireland as an academic rather than a popular writer.

Conor Cruise O'Brien might be called a playwright by accident. His Katanga experience led to his conception of Hammarskjold bringing about the downfall of Lumumba in the service of humanity and precipitating his own downfall in the process. *Murderous Angels* had its first production at the Mark Tapir Forum in Los Angeles in January, 1970. Clive Barnes described it as 'a rattling good play . . . exciting to watch and engrossing to think about. Forget all red herrings about whether it is true or not. The theatre makes its own truth, and as long as in our own minds we never confuse theatrical truth with historical fact, no harm will be done.'

O'Brien lives in a bungalow at Howth, a promontory overlooking Dublin Bay, with his wife Máire, a poet and daughter of a former Government Minister. When we talked to him, his play *Murderous Angels* had been rejected by the Abbey Theatre.

*　　*　　*

In a sense I have never really left Ireland. In all my fifty-one years I have never spent an entire year outside Ireland. During the last eight years I have spent most of my time away, but I have not come back as a stranger or in any way been greatly surprised at what I have found.

I went to the Congo in May, 1961, after the death of Patrice Lumumba. I naturally had occasion to think about the Congo a good deal and its connexions with more general issues: with the great problem of relations between races and specifically the relation between white and black. When I wrote my play, *Murderous Angels*, I thought of Lumumba partly in that connexion. Lumumba is a symbolic figure representing the aspirations for black power and the liberation of the black people.

There is no doubt that Hammarskjold could have saved Lumumba from his fate. This has been documented in *The Congo Since Independence* by Catherine Hoskyns, published by the Royal Institute for International Relations. You will find there the official instructions when Lumumba left the protection which had been provided for him at his villa and started to travel across the Congo. The instruction given was that there was to be no interference between Lumumba and his official pursuers, as the term went. I did not become aware of the full extent of the involvement of the UN Secretariat in the events which precipitated Lumumba's downfall until I read Miss Hoskyns's book; nor was I aware at the time of the extent to which they took care not to intervene to save his life. I am not saying that they knew he was going to be murdered, still less, of course, that they desired his murder. But as the old saying goes, they did not strive officiously to keep him alive.

I think a part of one's life is spent in the process of shedding illusions, and it is true in a sense that I shed some illusions in the Congo. I did not become disillusioned, if by that one means bitter and cynical; but I became more and more interested in how international affairs work. I have never taken, and I know I never shall take, a stand against the United Nations. I think the UN provides a very imperfect set of safeguards; however bad the world is now it would be in an even more dangerous condition if there was no such meeting place. When I wrote *Murderous Angels* I tried to take *Markings*, which was Hammarskjold's spiritual diary, and the record of his actions in the Congo partly as I experienced them myself, but mainly as they appear from Miss Hoskyns's detached narrative, to produce a dramatic character who could credibly be the same man who wrote *Markings* and also acted in a distinctly Machiavellian way (and I'm not using Machiavellian in the purely curse-word sense). I certainly wasn't trying to be either hard or easy on him; I was trying to see just what this man was. Lumumba could only have lived if the international forces surrounding the situation had been different. But those international forces called for his disappearance as a political force, and if you disappear as a political force in the Congo it isn't safe to remain there. So his death was inscribed in the logic of the thing.

Murderous Angels is a political play and a controversial play because you cannot have a political play that is not controversial. When Alan Simpson was appointed Artistic Adviser of the Abbey Theatre I discussed the play with him. He was interested in the play and through him I submitted it to the Abbey. The Abbey turned it down without much hesitation on the grounds, or so I was informed, that there would be some need for coloured actors and that it would be difficult to cast it here. But I felt that there was probably also a reason which they didn't state, that the play is highly controversial and the Board of the Abbey doesn't really like controversial plays. This is an interpretation on my part, but I think it is legitimate. An Establishment theatre that is receiving a subsidy does not wish to be embarrassed with an international issue which in turn might embarrass the Government. I think it undoubtedly true that the Minister for External Affairs would have made representation that this play should not be put on, but I was certain that eventually it would be staged in Dublin.

I have written two other short plays: one of them a dramatic monologue about King Herod, the other a treatment of the Salome theme. Some critics have made the point that *Murderous Angels* in particular is old-fashioned; the kind critics call it Shavian and the unkind critics sub-Shavian. It stems from that theatre because I think that no one who grew up in my time could help being influenced and stimulated, as I was, by Bernard Shaw. Among living Irish writers Seán Ó Faoláin influenced me more than anybody else when he was editor of *The Bell* by his astringent criticism, which was very good for me at the time, although I did not realise this immediately, and in particular by his example in combining the activity of a writer with social criticism. I think it was Harold Macmillan who gave Frank O'Connor some bad advice when he suggested that he keep out of public life at a time when O'Connor had been on the Board of the Abbey Theatre. His implication was that the writer should sit at his desk in an ivory tower. I think this advice may be good for certain writers, but not for all writers. It would have been better for Sean O'Casey if he had stayed in Ireland and become involved in politics and other aspects of the social struggle and written out of the experiences he shared. I have an almost total lack of admiration for everything O'Casey wrote after he left Ireland, including the autobiographies, the style of which I find extremely repellent. But his earlier plays, which probably will always be performed here and to some extent in other countries, suggest a considerable discrepancy between what he is writing and what he is thinking. To the end of his days O'Casey thought of himself as a revolutionary, but what his plays are talking about are the horror and pain and ignominy of such action. It is the tension between the writer and the man himself that makes his plays come alive.

I worked for something like twenty years in the Department of External Affairs. I was an official involved in the practical and, if you like, routine aspect of a part of the life of this country, so I do not feel a fish out of water by any means in Leinster House. My family has its roots deep in Irish politics. My grandfather sat in the old Irish Parliament from 1885 to 1918. Frank Skeffington and Tom Kettle were members of this family group. I grew up listening to politics, mainly Irish politics, and I suppose even in my youth I conceived the ambition to serve my country in this particular way. It may not be entirely useless for the Dáil to have among its members someone with the wide and perhaps unusual experience which I have had outside this country. I don't think anybody could be completely happy about the cultural climate of Ireland or any country either now or at any other time. Elizabethan England looks very bright in retrospect, but I don't know how it must have looked at the time. Ireland is certainly less mildewed and depressing than it was when I was fifteen years younger. Censorship-mindedness still afflicts us, but it has lost a lot of its power. Television has, on the whole, been beneficial in shaking us out of our very strong tendency to stagnation. That tendency is still there and it is probably the reason why so many young people leave Ireland and why those who remain are ageing and excessively conservative people. I have found a great respect abroad for our literary output of the past and perhaps an excessive disdain for our literary output of the present. I was asked in Stockholm when I lectured on Irish literature: 'Where are your Yeatses and your Joyces today?' I had to answer that you cannot produce a Yeats or a Joyce by an Act of Parliament.

Contemporary theatre, if it is to be any good, must have a considerable potential of social shock. The present Abbey Theatre Board wants the theatre to be a genteel place where nobody's feelings will be hurt, and therefore it must turn its face to the past. What I say may be imputed to the rancour of a rejected playwright, but I think that a cautious and a semi-official theatre management, which is what we seem to have at the Abbey, will always tend to go back to the past. I once wrote a film script about Parnell, which was never produced, and I don't think I would go back to it again. I have done a television script for the BBC on Casement's trial, and I've toyed with the idea of writing a play about Casement. But one toys with many more ideas than one takes up. When I am working really hard I get up at six in the morning and write until eleven and continue at that pace. I sometimes get up to write in the middle of the night. But this is not a general way of life. It took me three and a half months to write *Murderous Angels*, a relatively short time. People who take longer will tell me that their plays are better than mine, and I won't quarrel with them. I think one should be involved in a situation before one can draw on the material one needs to write about it. I am sorry, for example, that Brian Friel hasn't written about the North, which he presumably knows, instead of the South. I am very interested in the Northern situation, but I shall write about it in a treatise. The roots of that situation go deep. I have never belonged to the school of those who hold the North to be an artificial creation. The best hope of change lies in the educated strata of the younger Protestants in the North who could react against the system of caste discrimination; for it is a caste and not a religious system. My hope would be that this section would increase and that the Unionist section would become an anachronism. If such occurs I would see the opportunity for a growth in better relations among Irishmen. I do not see change in terms of blotting out a territorial border. The changes that are required must be in people's hearts and minds.

Bigotry is something which has existed for generations, but on the other hand, it might have been very difficult for people fifteen or even ten years ago to foresee the impact of the ecumenical movement. The spirit of man takes unexpected turns and jumps. Changes can come, and suddenly.

There is something profoundly wrong with society; not just Irish society, but world society. For lack of social awareness and responsibility society is heading in the last quarter of our century towards enormous disasters. The consequences of the population explosion have not been overrated. The West African country I know best is Ghana, with a population of seven millions. If present trends continue unchecked, which I think they will not, the population by the year 2500 will be something like two hundred and thirty-five million. The signs are that the population will be checked by the kind of disaster we have had in Nigeria and Biafra. The great massacre of the Ibos stemmed in part from the frustration and rage of a rapidly expanding population. Those who had power in the world allowed conditions to continue whilst going through the motions of attempting to develop what is called the underdeveloped world. The European nations and the United States have confined themselves to taking out of underdeveloped countries the resources which they need, with great indifference to the welfare and future of the inhabitants. Now the point has been reached where the growth of population in itself would not necessarily be all that bad if there were not a complete lack of opportunity for putting this population to productive use. In Africa and Latin America and most of Asia conditions are getting worse for infinitely larger numbers of people. Most of us shy away from this situation. I shy away from it myself. In America the slave trade has produced one of the greatest crises in history. All around you feel this fearful legacy of hatred and discontent among the descendants of those who were treated literally as objects to be sold and those who perpetrated that slavery. Sensitive Americans are extremely conscious of this legacy, particularly the youth movement in which a generation of Americans are facing this enormous skeleton in their cupboard.

It is a very curious thing that *Murderous Angels* has received a great deal of publicity in Britain and on the Continent, but in America, where it was published last year, there were almost no reviews. All those concerned with its publication expected mixed reaction, but the crashing silence which followed its publication is something for which I cannot adequately account. On this side of the Atlantic some reviewers have liked the play, some have been annoyed by it and a few have found it utterly boring. For what it is worth I think that American public opinion is broadly on the level of that of the leading Press reviewers: divided between liberals and conservatives. For obvious reasons the conservatives wouldn't like this play. The liberals wouldn't like it because it presents a not entirely favourable portrait of Dag Hammarskjold and United Nations' activities. The American right-wing has attacked the United Nations so unfairly that the left of centre has made of the UN a sort of sacred cow. My play doesn't treat this sacred cow with the appropriate salaams, if I'm not mixing up two great religions. There was embarrassment and uncertainty about how they ought to receive my play. I think the reviewers pushed it aside, not knowing quite what to make of it.

22

❧ ❧ ❧

Blakely : The North's Late Starter

THE PLAYWRIGHT SAM Thompson once described Belfast as 'a cultural desert'. Belfast, nevertheless, has provided a stage for the tradition of Northern Ireland dramatists; among them George Shiels, Rutherford Mayne, St John Ervine, Joseph Tomelty, Brian Friel, and Thompson himself. When Thompson's controversial play *Over the Bridge* reached the West End of London in the early sixties, one of the roles was taken by Colin Blakely, who later became one of the most outstanding of the younger generation of Northern Ireland actors.

A stocky figure who would pass unnoticed in a crowd, Blakely has performed in a wide range of parts from Christ for BBC television to Captain Boyle at Britain's National Theatre. Tyrone Guthrie, who had directed him in a number of plays, invited him to play the title role in the Abbey Theatre's production of Eugene McCabe's play *Swift* for the Dublin Theatre Festival of 1969, but the part went to Micheál Mac Liammóir because Blakely was busy filming for Billy Wilder. Like other Irish actors who have sought fulfilment outside their own country, Blakely likes to return to his birthplace. But when we met him it was in Dublin, where he was calling on estate agents in search of an Irish retreat not in the North but in the Republic. It was a visit which was to lead to his first appearance on the Abbey Theatre stage in Tom Murphy's *The Morning after Optimism*.

*   *   *

One day in Fortnum and Masons in London I spotted Alec Guinness among the food counters. When I walked over to him he tried to hide, but I caught him.

'Excuse me,' I said, 'you don't know me, but I'm twenty-seven and have just become an actor. Would you advise me to join a school or go into repertory?' He said: 'You haven't got much time young man. Go into rep.' But I couldn't get a job in repertory, so I returned home to Bangor.

I had started very late. Even before I entered the profession at twenty-seven, I had been an amateur actor for only two years. I was born in Bangor, not far from Belfast. My family had a sports goods shop and I had been in that business for eight or nine years. I was twenty-five before I joined a local amateur operatic group by chance; I was interested in a girl who was a member. My first line on any stage was: 'Would you care for some more salad, Miss Oakley?' in *Annie Get Your Gun*. After two years the bug had caught me. I finally plucked up courage to say to my father, a hardbitten businessman: 'I want to go on the stage,' a line which I had been practising for weeks. His answer was: 'Go ahead, so long as I don't have to support you.'

I headed for London because I was determined not to join the Belfast theatre in which the Arts Theatre were staging good plays on a shoestring and the Group Theatre folk plays which all seemed to begin with the reading of a will. I had never seen plays in Dublin. I might have gone to the Abbey Theatre, but I understood that they wanted only Gaelic speakers there. So I boarded the Liverpool boat to see what I could find on the other side. I had very little money, but the shop agreed to let me have six pounds a week until I found work. James Ellis introduced me to an agent who found me a job with a group which presented plays in schools. I drove the van, played Hansel and Gretel's father and put up the scenery and took it down again. They paid me six pounds a week for this and I loved every minute of it. Then I was out of work again. I tried to join the drama schools and they told me: 'Well, you're a bit old for us.' I realised that a course would take two years and by that time I would be twenty-nine. I was also wary of joining a class full of seventeen-year-olds.

It was then I met Alec Guinness, and, having failed to find a job in repertory, I returned to Bangor to see my parents. It was midsummer and I had been away only a couple of months. On the morning I arrived home an actor with the Group Theatre, which was playing a summer season in our town, fell from his motorcycle and broke an ankle. Harold Goldblatt, who somehow had heard of my arrival, asked me to take over the part for a pound a week. My price was going down, but I said yes and I was on the stage the following night. The play was *The Whiteheaded Boy* and I remember Jimmy Devlin spoke my lines for me. Notwithstanding, they kept me on and James Ellis joined us shortly afterwards. By this time the Arts Council of Northern Ireland was helping out and the group was able to widen its repertoire. We presented *The Diary of Anne Frank*, *Picnic*, and *The Summer of the Seventeenth Doll*. In a way the Group Theatre was Ulster's National Theatre, although since those days the Arts Theatre and the Lyric Theatre have both developed. I was being paid twelve pounds a week and enjoying the life, but there was no future. I was living at home, I hadn't married, and I believed that I was not progressing in any way. After two years I decided to leave Ireland for the second time. It was 1959 and Jimmy Devlin helped me to get a part in O'Casey's *Cock-a-Doodle Dandy* at the Royal Court Theatre. After that I got a part in *Serjeant Musgrave's Dance*. I received my first notices when I appeared in *The Naming of Murderer's Rock*, one of those Sunday night productions at the Royal Court in which aspiring actors played for two pounds. In *Cock-a-Doodle Dandy* there was an all-Irish cast, apart from Wilfred Lawson, which included Patrick Magee, Norman Rodway, Eamon Keane, Joan O'Hara and Jimmy Devlin. In *Serjeant Musgrave's Dance* I appeared with Ian Bannen, Alan Dobie, Donal Donnelly, Frank Finlay and Freda Jackson with Lindsay Anderson as director. George Devine, who was still running the Royal Court at this time, had directed the O'Casey play. Those three plays were presented over a period of some six months, after which I went to the Arts Theatre to play the father in *A Moon for the Misbegotten*. Although I hadn't realised it when I went for the audition, they wanted me for the small part of the son, who has the same name as the character of the father. When they asked me to read the son's part I refused and said I wanted to play the father. After half an hour I had talked them into giving me the part.

It was in the following year that I played in my first film, a small part in *Saturday Night and Sunday Morning*. A succession of tiny parts followed until Lindsay Anderson gave me my first worthwhile part in *This Sporting Life*.

I was on location with a film in Yugoslavia when Peter Hall wired me an offer to play Touchstone in *As You Like It* which Michael Elliot was to direct for the Royal Shakespeare Company. William Gaskill also wanted me for Hastings in *Richard III*, and it was Gaskill who afterwards invited me to join the National Theatre. I didn't like playing Touchstone much. I don't like Shakespeare's clowns; they give me a pain in the arse. My favourite parts have been the Captain in *Juno and the Paycock* and Proctor in *The Crucible* at the National Theatre. I enjoyed *Hobson's Choice* and *Volpone*. The repertory at the National is enormous and varied and the auspices could not be better. It is a properly subsidised theatre. The National did not exist when I started out to be an actor. I wanted a crack at the classical actor's repertoire and I could see no way of doing this in Ireland, so I went to London where I believed the opportunity was. Although I have played Irish parts, I wanted to be known in London as an actor, not as an Irish actor. I did not want to end up playing drunken old men and tagged with the label 'the veteran Irish actor, Colin Blakely'. I came out of the National Theatre after three years because I needed an actor's instability. I did not want to remain a company member for years and years until I was bored. Company theatres carry a built-in self-destruction. Once a group of people come to know each other too well, their company becomes a cosy club. No matter how honest you are or how hard you try, the edge has gone. I have gone back to the National Theatre for an occasional play. We have an understanding that when they want me for a play they 'phone me and when I want to go back I 'phone them. The Royal Shakespeare and the National are sometimes called the introspective and the athletic theatres. This may be a silly label, but the National is probably more heroic in style than the Shakespeare.

I had long wanted to play in Chekhov but never had an opportunity until Anthony Page called me up at the end of 1969 and asked me to play Astrov to Paul Scofield's *Uncle Vanya* at the Royal Court. Scofield and I had worked together once before when I played his servant in the film *A Man for All Seasons*. But Chekhov was a wonderful departure. We performed the play very simply, with everything happening within the minds of the characters. At the beginning of rehearsals we sat down every day for two weeks and just read the play. After that we moved on stage when it became necessary to move. Tony Page, a courageous director, allowed the play to grow each day. By the time *Uncle Vanya* reached the first night there was no sense of production. The audience felt guilty as though they were listening to a private conversation. They were drawn into the play instead of having it thrust at them. Scofield had played Chekhov some twelve years previously in the usual move-it-about, make-it-interesting approach which Chekhov does not need, but never as carefully as in the production by Tony Page.

Olivier is marvellous to watch. His style of acting is quite different to Scofield's, yet absolutely valid. Olivier is an idol of mine, but for a model I am drawn towards Scofield. I played with Olivier in *The Recruiting Officer* and *Love for Love*, and he directed me in *Juno and the Paycock*, one of his favourite plays which he had seen at the Abbey Theatre with Sara Allgood and F J McCormick and the other early Abbey Players. Except for Joyce Redmond, who comes from County Mayo, and me, he cast his production with English, Scots or Welsh players in the belief that O'Casey, who hasn't been performed much in England, should be given his international place. Eileen O'Casey, the playwright's widow, sat in during rehearsals, and Harry

Hutchinson was the technical adviser. Much of the idiom was lost, of course, but the essential quality of the play came through. What I have learned from Olivier is actual stagecraft; what I have learned from Scofield is interior acting.

At the National Theatre I had appeared with Robert Stephens in many plays, including *The Royal Hunt of the Sun*, *The Recruiting Officer*, *Hamlet*, and *Love for Love*. When Billy Wilder was looking for actors rather than stars to play Holmes and Watson in his film *The Private Life of Sherlock Holmes* he chose Stephens and me because I think he believed he had found a pair who would work well together. He wanted the public to think of Holmes and Watson rather than of, say, Cary Grant or Jack Lemmon. Wilder has said many times that if there is a theme in his films it is the relationship between men; not homosexuality, but the natural trust between men who respect each other. He chose one of the most famous pairs in literature and explored their relationship with a naughty eye.

Wilder is the most accomplished cinema technician I have met. In modern terms he could be called old-fashioned. 'I know they call me so,' he says, 'but I shall stay old-fashioned, thank you, because I think it is better.' He dislikes camera tricks, so that if a shot is framed five inches above the chin of an actor in such a way that it distorts the face and makes its own comment, he will retake the shot. 'We'll find another way,' he will say: 'Let's hear the lines.' Every line in our script was polished like a jewel. Wilder had been preparing his film for four years and not a word was out of place. He has a sense of humour and a cruel wit. When I played a scene in which Watson gets tight at a party and dances with members of a ballet company, Wilder said to me at the end of the shot: 'Well done, Colin. You're a cross between Laughton and Nureyev. You act like Nureyev and you dance like Laughton.'

I think of myself as an Irishman but not as an Ulsterman. I am disgusted with the whole acreage up there. Being a Protestant makes no difference, but being born in Ulster does make a difference in that one is a hybrid. For a long time Ulster reflected the aura of the successful hardheaded businessman; but now that Dublin is booming that particular charisma has been lost to the North. Since the decline of the shipyards the scene has changed. Those in power won't allow it to change, but change it must. Twice a year I return to Belfast. My parents are dead now, but my brother still lives there. I drive through the battle centres of Falls Road and Shankill and Sandy Row, and five minutes later I have arrived at my brother's house and all is peaceful. People agree with you: 'Isn't it sad? Isn't it a terrible shame? But wait and you'll see now, it'll be all right.' One is dealing with completely closed minds. You imagine that if you could get Paisley to yourself in a corner for a few hours he would see your point of view. But I don't think he would. It's not a question of politics but of blind conviction.

My own home town of Bangor is one of the most well-to-do and liberal towns in Northern Ireland, but you don't come face to face with the blunt realities there as you do in the poorer districts of Belfast. My father was an Orangeman, but I was brought up in a fairly liberal way. To my father Orangeism meant going out and having a few jars and coming home in good order. But he stopped being an Orangeman after a time and none of my family is a member of the Orange Order. I was approached to join the Order when I was twenty-one. I was not politically grown-up then, yet I knew that something stank about Orangeism and I refused.

In Belfast I found that most of the people in the theatre were Catholics. Yet the artistic world was more equally shared by Catholics and Protestants than the commercial world. Perhaps the artistic people are a wee bit more sensitive to what is going on.

I knew Sam Thompson quite well. He was a good playwright. The only occasion on which I played in the West End of London was in his play *Over the Bridge*, which lasted three nights. Thompson was the first writer to come out fair and square with the Ulster problem instead of writing folksy plays. *Over the Bridge* confronted the Catholic and Protestant attitudes in the shipyards of Belfast, a centre of strife for many years, and pleaded, Stop it, you fools! The play was about the community in which redhot rivets were thrown and men flung into the Pollock Dock and drowned. During the troubles of 1969 the shipyards, ironically, were the only centre to remain calm; the first sign of hope, I thought. When the play went on in London eight years previously it had meant nothing to the audiences. It said nothing very new in psychological or universal terms; it was simply a plea for understanding and tolerance in a particular situation. Today the play is as topical in Belfast as it was then.

I have found no prejudice against my being Irish in London. They could not care less what you are so long as you don't frighten the horses. My children have been brought up in London, but I would like some part of them to be Irish. A year ago I had thought of looking for a house in Northern Ireland; today I have decided to find a house in the Republic. I would rather live in Ireland than die in Ireland.

23

❧ ❧ ❧

Huston : The Call of St Cleran's

JOHN HUSTON'S STUDY looks out on a terrace where a fountain plays.
Beyond the terrace stony fields stretch as far as the eye can see. The
film-maker's home is a Georgian mansion built on the site of St
Cleran's, an eleventh-century monastery in the West of Ireland. The
house is filled with mementoes of his travels: pre-Colombian figures,
Japanese screens, a head of Robert Flaherty discovered in Epstein's
studio; paintings by Monet and Jack Yeats; lifesize statues from a
ruined Mexican church; a medieval Christ found in a Paris dealer's
shop.

Huston's house-guests have ranged from Carson McCullers to
Marlon Brando. One evening when Sartre was working with Huston
on the script of *Freud* ('fashioning it like a syllogism') a distinguished
cleric, a neighbour, called. Sartre and the cleric conversed in
French, but Sartre was convinced he was talking to the parish priest.

John Marcellus Huston made his home in Ireland after a lifetime
of wandering. He was born in Nevada, Missouri, in 1906. His father
was the actor Walter Huston and the young Huston travelled con-
tinually with his parents, starting in a dozen schools and finishing in
none. He was boxer, painter, and newspaper reporter before becoming

a Hollywood screenwriter. His first screen credit was on William Wyler's A *House Divided*. When Jack Warner gave him *The Maltese Falcon* to direct he substituted his friend Humphrey Bogart for George Raft, who had refused to appear in the film under a tyro director.

As the forties drew to a close Huston moved his operations to Europe and directed a number of major films in quick succession. Since becoming an Irish citizen in 1964 he has spent all his time between films at St Cleran's. Huston is the reverse of those actors, playwrights and directors who have left Ireland since the turn of the century; he has come to live and, he hopes, to work in Ireland.

He enjoys the confidences of the Irish Cabinet and persuaded the Republic's Prime Minister, Jack Lynch, to set up a committee to advise how best an indigenous Irish film industry might be established. When we met him at St Cleran's, the stooping, silverhaired veteran of the cinema was planning with novelist Gerald Hanley to make a film about Ireland's 1916 Rebellion.

*   *   *

I first came to Ireland twenty years ago. I had travelled all over Europe, but, extraordinarily enough, never to Ireland. I had finished *The African Queen* and was working on *Moulin Rouge* in London when I was invited by Lady Oranmore and Browne to stay at Luggala during Dublin Horse Show week. There was a Hunt Ball at the Gresham Hotel that night and afterwards they drove me to Luggala. It was the most beautiful sight I had ever laid eyes on: a dark lake and a piece of granite rearing up into the sky. I began to come back for the hunting. I had hunted in the United States and France, but never in Ireland. I began to seize every opportunity I could to come back to Ireland, and after a few months I decided to live here. I had been living in France, having sold my house in California, when I came here and rented a house in the County Kildare, where we lived for two years.

We hunted over parts of the country and came to County Galway with the Galway Blazers for a day. We saw this house, St Cleran's, which was not for sale then. Some time later I heard that the Land

Commission had acquired it and were about to pull it down. I bought it. I had to tear all the wood and beams out until it was just a shell, and then rebuild it. It is a house of varying ages, the last part Georgian.

When I was living in Kildare I went scouting for locations in Ireland for *Moby Dick* that would look like New Bedford. The American seaboard doesn't look anything like it did in the nineteenth century, but I found the nearest resemblance to it in Youghal in County Cork. It was a marvellous experience and the people were extraordinary. Now I use every chance to make pictures in Ireland. These have been pictures with natural backgrounds that weren't necessarily Irish, except *The List of Adrian Messenger*.

After I came to Ireland the McCarthy investigations were under way in the United States. I didn't have much use for any of that. I had no part in the investigations and had never been named, although I had something to do with a protest against Parnell Thomas, who was Chairman of the Un-American Activities Committee. I had no axe to grind, except that the business seemed to be highly unconstitutional and as an American I objected like hell. I had no Communist affiliations and was so detached that I could speak freely without fear of recrimination or assault. I was not in contact, but I sympathised, with those who had been named. It was a witchhunt which destroyed careers, and in some instances even people's lives. This kind of thing soured me. I remember pointing out at the time that the Irish Americans were among the most reactionary elements and I asked an American journalist who was in Ireland at the time to tell the Irish Americans how the Irish felt. I don't think he took up my suggestion; at that moment everyone was afraid to raise his voice. This perhaps had something to do unconsciously with my feeling of separation from the United States and my wanting to live away from it.

After spending ten years in Ireland one day I said to myself: 'This is my home and I would like to become an Irish citizen.' It was as simple as that. Now the money I pay in taxes goes towards education and hospitals, which are fundamentally more important than the things on which America is spending its money.

At the time I left the United States I was making motion pictures independently. I wasn't under an employment contract to any single studio, but I would undertake to make a film for a particular company. I always took my own line of country. After the war almost all my pictures were made on location; some in the United States, some outside. They were among the first feature pictures to be made on distant locations. The studios went along with that, so it wasn't to extricate myself from the clutches of the major studios that I moved to Europe. I still work for major studios, but picture by picture rather than as an employee. I must have the consent of the studio as to where I am going to shoot my picture; I get the studio to call the tune.

It was whilst I was making what really amounted to a foreign film in Ireland, *Sinful Davey*, that I spoke to the Taoiseach, Jack Lynch, and pointed out that *Davey* was a foreign film; it wasn't an Irish film just because it was being made on Irish locations. There were considerable advantages so far as Ireland was concerned with this and other such films. Outside companies spend a lot of money here and enlist Irish talent and educate Irish film-makers. But such advantages had very little to do with what I foresaw would be forthcoming from an Irish film industry which would employ Irish talent; not simply Irish labour, but Irish technicians, writers, directors and actors. An Irish film would be a film written by an Irishman, directed by an Irishman, with Irish actors in the roles.

I can see a lot of changes in Ireland since I first came here, not all of them good. I don't mean to be sentimental about the old Ireland, but there is a price that must be paid when you turn a country into a tourist resort. The advantages are certainly obvious, but there is a price not just in congestion on the roads, but in the attitude of shopkeepers and hoteliers. One can see a commercialism taking over that is contrary to the world's idea of Ireland. It wasn't here when I came to Ireland originally; at least it wasn't obvious, but it is becoming obvious now. I think Ireland must protect her resources better than she is doing.

I live isolated out here and go to Dublin only on occasions, so my observations are really limited to this part of Ireland. Ireland's assets are not those of England or France or Italy; they are of another colour. We have no great cathedrals or national monuments; but we have the country and we must not allow it to be spoiled. The character of the country and the hospitable character of its people must be championed and maintained.

I don't find it strange to commute from Ireland, because I do so much of it now; but I find St Cleran's a marvellous place to come back to and lick one's wounds. People have fallen in love with St Cleran's, and Americans, not only those who have been here, but strangers, write to ask me if they can acquire land in Ireland or find employment. These are people who would love to live away from the complexities and turmoil of life in the United States. When Marlon Brando stayed here he went walking alone one night, took a wrong turning and was lost. We had to go out in the rain to look for him. Monty Clift came here before we made *Freud: The Secret Passion*. His health was very bad. He had cataracts, but didn't know it. He had emotional problems and I think these derived considerably from the condition of his eyes. He didn't know that he was half-blind. His last film was a great effort and strain for him.

I think I remain fairly detached when I am making a picture. I am thinking about what is best for the picture and of nothing else. Sometimes I am mistaken, of course. Every day there are crises on a picture, but you discover that each crisis is not the end of the world. I have always had this approach which I think is in my nature. The people I choose for my pictures are the ones I think best for the parts. Economy doesn't enter into it; in fact, many movie companies are happier with a big name because they think this ensures an attendance. I brought Humphrey Bogart and Katharine Hepburn together for *The African Queen*. There was no opposition to my casting; everybody thought it was good chemistry. To my mind each of them was perfect for the part. I never look to a picture as a vehicle for a star. I don't begin with an actor and then make a picture; I begin with the story and cast it as best I can, and whether I cast a star or not makes very little difference to me. When I cast John Hurt as *Sinful Davey* there was some opposition on the part of United Artists because they didn't consider him a name. But I was able to insist on having him. In such matters I require a say.

There are two or three pictures I haven't been able to make because they have gone against the grain of the major studios. There was resistance at the time I wanted to make *The Lonely Passion of Judith Hearne* because I wanted to put Katharine Hepburn into the part, and her stock was rather low at that moment, as low then as it is high now. The people who owned the property and wanted to produce the movie asked me to put Rosalind Russell in the part. But I said I would rather not make the picture. I thought it was a wonderful part for Katie and saw her as my ideal Judith. Now I think they are going to do the picture with Deborah Kerr. I love Deborah and have a great admiration for her. Ava Gardner I have found delightful. Elizabeth Taylor is perhaps too much of a star for my kind of operation. But when I make a picture I prefer to use actors whose personalities reflect a role rather than those who through technical ability are able to put themselves into a part.

Every time I have been approached to remake a classic picture I have said no. I don't think good pictures should be remade. Bad pictures should be remade, and I would like to remake some of my own bad ones. When you remake a classic not only are you bucking the picture but you are bucking people's fondness for a picture which was made some twenty years ago. They probably think it was a better picture than it was. I was not satisfied with three or four pictures. One can have excuses, but the director is almost always responsible when a picture is bad. When I made a film called *The Roots of Heaven* it was taken with too great haste. It required much deeper consideration than any of us gave it. I had pictures that were tampered with by the producers after I had made them. I understood what they were up against with *The Red Badge of Courage*, although I am not sympathetic to what happened. In a couple of instances I don't even understand why producers have interfered. *The Barbarian and the Geisha* was knocked about after I had turned over the finished picture and gone to Africa. They cut it and shot certain scenes again and it turned out to be a mess. Until *The Red Badge of Courage* I had always been present when the picture was being cut until it was finished, but one of the disadvantages of not being with one company is that it takes some time to prepare a picture for exhibition and during that time the director very often finds himself away making another film. The issue of *The Red Badge of Courage* was blown up to something more than it really was. When I read Lillian Ross's book I found she had an extraordinary memory for detail without ever having taken a note. The only time I ever saw her with a pencil in her hand was when it was a matter of statistics. She repeated from memory conversations she had overheard which struck me as verbatim when I read them later.

One would think the day had gone when producers could fool around with a director's picture, but it happens occasionally. So much time elapsed before *Sinful Davey* was released that the producers wanted to keep their hands busy. They did not just cut the film; they changed the order of scenes and gave the film a random, erratic shape. This was the first picture I made entirely in Ireland, but I would not have had anything to do with it if I had known what was going to happen. When I finally saw it on the screen I was very disappointed, almost to the point of taking my name off it. But I didn't do so, because I did not want to become involved in litigation. When I edited *Sinful Davey* and sent it to the producers, I was told that one or two slight changes were being made; but I was unable to be present because I was away making another film. If I had known what was going on I would have raised all kinds of hell. When I saw the film there were more than one or two changes; there were a dozen and they threw it all out of kelter. What happened to *Sinful Davey* was as unthinkable as if somebody had taken a painting, cut it up into little squares and re-arranged them. It was a less understandable experience than *The Red Badge of Courage*. At least I was present at the preview of *Red Badge* and saw the audience reaction. It was a bad experience. I suppose a third of the audience left the preview before the performance was finished. In retrospect, I believe it had something to do with the period. It was during the Korean War when one used to turn over quickly the pages with war photographs in *Life* magazine. *The Red Badge* was a realistic picture about war which struck very deeply, and people didn't want to look at it at the time. It was during certain scenes that the audience at the preview got up and walked out. The producers thought that these scenes were too much for audiences to take and this is what motivated them to drop them from the film. It didn't make any difference so far as the success of the picture was concerned; it wasn't a success at the time, although it later became a classic. The critics liked *Red Badge*, but audiences didn't, and it's only over the years that it has acquired an audience. I have seen this happen to a number of my pictures. *Beat the Devil* had no success when it started out, but now it has become a cult picture at which audiences throw the dialogue back to the screen. *The Asphalt Jungle* had no great reception from critics or audiences at first, but now it has found its place. I think one of my best pictures is *Reflections in a Golden Eye*. I made it in a new kind of colour. I thought the picture very successful, but the distributors decided it would be better to release it in straight Technicolor and there was a bit of a battle over this. It was a battle in which the spoils were divided: in some places *Reflections* was released in my colour, and in others in Technicolor. I think that straight Technicolor is damaging to certain pictures of a psychological nature. In the case of *Reflections* the head of the sales department at Warner Brothers was dead against my idea from the word go. In certain pictures the eye reflects on the colour when it should be looking through to the thought, and in *Reflections* the colours were muted so that they would not take away from the ideas. We shot the picture in Technicolor and the colour mutations were a later laboratory job. I oversee this sort of project very closely. At the Rome laboratories, where they are very inventive and creative, they worked for weeks until they found a highly successful formula, which I hated to see discarded. Such experiences incline me to take precautions on the next picture. But you can only go so far, and finally all you can do is take your name off a picture, and as this entails all kinds of unpleasantness I have never done it. On a couple of occasions I wish I had. Among my better pictures I think my affections are pretty well divided, but there are certain pictures that carry with them particular memories. *The African Queen* and *The Treasure of the Sierra Madre*, in which I directed my father, I remember with a particularly dear feeling.

The shape of my life has had a different pattern to my father's.

One of the reasons I came to live in Ireland was because I wanted security for my children. I think this is one of the few countries in the world where a girl can go on a walking trip alone and be perfectly safe. Ireland has a moral climate. There are obvious physical advantages in spending your childhood in a country atmosphere. My children were riding horses when they were five years old and my boy is an expert fly fisherman. They consider themselves as Irish; they both learned to speak Irish, but I think that can be inhibiting. Donogh O'Malley once told me of his plans for the Irish language and I concurred with him. I had a great respect for the Minister for Education and his death was a disaster for this country. He did not wish to diminish the importance of speaking Irish, but he did not think it should be a requirement for civil employment; as I recall, he thought it should share in importance with Irish literature and history and art. A student's career should not depend on his being an Irish speaker, and this was the idea he was going to promote.

I am against censorship in any form. The only true censorship is that which the artist exercises. I think the rejection in Ireland of my film on Freud is a kind of paradox, because I have discovered a great degree of tolerance in the Irish people. I know that motion pictures and books have been the chief target of censorship but matters have improved. On the other hand, the stage has been quite uncensored. Freedom of thought is something which delights me in Ireland. One can have views of any kind. The eccentric does not exist in Ireland because everyone is highly individualistic. The climate that drove Joyce and so many others away from Ireland also brought their talents to fruition. This is an important distinction which must be made. I think you could make any sort of film in Ireland, but whether it would be screened or not is something else. You could write any kind of book in Ireland, but whether it would be published here is another matter. However, I think there is a lessening in the severity of censorship. I often wonder if emigration from Ireland isn't so much a matter of escaping from something as expanding one's horizon. I am all for Irish emigration; people are one of our best exports. Right now I think Ireland has an ideal population. This is one of the few countries in the world which is not overpopulated. The older I get the more time I want to spend in Ireland. I have a little two-roomed cottage at Lettermullen in Connemara where I occasionally spend three or four days during the summer. It's charming.

I have got to go on making pictures to afford to live here. I am probably working as hard as I ever did, but that's my life. I think of making pictures as a painter thinks of painting. You don't stop because you grow older. If I live to be as old as Titian I hope to be making pictures then.

253